ALASKAN PIONEER GIRL

A MEMOIR OF AMERICA'S LAST FRONTIER

Judy Johnson

TSL Publications

First published in Great Britain in 2022
By TSL Publications, Rickmansworth

Copyright © 2022 Judy Johnson

ISBN / 978-1-914245-91-6

Cover Design: Suzanne Labi

Contents

For my late Mom and Dad

and

My Siblings

Introduction

In December, 2015, I visited Mother for the last time as she lay either in her recliner or in a hospital bed set up in my youngest brother Brent's living room. He and my sister-in-law, Judy, were her carers. Their house was just around the bend of the L-shaped Porcupine Lake and was on part of our original 160 acre Alaskan homesteading claim made in 1959. Mother had instigated our move from town into the wilderness just as generations of American land seekers made the journey from East to West after Abraham Lincoln's Homesteading Act in 1862. She had lead the way for me and my young brothers, Brent and Jerry, over the recently blazed trail through the rugged Alaskan terrain made by my father and older sister, Gail, only days before in an army surplus dump truck with winch.

Now the strong and forceful pioneer could hardly stand or talk. She was hunched over and communicated mainly with her eyes, movement of her head, and hands. She was ninety-six years old and had been in relatively good health until the last few months. I had skied across the lake from her home next to our old homestead cabin to come for lunch. She responded to my request to get up in a wheelchair and help prepare Crab Louis for the family gathering.

Brent asked me, "Can she help?"

"Yes," I said as I rolled Mom to the kitchen dining table and handed her a hard-boiled egg to crack and peel. She looked at me with eyes full of appreciation, but was unable to speak.

Mom had taught us to love Crab Louis back in the tiny cabin. There was a beam running along the downstairs ceiling with a shelf attached holding our books, including the *Joy of Cooking*. I could remember her stretching on tiptoes to pull the cookbook down for the trusted recipe. This happened whenever we had sourced enough Alaskan King Crab from our fishermen friends, trading it for our wild salmon or moose meat. Guided by the recipe, I would help lay the cooked, shucked, crabmeat onto a large platter on top of Bibb lettuce leaves. I made the sauce by stirring together mayonnaise, ketchup, chopped red bell peppers and green onions, a squeeze of lemon juice, and a dash of salt and black pepper. We poured the sauce over the crab and lettuce. Mom boiled two eggs for ten minutes and then had me immediately immerse them in a bowl of lake ice water from the kitchen bucket to keep the yolks from turning green. We sliced and garnished with the cooled eggs and snipped chives.

On this, my last visit with Mother, I yearned to indulge in the Alaskan favorite. She took the egg from my hand and very gently tapped it on the table. It did not break.

"Give it a real go, Mom," I encouraged.

She smiled and tried again with shaking hands that had once pulled in nets from the Pacific, and was successful. We looked at each other, and I held back the tears. I knew that she would pass. The recipe would live on.

This is my story, but also hers.

Crab Louis
(Serves 4)

Heap 2 cups of Alaskan King Crabmeat on top of plated Bibb lettuce leaves and pour over the sauce given below.
Garnish with slices from 2 hard-boiled eggs and snipped chives..

Sauce, blend well in a large bowl:
1 cup mayonnaise,
¼ cup ketchup,
1 cup chopped red bell peppers,
a bunch of chopped green onions,
squeezed juice of one lemon,
salt and coarse ground black pepper to taste.

My Parents' Romantic Flight

Mama and Daddy had eloped after a whirlwind romance, having met on a Chicago ice rink. A reckless skater knocked her down without a backward glance, Daddy helped her up, and a sixty-year relationship began. They did not know it then, but ice skating would become an enjoyable hobby in Alaska, as they skated again together on Porcupine Lake.

It was not a direct route from Chicago to the Porcupine Lake homestead in Alaska. Mom and Dad traveled to St Louis, Missouri, to marry; took a train through endless wheat and corn fields to the coastal city of Seattle with high-rise buildings to get their bearings in the Northwest; and then onto Juneau by steamer to settle in the Great Northland to become Alaskans. My parents' journey to the wilderness was influenced by the spirit of adventure, romance, difficult relatives, the army, tragedy, and a rejection of small town mentality. The overriding reason to remain after World War II was to acquire land.

While courting, they took in a Mozart concert, but with limited funds they mostly chose less expensive dates. Singing *Don't Sit Under the Apple Tree* and *Chattanooga Choo Choo*, they would stroll hand in hand around the streets of Chicago to smell sweet lilacs blooming along the sidewalks in spring. Years after, Mama told me and my brothers about how they read the newspaper, and listened to the radio to keep up with the Cubs' games at Wrigley Field. Enjoying baseball was part of being an American. Mama suggested a trip to the Chicago Institute of Art, but instead, Daddy dragged her to the Chicago Automobile Show. GM's first dream car was on display which coincided with his big car yearnings, and he was thrilled with its hidden headlights and no running boards. Mama admired the top that folded into a compartment behind the bench seat as she was always interested in practicality of organization with everything in its place. The closest she would come to a convertible was an open top army surplus jeep years later on the homestead.

My parents tied the knot in a low-key ceremony in St Louis, Missouri. Mama was aware that she was rushing to marry after only a three month courtship. Her Grandmother Schroeder's words resonated and spurred her on: "Ruth, you were twenty-one-years old last year—an old maid. It's time to get on with it." As a slim twenty-two-year-old peroxide blond, Mama wore a light blue dress with matching jacket. Daddy, dressed in a freshly ironed shirt and trousers with his dark curly hair and Swedish blue eyes, was striking at nineteen. They had to marry over the state line because Illinois required one to be twenty-one to tie the knot. No witnesses were present in the home of the officiating Justice of the Peace. This made Mama anxious wondering if she really was Mrs. Henning Johnson. The ceremony was over in minutes. Daddy paid the registration fee, and left holding the marriage certificate in one hand and Mama's waist with the other. So eager were they to consummate their union, they were breathless by the time they had walked into their small hotel. Mama suddenly remembered and said, "Oh…suitcase with my new nightgown…back in the car." Unlocking the door to their room, Daddy laughed and threw the key on the bed. He lifted up his bride and waltzed her over the threshold. "Wear it tomorrow night."

Daddy proudly drove them back to Chicago in his secondhand Plymouth that he had bought with the $1,000 inheritance from Uncle Harry. Mama smiled, snuggled up to Daddy in the front seat, and they listened to current songs on the radio such as *I've Got a Gal in Kalamazoo*. While they listened, they smoked cigarettes that were habits begun in early teens. He was three years younger than she, but had charm—a trait that her own father totally lacked. When *Night and Day* came on, they sang along with Frank Sinatra. With his own large car, and a blond and devoted wife from a middle class family, Daddy had achieved more than most nineteen-year-olds. This he would soon discover, was not enough to impress the in-laws.

Mama's father, George Dabbert, had worked for Goss Printing Press decades as an electrician, and did not warm to a happy-go-lucky son-in-law without a trade. Their lives had been very different. George was the son of hardworking German immigrants. In the depression he not only held down his regular job, but also bought repossessed houses and renovated them. He resold these homes making a handsome profit. One day George would make his own unique contribution to WWII.

During the war, Mama's father won a Presidential Award for inventing a "Magnetic Chuck" working on the Manhatten Project at Hanford, Washington. His magnetic chuck released bombs more quickly. *The Chicago Tribune* headline was "Electrician Wins Tribune's First War Worker Award." Asked how he had developed the device, George said, "The idea just came to me. The only way I can help win the war is to do my own job. I want to help in my little way to defeat our country's enemies." As an adult, I read the article Mama had saved and sent, and wondered if Grandfather George, born in the U.S. but whose own grandparents were German immigrants, had misgivings about helping to release bombs more quickly over Germany.

Mama was well aware of her father's firm, no-nonsense characteristics. She told Daddy, "My German American grandparents felt the role of a woman was to be a wife and mother. That's as it has been for women in our families through the ages. Dad refused my request to go to university...No need. You will marry and run a home. Roy should go." Mama's brother was eight years younger and not academic. "Roy did learn from our father, though, and made his own profit off me, letting me use his bike to ride over to our grandparents, and charged me a penny-a-mile."

Daddy's father, Gustav Johnson, was a Swedish immigrant, and had been less successful. The 40-acre dairy farm in Wisconsin was remortgaged to allow Daddy's older brother, George, to buy a chicken farm which went bust in the depression. As a result, Gus and Hannah also lost the family farm. Hannah never recovered from their misfortune and ended up in a mental hospital in Chicago. Daddy and his father, Gustav, moved to the city to be close to her and to ensure Daddy completed high school. They also would be near his three older half-brothers and their families. Hannah remained in the mental hospital until she died in 1947. "Today's medicine would have kept her with us instead of in a care facility for twenty years," Daddy sadly told me when I was a teenager.

Daddy brought his new bride to visit his mother in the hospital. They gathered around Hannah's bed in arm chairs, Mama wearing a brown pullover and wool skirt, and Daddy in navy blue pullover and dark grey trousers. Hannah got out of bed and warmly hugged Ruth to welcome her into the family. This made Mama feel accepted. Mother told me years later, "Hannah smiled, inclined her head with thick red hair, and said, 'Tell me about yourself, Ruth'."

"Well, I grew up in a large bungalow in Oak Park. I go back once a week to continue lessons on our grand piano. It is good to visit my parents and brother, Roy…"

"Such a nice family. Johnny, have you told Ruth about our family? About my brother, Harry?"

Daddy uncrossed his legs and leaned forward in his chair with obvious animation. "Uncle Harry? We took a train to visit him in Seattle when I was five. He had recently returned from an expedition. He gazed straight at me and told me about roughing it as a sailor on whaling ships around Barrow, Alaska."

"Whale's baleen for corsets," Hannah interrupted, "Ruth, and oil for lamps."

"Oh, my mother and grandmother wore corsets," Mama replied.

"Once Harry's ship became trapped in ice," Daddy cut in. "He and the other sailors made their way, stumbling over the frozen Arctic water in subzero temperatures with a freezing gale stinging their faces and coating their beards and moustaches with ice. Their hands and feet became numb."

"He suffered frostbite and lost two toes," Hannah added. "But Harry felt fortunate to make it into town. He witnessed one colleague fall through thin ice. They tried, but couldn't rescue him."

"Harry was brave and adventurous," Mama said with wide eyes and shaking her head. "My German relatives were tailors and carpenters. Lived right here in Chicago…"

Hannah laughed and said, "There is more…my sister Nancy and her husband have retired to a fruit orchard in Seattle. Earlier they spent years in Alaska as Gus worked as a chef during the tail end of the gold rush. He also appeared with Bill Cody on the *Wild*

West Show."

"Oh no...don't tell me...my life has been in Chicago—nothing adventurous," Mama said.

"Now you know why I love hunting deer and fishing lake trout," Daddy added.

Mama was pleased that Daddy arranged a few meetings with his mother which made her feel accepted, but was concerned that he did not introduce her to the rest of his family. There must be a reason.

Two months after visiting Hannah in the hospital, they boarded a Union Pacific train to the northwest without jobs, but were filled with excitement and love for each other. The thought of roughing it was of no consequence, and all uncertainty just part of the romance.

They disembarked in Seattle and found a small place to live. Mama immediately secured a job in the Henry Stewart White Building and the Walker Building as an Otis elevator operator. In navy blue mesh gloves (to cover bad eczema on her hands, a lingering condition from working as a hairdresser in contact with peroxide) and a brown company uniform, she was punctual and never missed a shift. The buildings were across the street from one another, and she worked partial days in each, going endlessly up and down between floors.

To Daddy, living close to nature sounded more appealing than in a Chicago suburban house. Preference for breathing fresh mountain and ocean air instead of fumes from factories and cars, fishing salmon from icy streams and the Pacific, and hunting moose in thick woods finalized his decision. He ordered Mama, "Put in your notice, we're moving to Alaska."

She took him to heart. He was her husband, and his every word was for her to follow. Plus, ascending and descending, doors opening, doors closing, had become monotonous. To Daddy's pronouncement, she exited the elevator—and Seattle—on a boat with him. On the boat she could still hear the supervisor yell, "The nerve to return your uniform after only three months on the job. A mighty poor investment—you, Ruth Johnson." As the lift's doors closed, another door opened. On the boat they mixed not only with *Cheechakoes* (newcomers in Inuit) to Alaska, but old-timers and Daddy had job offers before they made land.

The steamer took them to the rainy capitol—Juneau. From the deck, they saw a perfect scene for an impressionist painter. Pastel colored wooden houses were perched on mountains only partially visible through grey clouds and heavy mist. The Alaska Juneau Gold Mine's dilapidated buildings were scattered on one side. Mining had made the town—known around the world as the biggest gold find. Large machines were digging into huge blackish mounds of tailings (gravel), and unloading these dirty heaps onto a barge to be hauled out and dumped into the ocean.

The newlyweds settled into a house on steep "Cedar Tract," and replaced their smart Chicago shoes for rubber soled sneakers and laced up boots, called shoepacks, to hike up a long cleated board-walk to their rental. They arrived breathless at the top, even without carrying bags of groceries, but they soon achieved both and more. Daddy learned to hook salmon with a rod and reel as food for the table. Their fingers clutched freshly caught fish by the gills as they climbed to the front door. Descaling and cleaning out the non-edible bits in preparation for cooking the salmon for supper replaced Mama's afternoon piano practicing of Chicago life. Grilled Alaskan salmon became a staple.

John's first job was delivering orders for the Green grocery. All went well for a couple of months until he had a bust up with the owner, and left without having another job. He took the dismissal lightly saying, "I'll get out with my fishing pole tomorrow to land us a meal."

Mama yelled, "You need a job to provide for a family. You know that I'm pregnant for God's sake." Gail was born three months later. Mama worried that money would be short with neither of them employed. Despite their financial circumstances, my parents did not give up cigarettes. It was an age in which big stars of the day smoked, including Ava Gardner and Clark Gable. Mama had started at the age of fourteen, and Daddy also as a teenager. She loved to relax in a chair by crossing her knees and posing with a cigarette as Marlene Dietrich had in the film, *Morocco*. I grew up with packages of *Salem* cigarettes lying around the house.

Mama's financial concerns eased when Daddy found work with Morrison Knutson paving the airfield. Daddy labored with other pioneers to convert the gravel air strip to a major airfield for the territory of Alaska. It was a smelly job reeking of hot tar and asphalt, but he applied himself and was recognized and promoted. The supervising engineer liked him, and kept Daddy employed after the job was completed. He became Daddy's mentor, training him as a land surveyor. In a few years "Johnson Land Surveying" was started.

Life was challenging for Mama away from her parents with a tiny baby. She and little Gail were almost homebound. It was not an easy feat climbing up and down steep "Cedar Tract" with a baby to get to the shops in Juneau. Then Daddy went to work in Attu on the Aleutian Chain, Alaska, with the Army Corp of Engineers. The Aleutian Chain projects southwest into the Pacific from mainland Alaska. It was a good paying civilian job, and the closest Daddy came to action in WWII; but by the time Daddy arrived in Attu, in 1944, the enemy was mostly gone. He heard the fighting had been bloody because the Japanese would not allow themselves to be taken as prisoners of war. In June, 1942, Japan had seized the remote, sparsely inhabited islands of Attu and Kiska. U.S. troops fought fiercely through a blizzard of snow and ice during the battle on Attu in May 1943 to free Alaska of the Japanese. Alaska was the only U.S. soil on which the war was fought besides the bombing of Pearl Harbour.

He noticed that the Aleuts looked much like the few remaining Japanese with some of the same physical features: dark and thick straight hair, flat-wide faces, and almond eyes. This made him realize that with the earth's migration of peoples, there must have been movement between Japan and Alaska. On the mountainous island, with howling wind and snow in June, Daddy helped construct a tunnel to house a hospital on the island, another step for him becoming an Alaskan.

It was difficult for Mama to have Daddy away as she was pregnant again. Thirteen months after Gail's birth, second daughter, Sherry, was born. Daddy returned for the birth of his second daughter, but soon returned to Attu to work. Five months later, despite having two small children at home, he was drafted and moved nearly 900 miles away to Fort Richardson Army Base in Anchorage. It was 1945, and World War II still raged.

Mama was left alone with her young girls. She relied on neighbors more than she ever had in Chicago, and was thankful that all were chatty and interested in hearing about her willingness to leave city life for the Great North Land. Maria, a capable Finnish woman, of whom nothing remains except her meatball recipe, had been an Alaskan resident for nine years; and Ruth was interested in making her a friend as she was of Scandinavian background like Daddy and also at ease with Gail and Sherry. They filled buckets picking blueberries and cranberries until their hands were the color of the berries. Maria annually butchered and canned meat, and was willing to teach Mama to do the same. She introduced her to sterilizing Mason Jars in metal pans of boiling water on the cook stove—carefully. The Mason Jars sealed the cooked meat after four hours in a hot water bath. Mama came straight to Maria from the doctor's after being diagnosed with appendicitis. Maria smiled and swept her blond hair up into a ponytail and met Mama's worried eyes. "I'll take care of Gail and Sherry for you, Ruth. Sure. But hold on…you want to become an Alaskan? Act like one. Be strong. First, you have to help me butcher my half of beef. Tie this apron on and wash your hands. Let's go over to the cutting boards. I've already cooked a meatball supper for us and your little girls."

It worked. The experience made Mama shake off her Chicago identity and become an Alaskan.

Mama and my sisters moved from Juneau and joined Daddy in Anchorage soon after her appendectomy. They rented a house in a suburb, and life in the territory's largest city was easier. Mama had Daddy evenings again to help with their young daughters. Friends were army families—couples who were also from the Continental U.S. Working alongside these army buddies was the closest Daddy would get to action in the war.

As Daddy always said, "I fought the Battle of Anchorage." It was his way of saying that he did not do much in World War II—most of his time was spent in the fire station. Mama and Daddy followed different paths after arriving in Juneau, but in the end both became Alaskans.

Grilled Salmon

The bright red color and firmer meat, of wild fish are brought about by a diet of shrimp, and swimming thousands of miles in cold Pacific waters, resulting in strong muscles—preferable over all other sources of salmon to me.

To serve approximately five, ingredients:

One side of wild Alaskan salmon, filleted
Fresh lemon to serve with cooked salmon

To grill/broil, remove the salmon, place on an oiled foil covered grill rack, skin side up facing the heat. Grill for about 3 to 4 minutes (until skin is brown) under a pre-heated grill and then turn. Season with garlic salt or salt and coarsely ground black pepper. Grill for another 1 to 2 minutes or until just cooked. Remove from the heat and place on a serving platter. Garnish with Samphire or parsley and freshly cut lemon. Wild Alaskan Salmon is also great in stir-fry and Sushi.

Maria's Family Meatballs

Best with moose, but beef will do.
½ cup dry bread crumbs
½ cup light cream, milk, almond or soy milk
½ cup water
200g/7 oz. ground moose, venison, or beef
200g/7 oz. ground lean pork
1 teaspoon salt
¾ teaspoon ground allspice
4 tablespoons grated onion
1 egg, beaten
3 tablespoons butter

Mix the bread crumbs, cream or milk and water; set aside for 3 minutes. With your clean hands, mix together the ground meat, salt, allspice, and onion. Add the breadcrumbs and the egg. Shape into desired sized balls. Roast at 200C for about 15 minutes. Serve hot with boiled potatoes, and a tossed salad

Chugiak Pioneers

World War II ended. Peace was declared. Mama and Daddy, despite having two small children, decided, as many veterans in Alaska, to apply for a five-acre home site—free Government land. They knew that leaving secure military life was necessary. What they had not realized was that building a new community would be part of the package to obtain the land. Rugged pioneering life lay ahead. Not only did they have to locate their land, but also create the name for the place.

Where should their claim be staked out? They drove eighteen miles from Anchorage and had a flat tire. Both jumped out. With the jack, they lifted the car to put on the spare. Mama looked around and saw McKinley on the horizon. "What about the hillside right here?"

Daddy stopped, gazed around while lighting a cigarette. He inhaled, taking in the lush vegetation, and then responded, "Yes...fine for a house after some trees are removed. Our drive could run above the highway."

That night after dinner and the children were in bed, they read the Federal requirements again: payment of $2.50 per acre with filing; no cultivation of the thick forest; residents had to build a livable house and live on the land for five years. A deed would be granted after a Federal inspector visited and agreed that the obligations had been met.

Mama and Daddy began by erecting an army surplus tent which they lived in while building a log house. Mama hung three wedding china platters over the inside door—gifts from her parents who had disapproved adamantly of her choice of husband. A wood-burning stove provided some warmth against the Arctic conditions of Alaska, but their physical and spiritual closeness strongly bonded them. Puffs of smoke seeped from the door of the stove when Daddy tended the fire in the night. On a draft, the smoke floated above the metal army cot where Gail and Sherry lay sleeping side by side. It hovered over two army cots shoved together for Mama and Daddy where Mama lay sleeping, and drifted through the canvas door as Daddy briefly opened it. Then the smoke rose upward through the trees to the moon and stars. Daddy crept back under the covers with Mama. In theory it was romantic living so close to nature. In practice it was hard—not the least because their physical closeness had produced two children.

The 16th of October a violent storm blew up. The flimsy canvas buckled, and the frame creaked and rocked as the tent threatened to part from its metal stakes. Would they, as Dorothy in *The Wizard of Oz*, be picked up in the wind and deposited in another state? Daddy stepped out to have a brief look and then quickly back. "We've got to get out of here, now."

Each grabbed a child and ran for their lives. Trees swayed, splintered, and crashed around them. Yellow birch leaves fell like giant confetti impairing their vision and lodging in their hair. Underfoot, fallen branches snapped as they raced. Mama stepped through the eerie blasts of frigid night air tightly holding toddler Sherry as she struggled to keep up with Daddy. He clutched Gail with one arm and a flashlight in his other hand. The weak beam of light danced up and down with his long strides. "Wait," Mama yelled into the wind, exhausted.

The Parks opened their door to Daddy's rap. They lived on the highway just below the building site. That night, and for the rest of the winter, Daddy and Mama stayed rent free in a cabin owned by the couple. The Parks were happy to lodge their neighbors at short notice. However, the unexpected refugees fleeing from the fury of the storm had caught the Parks just as—secretly—they were butchering a moose they had shot out of season. Heavy fines were given when illegal kills were discovered. Thus, Mama and Daddy were quickly ushered out of the main house and to the cabin before they could ask too many questions. Their silence was rewarded by grilled T-bone moose steaks for the night's dinner.

Spring arrived and they returned to the home site. On the 1st of May it was Zero F. It was unseasonably cold at this time of year even for Chugiak, Alaska. Heavy coats and wool socks inside lined boots were required. First they had to remove three trees that had fallen on top of the tent. Without the heavy trunks anchoring the canvas, it would have been blown away not only in the storm that they survived, but also by storms that followed in the winter when temperatures would dip to minus 30F and snow would fall and fall until over three feet had accumulated. Mama was heartbroken by what she saw, and burst out with, "Oh my platters...smashed to smithereens." Feeling sad, she knelt down and picked up the pieces.

She had to put her disappointment behind, and move her family back into the tent. The only way to get the land was to keep going. She and Daddy continued building the log house and basement situated on the bank with the highway about thirty feet below. At the same time the spot was being cleared, a long driveway from the main road was bulldozed by a neighbor who ran a heavy equipment company. The house would be small, but compared to the tent, it would be a mansion. Mama bought a book from an Anchorage bookstore that was a show and tell on home building. This—and only this—was both their architect and their master builder guide.

Daddy cut down mature spruce trees on the homesite with an axe and crosscut saw. He sawed off the branches, and then both he and Mama straddled the log using drawknives to peel away the bark. It was physically taxing, but they kept warm rhythmically stretching forward and then reclining as they worked. The smell of pitch and freshly cut wood permeated the air. Daddy sawed the logs to size for standing vertical around the floor of the house. After months, they put on his own handmade shakes for the roof. Daddy would like to have hired help, but the cost would have been prohibitive. New neighbors they had befriended were too busy building their own houses to offer much more than encouragement. My parents constructed a cement basement. The cement mixer was powered on site by gasoline. The basement was still unfinished when they decided to move into the log house with Gail and Sherry, ages four and three. Living in the new house meant that they were one step closer to owning the land.

On the 13th February, 1948, I was born in Anchorage at the Providence Hospital and came home with Mama after two weeks. A wooden crib on one side of the living room was my bed until I was old enough for a metal army cot with mattress in the same spot.

I have an early memory of Mama across the room reading Agatha Christie books while making herself cozy in the easy chair, feet propped up on an ottoman. Sometimes she knitted. For Christmas she made eighteen pairs of mittens for friends' children. The floral print slipcovers pulled and slipped as she shifted her body this way and that with concentration. She stood up and, with outstretched fingers, straightened the seams in perfect perpendicular lines, matching the wooden box seating across the room. I realized later that it was her German heritage that made her attentive to pristine order. Her parents' house in Chicago was always well kept, but they employed part-time help. In Alaska, Mama would rely on her daughters to assist her as soon as we were old enough; generally, by the age of four we were expected to do simple tasks such as set a table or make our own bed.

I was soon walking and running around our log cabin, eventually mastering the basement stairs to watch Mama fill the Maytag washing machine—with wringer and rinsing tubs. "Careful, Judy, careful..." she cautioned. On the ground level I tagged along beside my sisters and parents in the single large room. The family congregated in the handcrafted kitchen. Daddy had made the cabinets from Douglas-fir plywood. Wooden scallops ran underneath the top cupboards, and red countertops gave an appearance of warmth and welcome. Mama cooked on a gas range fueled from propane in cylinders positioned outdoors. The living room side of the kitchen counters led onto an open plan living area. Large front windows let in the sun and were adorned on the outside by moose horns from Daddy's successful hunts. A side window overlooked the road.

Mama had dyed cotton bed sheets green, and hung them on ceiling wires between the living room and bed to provide privacy for her and Daddy's nights on the double Beautyrest bed. The toy box and wooden filing cabinet sat by the curtain screen. Gail and Sherry slept nearby in bunk beds in a large alcove.

Initially there was no running water. Daddy or Mama went up the hill with a pail to a natural spring for drinking and washing water. Finally an over-ground hose to the house provided water at the kitchen sink in summer.

Heat from the wood-burning stove filled every nook and cranny. Mama prepared meals, cleaned, washed clothes; and our lives moved ahead. From the radio came songs: *Some Enchanted Evening, Buttons & Bows, Don't Fence Me In, La Vie En Rose,* and Nat King Cole's lyrics of "Chestnuts roasting by the open fire..." My parents sang along to all of these. Their happy voices and frequent smiles were reassuring to me.

Mama and Daddy ate at a small wooden table next to the open kitchen counter. Alongside, a little red vinyl folding table with chairs was set up for Gail, Sherry, and me. The cat curled underneath, ready for any food that we rejected. At Christmas the fully decorated tree was squeezed in between the tables, and the cat pawed at play breaking a few glass baubles.

They had chickens and planted a vegetable garden. Mama learned to make great meals from these vegetables, and also cooked moose meat from Daddy's annual hunts. Healthy appetites were assured by the physical requirements of daily life.

It was easier having a supply of milk at home rather than driving to the grocery miles away. My parents purchased a couple of goats for milking, Nanny Doat and Marzi Doat. Mama showed me how to milk one and let me have a go with my small, inexperienced hands. I squeezed and squeezed, prompted by her words, "That's how...keep going," but I only managed to get a tiny bit of milk in the pail. I gave up when she blurted out, "Watch your feet." I was barely able to side-step the goat's pellet droppings on the dirt drive. The goat heroically put up with my clumsiness. I did not want to try again and, thankfully, Mama did not force me. When the two goats ate wet laundry off the Parks' clothesline, that friendship was in jeopardy. Another neighbor came to the rescue by taking away the two darling Doats just before Daddy was ready to slaughter them.

Daddy's suggestion to name the town Chugiak was taken up in a community meeting. He stood and said, "I have been told by an old-timer, Athabascan, that Chu-ye-ak (meaning 'the place of many places') was how his people had referred to the area hundreds of years before the white man arrived. My name nomination is this with the anglicized spelling of "Chugiak".

Many of the couples on other nearby homesites were, as mine, parents with school-age children who traveled eighteen miles to Anchorage for classes. Gail missed the bus home one afternoon because she was watching ice skaters on a rink next to the Quonset Hut which housed her class. Worried, Daddy drove to Anchorage and found her before she became upset or isolated. Mama was beside herself when they arrived home. "That's it," she said grabbing Gail into her arms. "We need a local school. This is terrible. Someone could have taken you. I remember the Lindbergh kidnapping of the 1930s. You left alone on an Anchorage street...no, even more dangerous than the Lindbergh baby taken from home. Plus, the inconvenience of forgetting lunch boxes, collecting you when you get sick, or needing to talk to your teacher. Tomorrow I'll draw up a petition and ask neighbors to sign. Jim and Marie will help."

Mama was the leading campaigner in the fight to open a school. Jim McDowell left his wife, Marie, to run Moose Horn Garage; and drove Mama around the community to encourage everyone to sign a petition for a school and to write a letter to Territorial Legislature members and to the Governor in Juneau. When Chugiak School was built, Sherry and Gail were among its first pupils, and Daddy became President of the PTA. Jim said, "Ruth, you will take on anything with a vengeance if it will benefit your children."

The summer after leaving the military, Daddy fished salmon commercially with a neighbor who had a drift boat. They did not earn much, and Daddy's share of earnings soon ran low. He went to work as an engineer with the CAA and informed Mama that the job required him to be away. She was distraught, worrying about coping without him. The wood burning stove needed frequent feeding and the house lacked running water.

Daddy went to St Lawrence Island, which sits beneath the Bering Strait and is closer to Russia than the Alaskan mainland, for nine months. He returned home only one time for two weeks midway into the long assignment.

Mama carried on raising Gail, Sherry, and me and maintained

family life in the log house. It was difficult as a pioneer without her partner and being alone with three little ones. That winter she melted bucket after bucket of snow on the stove for drinking water and washing. Firewood was delivered and good neighbor Jim McDowell sometimes split it for her, but she often had to use the axe herself. She would collapse into her easy chair at the day's end and shake her head in despair. I remember her rubbing numb hands after coming in from outdoors and saying, "My God, I left Chicago for this…"

She read Daddy's letters aloud to us. One dated, April, 1950:

> Dear Ruth, Gail, Sherry, and Judy,
> Here I'm learning about Yupik culture and survival. Every part of a whale, walrus, seal, or polar bear is utilized. Animals are hunted for food. Whale gut is made into raincoats. Feathers and furs are sewn into clothes. Tallow is used to burn in lamps and for cooking. Sealskin is used to make mukluks (boots). I feel fortunate to live in the community and to learn about appreciating and conserving nature.
>
> Work keeps me busy, but I still miss you all very much. For company I've been given Kasiki, a Siberian husky whose name means stinky. He is only a puppy and very cute. I'll be bringing him home.
>
> The girls must be growing and I hope helping you, Ruth. Tell me about their latest exploits in your next letter.
>
> Before I close, I must share today's new food experience. Julian, the five-year-old son of a family I've befriended, introduced me to homemade blueberry ice cream. Blueberries and blubber. Ha.
>
> I ate it but declined seconds.
> Love, John/Daddy

When Daddy finally rejoined us, he brought the playful puppy Kasiki with him. Daddy was fun; he had also brought us (or was it really for him) seal skin Eskimo yoyos which he could whirl in opposite conjoining circles. I was too small to suspend them high enough, but Mama, Gail, and Sherry all attempted the difficult feat with some success and lots of laughs. Kasiki barked and wagged his tail.

Running my hands over the raincoat sewn from whale gut he also brought, I imagined Daddy out in a boat helping to harpoon the huge, spouting mammal. The Cormorant feather parka and sealskin breeches were soft and cuddly. Alaska was too hostile an environment to be careless with resources. If something died it then lived on in another form. Nothing was ever wasted.

Kasiki was playful fun for only a few weeks until he ran out onto the road below the house and was hit by a car. His leg was broken so Mama and Daddy took him to a veterinary surgeon who put on a splint. Poor Kasiki was so uncomfortable that he drug himself around and rubbed the device into his body. Infection set in and, sadly he died. I hardly remember Kasiki, but he was only the first of many dogs we had in the family.

Daddy resigned from the CAA on his return, and set up a land surveying business in Chugiak. I watched as he left in our Willys Jeep to survey in the Chugiak area each day. In the evenings he drafted plats, which were maps drawn to scale showing land divisions. I went to sleep with the tap, tap, tap of the typewriter as Mama typed his letters; and at breakfast, the business accounts ledger that she kept up to date was on the table.

We were settled, and after seven years, had the Government deed to the homesite and hoped to stay in the friendly community of Chugiak. My parents were no longer Cheechakoes, but Chugiak residents, the place they had invented as much as discovered.

Grilled T-bone steaks

Sprinkle garlic salt and black pepper on each steak placed on the rack of a grill pan. Cook under a pre-heated broiler (grill) until lightly brown on each side. Serve with baked potatoes and salad.

Roasted Vegetables

In a roasting pan, place chunks of these vegetables in one layer:

Carrots	Parsnips	New potatoes
Cauliflower and Broccoli florets		

Sprinkle with one to two tablespoons of olive oil, salt, pepper, ground cumin, coriander, and dash of cinnamon. Mix with hands. Roast at 180C/350F until tender.

Last Happy Summer in Chugiak

Thoughts of the summer of 1951 return to me now as a time of comfort and security with Gail, Sherry, Mama, and Daddy. How those days would unfold can be portrayed by one Saturday vivid in my memory.

I woke up and the sun was out after days of rain. Mama and Daddy were already in the kitchen making pancakes for breakfast. I quickly dressed with some help from Mama, putting on Sherry's old blue cotton trousers and white cotton blouse. Sherry wore Gail's hand-me-downs. Only Gail had new clothes of jeans and a floral blouse. The three of us girls took our places at the little table. We ate the pancakes served with butter and maple syrup. Then we helped Mama clear the table, and sat for her to comb our hair. Mine was always a bit tangled, and I reluctantly endured her pulling the comb through my natural curls. Sherry also squirmed with her curly hair being combed. Gail's hair was braided, and she had to sit still while that was done. Daddy said goodbye as he left for land surveying.

We put on sweaters Mama knitted—mine bright blue, Sherry's pink, and Gail's red—and ran out to play in the sun in front of the house. Mud puddles were still present on the drive after yesterday's rain. My older sisters showed me how to take a small board to lift soft mud beside each puddle and lay it onto larger boards. Mama came out of the house with our toy baking pans. She returned to the kitchen where she glanced at us from the front windows.

"Oh boy, mud pies!" cried Sherry. I worked to copy her and Gail, picking up hunks of mud with my hands and rolling it into a smooth ball. The wet mud felt soft and like clay against my fingers and smelled damp.

"Fill the pans like this, Judy," Gail said, "That is how Mama said to do it." The three of us rolled and patted until several pans were full of mud.

"Write names on the pies. Here, I'll help you, Judy," said Sherry picking up a tiny stick. Sherry, four years older, passed me the stick and covered my hand with hers as she wrote J U D Y. I copied my older sisters lining up the pans of mud to dry in the sun as we filled them.

Jim McDowell drove up in his pickup truck with his son, Bruce, beside him. Jim ran Moose Horn Garage half a mile up the highway. His wife, Marie, ran the garage café. Jim pumped gas, cleaned windshields, and checked the oil in cars. He also worked on engines and reeked of the smell of motors. Mother came out to say hi to Jim and Bruce before Jim drove off. Bruce was the same age as Sherry, with straight brown hair hanging into his eyes, and had his cap pistol with him. He was only interested in firing shots from it—not making mud pies. He kicked at the boards with his cowboy boots which shook the filled pans. This frightened me as well as the bang bang of the cap gun. It seemed he was demanding attention with bullying. I kept away from him and created more pies. Gail and Sherry each took a turn to fire off the gun. Acrid smoke drifted through the air from the fired caps. Bruce, Gail, and Sherry played cowboys running around mud puddles while I continued to make mud pies. I looked up and several times saw Mama watching us from the kitchen window. After a couple of hours, Jim returned in his truck to take Bruce home. He had a smelly cigar hanging from greasy motor oil hands, but took Bruce's hand to walk him around the puddles and into the waiting truck. Mother called us in to wash up for lunch.

After we ate, she read from *Alice In Wonderland*. Then, we played dolls outside by the mud pies until dinner time. I had my own Terry Lee doll who cried actual tears, and we bathed and dressed her as our Mother did us.

Daddy drove up at the end of his long working day outside, to the house in our Willys Jeep. He unloaded his surveying equipment of transit, tripod, axe, and saw while Gail, Sherry, and I helped Mama by setting the cutlery and plates at our little table. Gail also was permitted to set the glasses. The house smelled sweet from the roasting ribs basted occasionally by Mama. I dropped a table knife on the floor and quickly picked it up.

Sherry said, "Don't worry, Judy, give me that one and I'll get a clean one." She immediately replaced the knife. She was always looking after me and instructing me as was Gail.

Mama brought in the barbecued ribs, peas, and baked potatoes. We ate leisurely.

Daddy said, "I've worked up quite an appetite chopping brush that was on the boundary line. These ribs are great, Ruth."

Mama said, "You can pick up the ribs with your hands, girls, just like your Daddy as they are easier to eat than with a knife and fork."

"Daddy, Bruce came with his cap gun. Judy wouldn't play cowboys with us because she was afraid," Gail said.

"I made mud pies," I exclaimed, "and Sherry helped me write my name on one."

"What's for dessert?" asked Sherry.

"Cherry jello, but you have to clean your plates first," replied Mama.

We three girls helped clear the table, and Gail helped Mama and Daddy wash the dishes.

Daddy chose to read more from *Alice In Wonderland* before we went to bed. As the youngest, I nestled between Sherry and Gail on my bed as he read and remembered Alice escaping from the Queen of Hearts who had ordered Alice's head to be chopped off. Then Alice woke up and realized she was safely by her sister on the riverbank, and I nodded off.

With such idyllic days of my childhood, it was impossible to foresee the coming tragedy.

Barbecue Sauce

Sauté over a low temperature:
　　1 onion, chopped, in 3 tablespoons olive oil
　　1 glove garlic, sliced
Add and simmer for 30 minutes:

3 tablespoons Worcestershire sauce	1 cup water
1 chopped red pepper	2 tablespoons vinegar
4 tablespoons brown sugar	1 cup Tomato Catsup
1 teaspoon prepared mustard	1 stalk diced celery
½ teaspoon Salt	
tablespoon lemon juice	

Thanksgiving, 1951

While Mama and Daddy had made breakfast, Sherry, Gail, and I had clasped hands and bounced on our parents' bed. Sherry kept shouting, "Higher, higher." Laughing, we collapsed onto the Beautyrest covered with a beige chenille bedspread. Sherry yelled, "Again." Oblivious to the rumpled covers beneath our bare feet, we aimed to keep up with our mischievous sister. Blond curls flew around her giggling face as Sherry sprang up from sturdy, naked legs.

Age four, and obsessed with *The Lone Ranger* radio broadcast, I never missed a program. There was the thunderous pounding of hooves as the *William Tell Overture* crescendoed into our living room. I could almost smell the smoke as the sound of shots erupted, and visualized bandits falling from their mounts.

Listening, I rocked in my favorite chair while watching Mama and Daddy prepare the Thanksgiving meal; and daydreamed of them and us three sisters enjoying turkey, stuffing, cranberry sauce, and pumpkin pie. Over breakfast Mama had said, "I'll save pie dough for you girls to roll. Gail and Sherry, you can help Judy. Sprinkled with cinnamon sugar and baked...yummy."

Suddenly, there was a THUD, a loud screech of brakes, and the sound of long skidding on gravel. This came from the road below, drowning out the radio. I stopped rocking and looked ahead. My parents quit working and turned towards the kitchen side window. They hesitated and peered through the glass.

A man shouted, "Mr. Johnson. Better come down here. It's your kids."

Mama and Daddy sprung out of the door. Confused, I rose, stumbled from the chair, and began to cry. What had happened? I got to the window, but even standing on tiptoe and stretching I was not tall enough to see. What? What?

I stood under the kitchen window. Bright headlights beamed up. Shadows jumped in the room as the cars moved. Occasionally I heard shouts and murmurings. Nothing was familiar. Not one voice. I could not imagine what was unfolding below. Someone said, "We'll use my car…there…ok…careful now…"

I wanted Mama, but it was our neighbor, Marie, who came in and took me in her arms. "There, there, Judy dear," she said over and over as I nestled my tearful face into her unfamiliar bosom.

Returning home from school, Gail, Sherry, and a twelve-year-old neighbor girl had been let off at the bus stop below. I was excited waiting for my older sisters to return so that we could start rolling the promised pie dough. These had been my thoughts as I listened to the *Lone Ranger*, and my sisters were probably thinking the same as they ran to cross the road. They could not have heard the truck coming around the curve. The oldest girl remained at the bus stop, and only suffered a torn coat. Sherry was a little ahead of Gail when the truck hit.

Daddy thought he had been called out to retrieve our kid goats. He stood at the top of the thirty-foot bank shocked by the scene below. His children and their tin lunch pails were splayed on the pavement. The young driver of the transfer truck stood with feet apart, firmly planted on the road beside my still sisters. He gazed up at Daddy, shaking his head and holding up his hands, saying, "They just ran out in front of me."

Daddy came down the bank with Mama. What happened after that moment? The accident was never mentioned in the family.

I gleaned a little from overheard conversations and murmurs from the neighbors. Sherry, aged seven, had been struck in the back of the head and died instantly. Her body was removed to the Anchorage Funeral Chapel with Mama riding along. Gail was taken to Air Force Hospital with Daddy, and then moved by ambulance to Anchorage Providence Hospital. Daddy requested last rites administered for both girls—feeling guilty that he had not had them christened at birth. He had been raised a Lutheran by Swedish immigrant parents; Daddy now had my sisters baptized as Lutherans. Mama made no attempt to interfere even though neither church nor religion had been part of her German American upbringing.

Gail had a fractured skull; broken wrist, nose, and teeth; and lay unconscious for three days. Gail told me later that when she woke, Mama was by the bed, and Gail saw the immediate relief in her eyes. Gail asked, "Where is Sherry?" Mama said, "Home. She is home, Gail." Gail began to cry sensing that this was untrue. Mama tried to comfort her.

Mama, held up on one side by Daddy and on the other by his best army buddy, Ed Snyder, watched Sherry's coffin lowered into the frozen ground. I saw Mama's breath in the frigid air and tears roll down her distraught face. She struggled to hold up her head as her tears fell onto her severe black clothing. This was the first time that I had seen Mama since that horrible afternoon when my *Lone Ranger* program was interrupted.

With no Lutheran minister in the community, the Pentecostal one from Chugiak was asked to conduct the service. Gail and Sherry had attended Sunday school in his church. If Daddy was late picking them up, my sisters would return home telling me how terrified they became when church service began and members of the congregation started crying, shouting, and carrying on with "fits."

At the cemetery I stood shivering in my boots and lined wool coat, watching and wishing it to be over. I looked at the crowd and felt uncertain, alone. Adults huddled, glancing at Mama and sometimes at me; but most stood with downcast eyes, wiping away the occasional tear. Snow started to fall and intensified my chill. Snowflakes collected and transformed the grievers into monsters masked by low riding white hats and ice cloaks. Gail was in the hospital. Sherry? Daddy said that she would be here. Where was she? Why was I not allowed to see her? Awkwardly holding my hands together, I shut my eyes.

The winter's first snowfall a few days before the accident had provided my sisters and me with outdoor play. The three of us had rolled balls of snow in front of the house. My ball became so heavy that Gail and Sherry helped me by pushing on each side. The snow scrunched. It was cold on my tongue, but immediately melted for gulping down. "Enough," Gail said. "Good," Sherry agreed falling backwards and laughing. Moving her arms and legs sideways, she shouted, "Snow angel." Gail and I fell back and imitated Sherry. Together we stacked our three large snowballs. Mama and Daddy stuck in a carrot for the nose, raisins for the eyes and mouth, and wrapped a red woolen scarf around the neck.

Here at the funeral, Mama's layers protected her from the frigid temperatures, but not from her parents' decision to remain thousands of miles away in their retirement home in sunny Florida. All I can assume is that Grandfather Dabbert's estranged relationship with his daughter for marrying Daddy would not allow him to board a plane, even with the death of one of his granddaughters. Mama told me many times that her father gave people one chance and that was it. His first impression of Daddy was of a happy-go-lucky, worthless individual—and his opinion never changed. Not to attend his granddaughter's funeral, and to forbid his wife from going, showed how deep the hatred went.

In a heavy black coat and hat, the preacher read the "Twenty-third Psalm." The comforting words did not seem to penetrate Mama's grief because she kept up a relentless lament. She told me later that when the "holy roller" preacher ended the service by speaking in tongues, she was overwhelmed with irritation.

Back home, I remained confused and tiptoed around trying not to disturb Mama. As her youngest, before, she had cared for me closely. Afterward, my grief was more silent than hers. Was Sherry gone forever? Mama brushed away my questions. Mama mourned Sherry by spending time alone, often reading.

Daily, for three months, she drove the eighteen miles to Anchorage and back to visit Gail in the hospital. Mama would drop me at Jim and Marie McDowell's, who were neighbors and friends. They ran the Moose Horn Garage and Café down the highway from the end of our drive. Marie waited on customers with fried eggs and hash browns, and smilingly encouraged me to drink my bottle of root beer and finish the picture in my coloring book.

I watched Jim pump gas, clean windshields, and check the oil in cars. He also worked on engines; thus, the clanking of tools as he tinkered over the motors of Ford, Chevys, and Willis Jeeps. The forecourt reeked of gasoline and oil. It was a delicious smell drawing me as close to the gas pumps as Jim allowed. People emerged from their cars to make a pit stop, grab a meal, and use the facilities. From these customers I would get a quick "hello," or maybe, "nice picture" when I was sitting inside.

Gail had to have numerous surgeries, bones reset, and a new tear duct. Her body healed after three months and she returned home. Immediately, nine-year-old Gail was a witness in court with Mama and Daddy. My parents sued the twenty-three-year-old driver of the truck.

The Highway Patrol Officers reported that witnesses stated that the truck was not traveling at an excessive rate of speed, but they did believe the vehicle had faulty brakes. The driver said that he saw the girls on the left, and tried to pull to the right, but a parked car blocked him. Sherry was hit in the front of the truck and dragged a short distance while the rear end of the truck struck Gail as it sideswiped the car. The truck came to a stop several hundred feet beyond the point of impact. After two days, a jury of five women and one man found the death of Sherry Lee Johnson to be due to an unavoidable accident.

I rocked in my chair waiting for Gail. She came in silently weeping so I left her alone in the alcove that she had shared with Sherry. The legal formality of the court procedures made it hard for Gail and Mama as they were forced to relive the painful seconds when Sherry died and our lives were changed forever.

How Mama coped I do not know except I saw that Daddy held her tearful face and trembling body against his shoulder much of the time. She received no counseling. Comforting words from her own mother came in letters. There were no telephone calls. More than once she completely lost control of her emotions, grabbing plates off the breakfast table and smashing them onto the floor. Tears flowed down her face as she broke into mournful sobs.

She looked at Daddy and screamed, "You bastard. You couldn't even go down and take their hands to cross the road. God, my God. I can't bear it." Gail and I froze and then started crying. Gail said to Mama, "Don't hurt Daddy." He held Mama while we swept up the broken pieces. I was confused and did not understand until years later that Mama was consumed by guilt and lasting grief.

Mama and Daddy refused to talk about the accident—sidestepping my repeated question: "Where is Sherry?" We were forbidden to walk along the main highway. They made Gail and me take the back road, which was up the hill behind our five acres in Chugiak, to McDowell's store for groceries and cigarettes. I worried that I would fall when stepping in narrow car tracks in deep snow with my small feet. The dark Alaskan winter was made even darker by large trees blocking out light. I raced when sent out by myself in summer because I imagined being chased by a stranger, a moose, or even a bear.

The following summer my brother Jerry was born. Mama and Daddy were delighted with a son with blue eyes and light blond hair. Daddy picked him up and declared, "A Swedish towhead." Mama had knitted blue booties and a hat while she was pregnant— hoping. Marie and Jim and other neighbors brought baby clothes for THE boy.

Best of all was Daddy's announcement at the dinner table one evening. "We'll be making a long overdue trip to visit our families. I'll buy a new Willys Jeep in January to make the drive to Chicago. We'll help Grandpa Johnson celebrate his 88th birthday, and Judy's sixth. Then we'll drive onto Florida. Hopefully, Grandpa Dabbert will make us welcome."

Grandpa Gus Johnson treated me to Swedish pancakes for my sixth birthday. Despite the loss of his farm and his wife going into a mental hospital, he showed us how to make these thin pancakes which have remained a comfort food in our family.

My Dabbert grandparents were very hospitable in a different way. I noticed Grandpa Dabbert spoke less to Daddy than to the rest of us. Daddy promised to send wild Alaskan blueberries to Grandma because she said they were recommended in her diabetic diet. Grandpa frowned and said nothing. No blueberries were sent on our return home although we picked plenty, froze them, and made blueberry jam.

I followed Gail, creeping around in our grandparents' home looking into bedrooms. She startled me when turning to me and saying, "Maybe Sherry didn't die; maybe she was sent here to get better. Why should I live and not Sherry?" At six years of age I did not realize that Gail, like Mama, was also harboring overwhelming grief and guilt. Although Mama was with her from the moment

Gail opened her eyes after the three-day coma, I am not sure whether they discussed the accident—we never did as a family.

The radio played constantly when we returned home to Chugiak. One morning the song, *Cry*, came on while we were all in the kitchen. Johnnie Ray's words resonated as my parents prepared lunch.

"If your heartaches seem to hang around…go on and cry."

Mama walked to the window and said, "Every time I look below, I can't help think about that dreadful day."

Daddy stopped peeling a potato, put down the knife, and walked over to Mama. He wrapped both arms around her; pulled her to his chest; and said, "Yes, it's too much for us here, isn't it?" Their cheeks touched and with eyes tightly shut, they mournfully swayed to the rest of the song.

My parents had settled in Alaska as newlyweds. The war brought them to Anchorage, and afterwards, to Chugiak. There, nine years later, they received the deed for their free Government land. They had many friends in the community. Mama was instrumental in getting Chugiak School built, and Daddy naming the town. The trifling court settlement, which had been paid to Mama and Daddy as a result of the accident, was used to buy a piano for the Chugiak School. Sherry was commemorated on a plaque there. Gail received a few hundred dollars.

But, their decision to leave Chugiak remained firm. We made the trip to Florida and Chicago, and then we moved.

All-Purpose Crepe Batter
(Makes 10 to 12 crepes)

3 eggs   Dash salt
2 cups/9 oz./250 grams flour   1 pint milk
2 oz./¼ cup vegetable oil

Combine ingredients in blender jar and blend for about 1 minute or until smooth. Refrigerate 1 hour before cooking in a crepe pan. Serve rolled up with vanilla ice cream in the middle and sliced strawberries and whipped cream on top.

Moving On

I was relieved when Daddy pulled over to the lookout beauty spot on the top of the hill overlooking Homer. We were on the way to our new home. I could see my new life ahead. My legs ached from sitting so long in the back, and I had my usual car sickness. Yesterday was worse as we had driven six hours from Chugiak to Clam Gulch. We were guests in the home of the Howard Mc-Claughlin's, who were family acquaintances from army days. Their house and the general store with Post Office on the highway, appeared to be in the middle of nowhere. "Don't people live in Clam Gulch?" I asked.

"They do, but they are homesteaders…way back from the road," Daddy replied.

We left Chugiak to divorce ourselves from the accident site and to move the family on to the future. Mama was still on edge after Sherry's death. My parents walked away from their five acre home-site, but had every intention of acquiring more land in their new location.

This morning we drove another 90 minutes over bumpy gravel road—often like a washboard with us kids in the back being bounced around like dirty laundry in a washing machine. I pushed the front seat forward as Mama got out with toddler Jerry. The jump down onto dusty ground was Heaven. I was able to stand and stretch my legs, but I was irritated when the wind blew my unruly curls into my face. Gail had no such problem with her pigtails. The morning ritual was for her to sit erect on a high stool so that Mama could section her thick hair using a rattail comb, and with strong hands, braid two waist-long French plaits. "Ouch. Pulling," Gail would say.

"Then hold still," Mama replied.

Daddy and Mama walked forward with Jerry from the car. Looking over the town of Homer which was nestled along the steep hills of the bay, Mama swept out her arm and exclaimed,

"Artists come to paint this." Its blue waters and reflective skies inspired many artists. Mountains ascended from the ocean depths to soaring peaks, with snow lingering and one glacier prominent. "That narrow strip of land stretching out into the bay is called 'the Spit,'" Daddy said.

Spit…what a stupid name, I thought at age six.

"Oh…fishing boats coming in," Gail said, and walked closer to the edge of the 300 foot bluff.

"Get back, Gail," Mama warned.

"They are loaded with pink salmon—it's August," Daddy added, as he walked back to the car.

We drove down the hill into town, curious and eager to find a place to live. I saw a mixture of frame, cement block, and log structures making up the school, stores, churches, bars, and houses along the main street. After a five mile drive to the end of the windy Spit and back, Daddy said, "I am going to talk to the pastor we met as he may remember your mama and I from our previous trip."

"There's only one thousand here. I remember his church being across from the hardware store on the main street," Mama said.

Daddy set up his land-surveying office in our rental home in the parsonage on Pioneer Avenue—a gravel road. I had my own room upstairs, as did Gail, and one for Jerry. Each room opened to the next because there were no doors and no hall. The center walls around the stairs were covered with pliable Celotex board. The layout of the upstairs provided little privacy or secrets between us kids.

Gail quickly settled into fifth grade. Mama volunteered at the public library, taking along Jerry and me. The building was cold in winter so I kept my coat buttoned. I helped by entertaining Jerry, but at the same time watched and listened to the adults. People came in for a book and to chat which gave Mama the opportunity to get acquainted with a few in the community. Mama read stories to us between customers. I remember being frightened by listening to *Grimms' Fairy Tales*…three drops of blood from an old mother's fingers that had been cut by a knife and let to fall onto a white cloth.

Mama had frequent outbursts. Once, she hit the sharp corner of the built-in dining cabinet with her hip trying to get around to the table. "Damn this ill-conceived piece of junk. It will kill me yet. I'm black and blue." Daddy, with only a few forceful movements using a saw retrieved from his metal box under the stairs, removed the obstacle as if it was a rotten tree limb. "Thank God," Mama said rubbing her hip.

Looking back, I realize she was a very frustrated human being. Losing Sherry had been almost too much for her. With the loss, Mama carried the burden of guilt. She had not gone to the bus stop to take the hands of Gail and Sherry to cross the road that fatal day. Her despair was to be communicated in endless bickering and fault finding.

The 12th of January, Daddy said after dinner as we were leaving the table, "It would have been Sherry's birthday today." Spontaneously, I started singing "Happy birthday to you..." His hand reached over, and I felt an immediate stinging slap on my face. Gail went quiet, but there was Mama's,

"My God, Judy. Never..." This was the only mention of Sherry or the accident throughout my childhood and for decades following.

The year after we settled in Homer, I started first grade. School was less than a mile away, and Gail and I walked the short distance back and forth with friends. I met Tania Uminski on the way down Pioneer Avenue which was the town's main street. Tania was of Polish decent and her mother was from Chicago like mine. She was slim and tall for her age, with blond hair. Our walking was helpful to Mama because my younger brother, Brent, had been born. She had flown twenty minutes across the bay by bush plane to give birth to him in Seldovia since Homer lacked a hospital. Seldovia was a twenty minute plane journey away and was made up mostly of king crab fishermen and their families.

Another boy was an additional blessing for my parents. We were now a family of two boys and two girls. Brent was a little darker blond than towhead Jerry, but still his blue eyes and smiles won us over; and he received lots of cuddles from all the family as we sang to him—Daddy in Swedish.

"Two sons are going to be a big help on our future 160 acre homestead," Daddy said as he smiled at Mama. I began wanting more time to myself and friends, but now had Brent to watch at times as well as Jerry.

There was daily grocery shopping at the Homer Cash Store. The owner, Mrs. Walli, was a friend and an old-timer with strong political views. In her loose fitting shirtwaist dress, she amply filled a chair, with hips protruding as she leaned across our table to "guide" Daddy on imminent issues before the Public Utility District. He had been elected to this, the town's governing board. Mrs. Walli and Daddy devoured freshly baked brownies with coffee in the process as Mama hovered, served, sitting for a few minutes, and jumping up to put my brothers to bed. She resented the political entertaining and, increasingly, the small town mentality of Homer with her family on display.

I heard her mention homesteading to Daddy after these evenings saying, "Getting more free Government land is what we should do."

Daddy listened and said, "The surveying business must be established first."

Mrs. Margaret Anderson was president of the PUD board, and she and Daddy engaged in endless political conversations. These were not only at the PUD office in the Fire Department on Pioneer Avenue. Margaret and husband Fred lived with their two young children in a comfortable home with a flush toilet—we had an outhouse—and regularly invited us Johnsons and a few other families on Saturday. These evenings we enjoyed home-prepared foods of salmon, halibut, moose, mashed potatoes and gravy, plenty of vegetables, salads, and desserts served buffet style. Each family contributed by bringing a specially prepared recipe.

Margaret's and Daddy's banter and laughter, along with political points, rose above the rest of our chatter.

Then, wow, the easy friendship was blown apart. Daddy returned from surveying one afternoon saying, "I would like to give Margaret that ivory polar bear that I brought back from St Lawrence Island, Ruth."

Mama flew into a rage crying and shouting, "You gave it to me.

It was made for me. You bastard. Bastard. I barely coped with Gail, Sherry, and Judy all those months you were gone... melted snow for water. Without the neighbors...what would have I done? God, oh God. I can't bear this. I want to leave. Go to my parents." She rushed into their bedroom weeping. Daddy put the artifact back down with a thud. The tiny ivory salmon dropped down from the bear's mouth.

Mama retained the ivory bear and became more determined to leave Homer. I do not think the Andersons were made aware of Daddy's intensions to re-gift the ivory piece. It was beyond my understanding at the time, but in later years I realized the deep hurt Mama felt with Daddy's need to please Margaret, even to the point of giving her the handcrafted St Lawrence gift. I heard Mama's repeated threats of fleeing to my Dabbert grandparents. Would she take us kids? This thought lingered and worried me. I smelled strands of hair from the right side of my head. The curls straightened as I stretched them against my nose, and dampened them slightly by the vapour from puffing at them through my mouth. My dishwater blond curls became unbalanced: one side bouncy waves and the other straight as a pencil. Daddy asked me once, "Judy, are you nervous? My helper said that may be why you smell your hair."

My reply was to lean sideways on one foot, and look down. I did not discuss Mama's outbursts with Gail, Daddy, or my close friend, Tania Uminski. Jerry and Brent were still too young to pick up family tensions and seemed oblivious to all but their own play.

We lived in the rented parsonage for six years, but throughout this entire period Mama encouraged Daddy to search for a suitable 160 acres that could be claimed from the Federal Government. This was in addition to his land surveying with Mama helping with secretarial and accounting duties.

The 4th of October, 1957, even remote Alaska was excited by our expanded horizons—up into space. Daddy said, "Ha, we thought the Russians were way behind us, but look. They are the first into space." The Soviet Union had launched *Sputnik*. While others followed it on radio, Daddy spotted it with his transit—the main surveying instrument. The Space Race began.

That evening I was sent to Mrs. Walli's store for ice cream. We would celebrate men's achievements by sprucing up our usual diet of meat and potatoes, a diet which was not unlike the ordinary Russian workers whom I had learned about in my school *Weekly Reader*, except we also enjoyed vegetables and, tonight, ice cream. The ice cream was special because we had no refrigerator, and our freezer was a locker across the street rented from the hardware store owners.

Despite living a life not dissimilar from an ordinary Russian who did not enjoy the perks of Communist Party membership and the Russians conquering space before we did, I was convinced that being an American was best. I was taught that the U.S. democracy laid down by our Founding Fathers—George Washington, Ben Franklin, Thomas Jefferson, and others who had written the Constitution—was the greatest in the world. From this document our Government was formed making us the most fortunate people on the earth. Even in the territory of Alaska, we stood with pride in school assemblies, right hand over heart for the National Anthem. I remember Tania, Mary, and I standing together and looking straight at the flag, reciting the familiar words.

Gail and I were assigned after school and weekend chores to keep the house running. I washed the dishes. Sometimes I scrubbed and waxed the linoleum living room and kitchen floors on my own initiative when Mama was out. I sought the praise and adoration she gave Gail. My older sister did most things right. She was given a bike and took good care of it. The bike was a girl's English racer that was passed on to me. I fell trying to ride it because it was too big, and I could only stand rather than sit on the high seat. I damaged it with frequent falls. On and on...I the destroyer, and Gail the daughter who took care of her things. When waxing the floors, seeking Mama's praise, I failed to move the easy chair or footstool as I rushed to finish. Mama's frown and "Oh dear" dampened my joy.

A punishment my parents frequently employed was to withdraw my dessert. That was terrible because even though I was skinny, I loved homemade delicacies—lemon meringue pie my favorite. She or Daddy made a firm decision to hold my serving back after I had committed this or that crime, but eventually relented. Mama softened and said, "Ok, your Daddy and I want you to have this," as she pushed the pie in front of my tearful face.

Sometimes I pleased my parents but, more often, I was in trouble. Possibly I was regarded as very assertive, especially for a girl. I was interested in grabbing every opportunity. A day during Homer elementary years stands above the rest. Tania Uminski, my close Polish American buddy, and I were walking home from school. We parted at her parents' small department store where they lived behind the store. She had to be punctual for her piano lesson that day. I continued on alone. The Homer Drug Store was just down from our rental house, and there was a shortcut over fallen weathered logs almost to our door. My daily habit was to walk into the small store, saunter around peering at this and that, and "lift" a couple of Hershey bars from the rack by the door when making my exit.

This went on for a time without mishap…then Mr. Myhill, the owner, caught me. "Hold on there, Sister," came his firm voice projecting from a reddening face with furrowed brow, crowned by receding grey hair. He peered down at me from behind the counter. My eyes met his, and I turned to drop the confiscated goods back into their rightful box. He thanked me. I left with unsteady knees and a pounding heart while feeling his eyes follow me out the door which, even with a slam, refused to close. Dashing recklessly along the logs, I arrived home. Stepping in by the back door, I worried that my anxiety would show.

Mama was preparing dinner in the kitchen and asked me to wash my hands before setting the table. Jerry was playing in the living room. "Nrrrrrrr" came from him as he moved the toy truck by hand on "a road" in front of the easy chair and around the ottoman. Brent was blabbering and throwing soft toys around in his playpen under a window next to Daddy's drawing board. Gail came in carrying a load of books. After a brief hello to Mama and me, she ran up to her room to study. Her study time was usually interspersed with trying on clothes and reading the *Ladies Home Journal* or looking at patterns in *McCall's* and *Simplicity* magazines. I would never rat on Gail—my idolized older sister.

She had told me that she would like to learn to sew. "It would mean so many more clothes."

Daddy came in looking tired after romping through brush surveying. He and his helper had needed to chop and use the chainsaw to remove trees in the way of a boundary. He said, "Saw Myhill with a couple of his boys pulling away from the post office as I drove up. He rolled down his window and asked me to come by after dinner. Wonder if he needs a survey?" Daddy said to Mama. "Maybe so," she replied. I gulped and looked down at my hands as I laid the cutlery beside each plate. I sat at the table fidgeting and pushed my meat, boiled potatoes, and broccoli this way and that as the rest of the family ate and chatted. Mama served the cherry Jello dessert, and then Gail and I cleared the table.

Daddy roared our Willys Jeep up to the house after seeing Mr. Myhill. Shaking and trembling with fear, I knew what was coming. He yelled, "WHERE is Judy?" His feet thudded loudly as he strode into the living room. His belt was in his hand as he put me over his knee and walloped my behind. I cried and cried. It had hurt, but worse was being discovered. What a fool I was. I was sad that I had done it, but even more upset that I had been found out.

Daddy shook his head and took me in his arms as Mama hovered. "You can have candy bars, Judy," he said. "Just ask for money beforehand." I knew that Mama would not back him up on this, but I agreed anyway. I hated the embarrassment not only for myself, but for the family. Especially I hated Mr. Myhill. His son, Dale, was in my class...would he be told? If so, who else would HE tell? He chatted with most in our class and sometimes with me even though we were not close friends. Afterwards, Daddy rinsed as I did my usual dishwashing. He hugged me as we finished, and said, "You know that I love you."

Mr. Myhill must have kept my thievery to himself as no one at school mentioned it. In future years I would achieve positive recognition not only in Homer, as "Miss Homer," but statewide when pictured and written up in the *Anchorage Daily News*. If Mr. Myhill read the article, he might have chuckled remembering our little encounter in his shop during my childhood.

Daddy happily announced one spring, "I have taken seven and a half acres on the East Hillside. It is in lieu of payment for a subdivision."

42

"Subdivision?" five-year-old Jerry asked.

"I broke the big original homestead into lots for the owner to sell. I took some of those lots as payment for my survey," Daddy said.

The land had a stunning view of the bay and mountains; the blue of the bay being reflected on good days by the blue of the sky. The missionary log cabin on the property was too small for our family, and was the only house on the acreage that Daddy had acquired, but Gail and I played in it. We investigated the cupboards and found potent curry powder. "It is used in Indian cooking, but such foods give your daddy heartburn," Mama told us as she threw every speck of the "toxic" spice into the compost heap.

Below the cabin, Daddy rototilled the firm earth to loosen the dark soil for planting. Under duress, Gail and I helped plant rows of potatoes and vegetables. Afterwards, Mama said, "Each of you can make a flower garden." I hoed out a heart shape area hacking through the long grass, weeds, and firm earth for Daddy to till. Shaking the packet of mixed flower seeds into my hand, I then scattered them over the freshly prepared ground and lightly tapped in with both hands before watering. Blooms burst forth in a few weeks. "Well done. Forget-me-nots and poppies. How pretty," Mama said as she, Daddy, and Gail admired my fruitful efforts; perhaps I was good at something.

Summer changed to winter. At Christmas Daddy's gift to Mama, Gail, and me was an electric Singer sewing machine. Mama purchased patterns from Uminski's Department Store and ordered fabric. She had a special dress sewn for Gail and one for me by Easter. Gail soon was making some of her own clothes having asked Mama for advice. I looked forward to being mature enough to do the same.

Aged ten, I joined the Four H Group of America, a hands-on club for children based on farming, sewing, and cooking; and I received guidance to make my first skirt and matching top from checked blue and maroon light wool fabric. The white collar and cuffs were beyond me so Mama took over. All members entered completed garments for the end of summer Homer Fair. I received a white ribbon with a handwritten evaluation from the judges: "Looks like a different person put on the collar and cuffs from the one who made the rest of the two piece garment." It was embarrassing to have been found out again, but my parents beamed with pride at my completed outfit.

School continued with me often visiting back and forth with girlfriends. I and the rest of the family had moved on since the accident—except Mama. Her outbursts continued and nothing could heal the loss of Sherry for her.

Soon, a boy would enter my life.

Mama's Chocolate Brownies

In a double boiler, melt the chocolate and butter in the top pan over simmering water.

Preheat oven to 180C/350F/gas mark 4; Line a 20cm/8 inch with grease-proof paper

Ingredients:
120g/5 oz./½ cup plus 1 tablespoon unsalted butter or baking margarine
120g/5 oz. dark or plain chocolate, broken into marked squares
65g/½ cup plain flour
1 teaspoon baking powder
180g/6 oz./1 cup caster sugar
2 eggs
1 teaspoon vanilla

Margaret Anderson's Angel Food Delight

Prepare an angel food cake from a cake mix, using a tube pan for baking. Cool.

Slice strawberries and sweeten with small amount of sugar if desired.

Prepare chocolate sauce for spooning over servings of a slice of cake, heaped with prepared strawberries, and topped with a bit of the sauce.

Chocolate Sauce

Combine and stir in a small heavy pot until smooth:
2 bars (100g each) Belgian chocolate;
50g plain chocolate;   150 ml double cream

Lemon Meringue Pie

First prepare a single baked short crust pie shell.

To make the lemon curd, combine by stirring together in a 2 quart or 2 liter saucepan:

1½ cups/11 oz./325g granulated, white sugar

6 tablespoons cornstarch

¼ teaspoon salt

Gradually stir in:

½ cup/4 fl. oz. cold water

½ cup/4 fl. oz. lemon juice

When well incorporated, add, blending:

4 beaten egg yolks

2 tablespoons of butter

With constant stirring, gradually add:

1½ cups/l2 fl. oz. boiling water

Bring the mixture to the boil while continuing to stir. When it starts to thicken, reduce the heat and let it just simmer one minute. Remove from heat and stir in roughly grated zest from one lemon. Pour into the baked, cooled, pie shell and top with the soft meringue from following recipe. Bake as directed. Let cool before serving.

Soft Meringue Topping

Ingredients:

4 egg WHITES, at room temperature,

¼ teaspoon cream of tartar

100g/4 oz./½ cup caster sugar

½ teaspoon vanilla

In a mixing bowl, beat egg whites and cream of tartar on medium speed until soft peaks form.

Add sugar, 1 tablespoon at a time, beating after each addition.

Add vanilla and beat on high speed until peaks are stiff but not dry.

Spread the meringue over pie filling, securing it to the edge of the crust. Make a spiral design for fun. Bake in a hot 220C/450F oven for 5 minutes or until golden brown.

Love and Loss

He pushed open the door on day one, stood behind all of us seated students and asked, "Is this fourth grade?"

Miss Edwards, the heavyset teacher from South Carolina drawled, "Weell, yeas it is."

"Good. I'm Jack Collie from Illinois, and I'm in this class."

Jack's dark hair, twinkling eyes, ease of manner, and cocky smile captivated me then and for years to come. He was from Mama's home state, and charmed his way into our lives just as confidently as he stepped into the classroom that first day. He won marble games played with other boys, and his pockets bulged as proof. In front of the class he would keep our attention whether reading a book report or telling about the latest cowboy film he had seen. From the beginning we joked and laughed with each other.

One day in spring, he sauntered down the classroom aisle to catch the bus; but side stepped other students, and made a beeline to me. He smiled as he dropped a folded paper onto my desk. "Bye, Judy," he said, and he was gone.

Inside was a handwritten message: "Judy, this is for you. Love, Jack." A silver-plated pocketknife on a chain fell comfortably into my hand. Surprised—and delighted—I skipped home.

I wore it around my neck underneath my dress or pullover for a few days. Sadly, I lost Jack's treasured gift walking home from school after only a couple of weeks. Retracing my steps to hunt for it, I was met by the huge Road Commission grading machine with blade down. The driver moved along to scrape the gravel and dirt to fill the potholes on the road. Heartbroken, I slowly returned home. Gone was Jack's proclamation of our love. I was sad that I had lost the knife and long chain; and did not tell anyone, even Jack. He must have wondered why I did not wear it, but never asked me. In fact, this should have weighed on my mind, but I was too busy being naughty.

I was often in trouble in fourth grade, and Miss Edwards called in Mama for a conference. It worried me but Mama told me that although my behavior was often bad at home, she thought I was better in public; and the teacher did not impress her. Mama showed up for the appointment, but the teacher failed to. The issue was dropped.

Jack and I were promoted to fifth grade with the other students commencing in September with the one exception of Edgar, a boy I had hardly noticed, but would remember forever. His family had moved away. Edgar was popular: a slim, eager, blond-headed boy. His desk was in front of mine; and if I lost my pencil, he had one for me and vice versa. He could shoot marbles, play baseball, or horse around with Jack and the other guys, but with a smile and low chuckle rather than boisterous outbursts. I remember him in a beige soft-looking wool pullover with hands in jean pockets—his eyes looking full of eager pleasure as he crouched around a marble game between Jack and Stevie Walli on the dirt playground. I stood waiting my turn between Mary Rearden and Tania Uminski in the girls' jacks game nearby. Edgar slapped Jack on the back when Jack won a big glass Cats Eye Blue agate. He proceeded to raise Jack's hand and hug him like a brother. Other boys joined in the hugging.

Mary Rearden had moved to Alaska from California, where her grandmother remained. Mary had dishwater blond hair, was of medium build, and wore glasses like Tania.

The school year ended in May with a class picnic at Green Timbers on the Spit. We each devoured our packed lunches, and then played chase and hide and seek around the spruce trees. The day ended with a bus returning us to school and short term good byes for we all were confident of meetings during the weeks ahead.

Then Daddy returned home late one summer day and pulled Mama, Gail, and me aside. "There was a tragic accident in yesterday's storm. The family fishing boat of one of your classmate's sank, Judy. Edgar...search parties are out."

"He is only a kid like me. Ten years old is too young to be working on a fishing boat in Cook Inlet," I uttered.

Mama's reaction was, "Oh, my sainted aunt. How terrible. The poor woman...a son and her husband both missing."

Daddy continued, "His older brother would have gone but was sick, so Edgar took his place. The storm came up and got bad...prevented them getting back."

The concern shown by my parents paradoxically increased my misery. With the benefit of hindsight, coping with my friend Edgar's drowning gave me fortitude. The hidden seed germinated within me after my sister Sherry's death and grew into a tree after Edgar was swept out to sea.

I think Mama and Daddy would have hugged me if I had hung around. I was confused and unsure of what to do. We were not a demonstrative family. With German and Scandinavian heritage, we physically held back. We made up for the lack of kisses upon greeting one another and impromptu embraces with preparing special foods for a loved one who had a special occasion or whom we wanted to reward. I was preparing brownies from Mama's recipe at age nine.

I climbed the stairs and curled like an infant on my bed. Gail stood at a window in her room looking out to the street and neighbors as she rested both arms on the sill. She turned and hesitantly came into my room, sat on the edge of the bed, and put one hand on my shoulder.

"Terrible about Edgar, Judy. Terrible. Sad. So unfair."

My sister then hugged me close, lingering with her arms holding me. I felt the beating of her heart and was comforted by her physical warmth. More than that, I felt Gail completely understood. Just because I was not crying out loud did not mean I was not hurting inside.

Rescuers searched the beaches on foot and the bay in boats for days. His father's body was found tied up in fishing nets that washed to shore. He knew securing himself to the fishing gear was essential for being recovered later, so had done so in the bad storm. Edgar's body was never found. He may have been below deck clinging to his bunk while his father was on deck being tossed about and unable to help his son. At age ten, Edgar likely did not have the knowledge of tying the net around himself so that he would not be lost at sea.

Summer ended and the day came for us to return to school. I

did so, eager to see my friends daily, but unable to forget thoughts about Edgar trapped in the fishing boat.

Mrs. Johnson, our new fifth grade teacher, changed that. Slim in a below-the-knee, blue wool dress she stood by her desk and addressed the class. Her shoulder-length brown hair moved as she looked around taking in each of us. She started with, "I heard that you were an unruly bunch last year. Perhaps that was due to you being housed in the basement of the church up the road, away from the main school."

She did not look as if she believed this explanation. "I expect all of you to behave in my class. I do wish to say a few words about someone on all our minds." She slowly walked to the front of the class, stopped, and then retraced her steps while looking into our attentive faces. There was warmth from her heart and in her eyes as she said, "You have all heard about the death of Edgar. If you need to talk…want to come to me at any time…you can."

Pent up tears rushed to my eyes. I wiped them away with the back of my hands, and through sneaked glances, saw others do the same. She continued to speak about our kind, brave classmate and explained that Edgar's family had left Homer and Alaska to be with relatives "in the south '48." I understood their need to leave as living in The Last Frontier required a strong man as provider.

Mrs. Johnson was not a mother, but this did not stand in the way of her becoming my favorite teacher. From that day, Mrs. Johnson held "Outstanding Teacher" in my memory for what she said then and motivated us to do the remainder of the year. She had virtually no discipline problems with us reputably unruly students. Best of all, she was inspirational. I loved her geography class because it made me more aware of a world beyond the territory of Alaska and the U.S.A. We made maps using plaster of Paris to form mountains on continents, and blue paint to brush expansive seas and oceans.

For the end-of-the-year program, we performed dances of states or countries that interested us. Jack and his friends acted out the Russian Cossack. Jack crouched low and kicked out one leg at a time while keeping arms folded and his head held squarely on his shoulders. His eyes looked straight ahead at the boy in front. He wore a big grin on his face which made me think that he might erupt into laughter at any moment. They danced in a circle and practiced and practiced so that no one toppled on the day. As they stepped alongside me, Jack chanced a quick glance and wink. I smiled and warmth flowed inside.

I led the girls of our class in the Hawaiian hula. Gail and Mama had taken lessons in Chugiak a few months after the death of Sherry. Gail became proficient after we moved to Homer by dancing to records Mama bought. Gail had performed the hula for the entire Homer School student body and was invited to perform in schools up and down the Kenai Peninsula.

"Uminski's will have material and a patterns we need," Mama announced. She sewed green satin bikini tops for me and the other girls in my class. With the help of our mothers, we assembled imitation crepe paper grass skirts. My accomplished sister, Gail, played the record *My Little Grass Shack in Kealakekua, Hawaii*, while demonstrating how to sway our hips gracefully and to move our hands and feet to the music.

That night I rode home with all the family still singing the Hawaiian song and swaying in the jeep:

> I want to go back to my little grass shack in Kealakekua, Hawaii
> I want to be with all the kanes and wahines that I knew long ago
> I can hear old guitars a playing, on the beach at Honaunau
> I can hear the Hawaiians saying *Komo mai no kaua I ka hale welakahao*
> I want to go back to my little grass shack
> In Kealakekua, Hawaii
> Where the humuhumunukunukuapua's
> Go swimming by

The Hawaiian song reminded me of Mama's pineapple upside down cake and the fields of pineapple in Hawaii she had told me about. The friendships formed would become long distance, but songs and dances would not continue.

Life with Gail, Jack, Tania, Mary, and other friends and classmates in Homer, as I knew it, would end. My parents had sold the five-acre home site in Chugiak due to the accident, and ever since had wanted to acquire more of the Government land available. Daddy and Mama had considered homesteading for years. The longer we lived in Homer, the more adamant Mama became to make a land claim and move. She was desperate to leave Homer and to remove Daddy from its politics and Margaret Anderson. The subject came up at the dinner table. "I've had more than enough of entertaining your Public Utility District cohorts," she said. "Homesteading is our escape from this small town. We can sell the land afterwards and make some money."

Daddy looked over at her and nodded in agreement. "You're right, we have to act."

Alaska had become the 49th state that year, and the homesteading rule had changed from it being a territory. It was the last year a claim could be made.

Mama stood and began clearing the table. "Let's look at the Kenai Peninsula map again," she said as she asked Daddy to bring the much creased map to the table.

Pineapple Upside Down Cake

Preheat the oven to 350F/180C. You will need one 9-inch skillet or cake pan.
Ingredients:
20-ounce can of unsweetened pineapple,
9 tablespoons unsalted butter or margarine,
¾ cup/200g packed brown sugar,
7 maraschino cherries,
approximately 12 pecan halves,
2 eggs,
8 tablespoons Buttermilk,
½ teaspoon vanilla,
1 cup/150g plain white flour,
¾ cup/200g white granulated sugar,
1 teaspoon baking powder,
½ teaspoon baking soda, and a dash of salt.

Drain 7 slices of unsweetened pineapple on paper towels.

Place 3 tablespoons unsalted butter or margarine in the skillet or pan; heat to just melted in the oven. Brush to coat sides.

Sprinkle the brown sugar evenly over the melted butter. Arrange the pine-apple slices in the pan, starting with one in the center. Place one maraschino cherry in the center hole of each pineapple slice; and 1 to 2 pecan halves between the slices.

In a small bowl, blend thoroughly:

    2 eggs,

    2 tablespoons Buttermilk,

    ½ teaspoon vanilla.

Sift together:

    1 cup plain white flour,

    ¾ cup sugar,

    1 teaspoon baking powder,

    ½ teaspoon baking soda, and

    a dash salt.

Mix into egg mixture with an electric mixer, on low speed; add 6 table-spoons unsalted butter or margarine, melted, and 6 tablespoons buttermilk. Slowly increase the mixer speed and beat only briefly. Spoon batter over the fruit/nuts in the skillet and spread evenly. Bake 35 minutes in the center of the oven. Use the toothpick doneness test (remove from the oven when the inserted toothpick comes out clean). Cool for about 3 minutes and then loosen sides of cake with a spatula. Invert onto a serving platter, by placing right side of dish over the baked cake, and turning the pan upside down. Delicious on its own or with vanilla ice cream or whipped cream.

Swimming in Porcupline Lake

Homesteading Claim on Porcupine Lake

"I won't go; I won't leave my friends; I want to stay with Gail," I said, stomping my foot and screaming. This did not sway my parents. As I was older now, Daddy and Mama had become Dad and Mom.

School was soon to start the summer of 1959. Dad had initiated the pursuit of "making a claim" on the one hundred and sixty acres he and Mom wanted to homestead in the Alaskan wilderness. At eleven I felt outraged to be uprooted. I was coming up to my teens and looked forward to a busy social life in town, following in the footsteps of my older sister Gail. After school she was with friends sipping sodas in the "Dairy Delight," the town's one burger joint, while playing the latest Connie Francis hits on the jukebox: *Where the Boys Are, Who's Sorry Now, Stupid Cupid,* and *Lipstick on Your Collar.* She hummed and sang the tunes around the house and I joined in. Soon I intended to spin my favorite hits on the same jukebox. However, Mom and Dad had a different plan—they were determined to take up the opportunity for free Government land.

The part of the Kenai Peninsula chosen had many swamps and lakes with billions of mosquitoes. There was a dirt track for a mile and then no road, so Dad's plan was to drive with Gail in our 4 x 4 army surplus dump truck, which had a winch, to the site. He and Mom loaded basic start-up supplies onto the back of the truck including lumber, tent, and food.

Jerry asked, "How will you know where to turn off the highway, Daddy?"

"There is a small log cabin with a green roof exactly at mile point 63.2. That is where we start through the woods."

Mom said, "Don't take all the canned moose. Leave some for us."

Dad replied, "Have Judy run to the store."

"For God's sake, John, I need Judy to help with Jerry and Brent.

I'm still not up to scratch—have only been out of bed for a few days."

They were constantly bickering. In the end, more than enough was on the truck for the few days ahead. At last they were ready. Mom, Jerry, Brent, and I waved Dad and Gail off as they drove onto Pioneer Avenue to begin the sixty-mile journey on gravel road.

Three days later we had not heard a word. Mom was anxious that they had not yet returned.

"I think we had better go investigate," Mom said at breakfast, slumped in her chair wearing her old dressing gown. "We'll drive the Chevy to where they left the highway. From there we'll walk in."

"Do we need boots?"

"Yes, get Jerry and Brent into theirs. It's good weather, but we need jeans and sweatshirts…and put on mosquito dope," she said, rising slowly from the table with her teacup and plate. "Help me, Judy. I'm a bit under the weather."

"Can Scamp come?" I asked. Scamp was our brown Chesapeake retriever.

"Of course. Get him into the back of the car. We won't take the cat though. We'll leave her extra food."

We drove up the highway along the Cook Inlet coast. On the left, blue mountains soared from the ocean. On the right, I could see various shades of green, including abundant grey-barked spruce, silver-birch, and tall mottled cottonwoods. These broke up the stretches of brown swamp. Mom and I rolled down our windows to let out the odor of Scamp's panting breath. He was wedged between Brent and Jerry in the back.

In a couple of hours, we arrived at mile point 63.2 where Dad and Gail had driven the truck off the highway. The log cabin with a green roof was right beside the gravel Sterling Highway. I opened the door, and Scamp leaped out making his way to a tree for a pee.

Getting through the thick forest and wet areas was like following Hansel and Gretel's bread crumb trail. I trudged along and thought back to the bombshell announcement Dad had made at dinner one evening before he took us into the middle of nowhere.

"You kids will love living on Porcupine Lake. Swimming in summer and skating in winter," he said. "I was infatuated by the spot yesterday when I flew in on the pontoon plane. Ideal. Reminds me of Wisconsin."

Brent and Jerry were excited about the adventure. At four and six, they were not leaving behind established friends. Most importantly, they would continue to have each other as playmates. In contrast, I felt wrenched away from my many friends. The fun of easily arranged visits to my home and theirs—all finished. Skipping freely down the street from school to home would be replaced by trudging in and out on this two and a quarter mile rough track through the woods. Running to a shop to pick up something—completely gone. This long, isolated trek through forest and watery terrain would mean even fetching the smallest item would have to be a carefully planned undertaking. With each step I recalled Dad's excited pitch of the great life ahead. "There will be fresh air to fill your lungs, rainbow trout to fish, and beavers to watch." Resentment grew as I became weary winding between thick trees, over bogs, and continually swatting buzzing mosquitoes in spite of heavy doses of smelly repellent.

Poor Mom was walking slowly. She was doing her best to keep up, but was still recovering from something that initially I could not understand. While bedridden, she had called me in for a private talk. Lying under covers and looking weary, her eyes met mine. "I won't be having any more children, Judy. I've lost twins."

I felt embarrassed and remembered the doctor had come to see Mom a few days before. They murmured behind the closed door of my parents' bedroom. He emerged carrying a small newspaper package and made his exit without a glance or word to me. His visit left me wondering about Mom. Gail had whispered, "Miscarriage," but I had never heard the word before and did not want to let my ignorance show.

Mom maintained a concerned cheerfulness trudging along on the rough path. I knew she was worried. There were bears, moose, and even wolves in the woods. We had to sidestep moose droppings which made me think a huge beast with horns could step out of the patch of twisted alders ahead. My own thoughts were still miserable as I sunk into the springy moss with my boots, and nearly stepped out of them when they lodged into the wet ground. Scamp leaped ahead exploring the newly blazed trail.

"They can't be far now," Mom said several times.

The romantic idea of living off the land was closely shared between Mom and Dad. To me it was an outlandish plan. I had learned in school history classes that homesteading claims enabled the western United States to be settled. Probably the ghost of President Abraham Lincoln would jump out from behind the next spruce to congratulate us for taking up his proclamation even in remote Alaska. He had rewarded the Union War veterans with similar tracts of land. Fine for those early pioneers to rough it. Why were my parents so eager for "free land" when it meant hardship for us—and especially for me—in the outback?

We trudged through the forest not seeing even a house or dwelling. I had been told that other homesteaders lived in these woods, but there was no sound of even one family.

We finally reached Porcupine Lake. I felt relief to see the blue sky reflected in the steady movement of waves partially screened by spruce and birch that surrounded the lake—about half mile away. Gail and Dad stopped their work around the tent. They seemed surprised to see us. Dad walked forward and embraced Mom saying:

"My word, you walked all the way…in your condition, Ruth. Hi, kids. Ruth, you amaze me. We're nearly finished. Planned to leave soon."

Mom replied, "I expected you back yesterday. I was worried. So? Show us what you've done. First, can we have a drink? I'm thirsty. Kids?"

"Ok. Need to fill up," he said as he swung the stainless steel bucket and ran down to the lake. He returned with water spilling over the brim as he set it down. "Here…drink up." He dipped and filled tin cups.

I drank mine and felt refreshed. Mom sighed with pleasure. Jerry and Brent swallowed big gulps. We looked out at the lake. There was still a slight breeze making waves. Green lily pads with yellow blossoms grew around the shore. We put down our cups and stepped up to the tent behind Dad and Gail.

"So good…the taste of pure lake water. Like from our spring in Chugiak. But, ok, let's hear about your building," Mom said.

"Come into your canvas palace. Here, at the front window you'll see loons and ducks swimming. There are still a couple of things to finish, of course. We had to make the floor twelve feet square…the size of the tent."

Gail interjected, "Dad and I tramped into the woods scouting small trees for footings. We attacked the woods, and hordes of mosquitoes attacked *us*."

"The chainsaw was priceless," Dad said.

"I chopped off branches. Used a hatchet," Gail said exuberantly. "The smelly pitch oozed everywhere…sticky stuff got all over me. Carried the logs on my shoulder—sweat dripping."

"She worked like a trooper," Dad said, beaming. "Dug and hammered the logs in." He pointed to the shovel and sledge hammer standing in one corner. "We'd cleared the space beforehand."

"Pounding the floorboards over the footings was easy," Gail said as she bent her knees and jumped up and down. Jerry and Brent copied.

"Ha," Brent said confidently. "I can hammer."

Jerry quipped, "You've only used a toy one. I could have used a real hammer. I…"

Gail cut him off, "We struggled for hours setting up the tent over the floor."

Looking at Mom and us kids, Dad said, "I bought the tent from old Nordin. Paid enough. Discovered here that it had rotted in places leaving scraps. What an ordeal. We eventually managed to overlap the pieces to make it watertight. I cussed Nordin. Friend?"

"We slept here," Gail said walking to their sleeping bags on the floor. The wood smell filled the tent."

"I smell it," I said, taking a deep breath.

"It's still in the air," Dad said as he walked to the door of the tent and stepped out.

"Have to tell you about getting in with the truck. Sit." He said, and pointed to the cut logs.

I perched on a stump. Dad, Gail, Jerry, and Brent did the same. Mom stood, leaning against a birch, smiled and nodded for Dad to begin.

He told us that they drove the truck off the road and plunged into winching across swamp and forest. Gail took the hook on the metal cable of the winch and wrapped it around a tree for a pull. The truck moved toward the tree, rolling and heaving over the damp moss and mounds of muskeg which were covered with cranberry bushes. It was necessary to drive slowly over the uneven ground, and at a speed which meant the cable could be attached without tangling on the rolling spindle.

"At just the right moment, I yelled, 'Unhook it. Tie a red flag on the tree.' Gail always sprang to action. I was relieved each time that the winch and tree were strong enough to hold up."

"We went for over a mile after leaving the dirt track. You just walked in on the trail. It took us all day. Finally, we got here," Gail said, getting up from her log stool and looking out at the lake.

"I was exhausted, but went for a swim with Dad. The cool water felt like Heaven. Made my mosquito bites stop itching."

"There was the call of loons swimming. Eerie. Only sound," Dad reflected, getting up to join Gail looking at the lake. The waves kept moving along from shore to shore, ignoring the lily pods proudly emerged in an inner circumference ten feet from land.

"It was 9:30 at night; the sun was setting. The sky lit up in brilliant pinks and flaming oranges that reflected onto our lake," Gail added, stepping back to us.

"We rolled out our sleeping bags here by the fire. I fell right to sleep. A hooting owl woke me."

"I've slept under the stars on moose hunts, but here was Gail's first," Dad said as he walked back to his stool.

"My hair and skin smells of campfire smoke, and..." Gail started.

Jerry and Brent ran off out of earshot. I saw them lift a board onto a stump and began to seesaw.

Dad interrupted, "I must admit that when Gail arrived as a baby...I was happy, but disappointed that our first born was not a boy. Stupid me. She's been better than a son here. Gail has been cooking our food from opened cans on the fire and best of all, rainbow trout from the lake. She helped build a house and cooked, too."

"Brilliant, Gail." Mom said, smiling.

"Oh gosh. Thanks." Gail quipped, beaming, shaking her hair which was now cut short and permed rather than in braids.

"Well, back to work…there are a few things to finish…" Dad turned and motioned for Mom and Gail to follow.

I watched my parents and Gail go, and then ran to join my brothers on the seesaw. I shoved at Jerry saying, "Let me have a turn with Brent."

Brent and I did a short spell of seesawing. "Let's liven things up," I said laughing. I proceeded to slam my end of the board down to the ground and sent Brent flying. He landed on one arm and immediately burst into tears. Jerry and I helped him up and over to our parents as he clutched the injured arm. I kept my head down to hide my fear and shame.

Mom and Dad quickly decided that it was broken and needed a doctor's attention. I was surprised and relieved that my parents did not reprimand me. Perhaps they thought that all energy needed to be saved for the trip ahead. It meant some of us bundling into the truck and the rest walking behind to make the slow journey back to the highway where our car was parked. No winching was required as the load of supplies had been removed from the back of the truck. Plus Dad recognized which spots to avoid. I was pleased to escape, but knew that our labored exit from the wilderness would be temporary.

Hearing Brent whimper in the car as we drove back, I worried that later Mom would really scold me. She might ask Dad to give me the belt. We arrived into town where Brent's broken arm was set. No punishment ensued, and I went to bed and slept soundly. The building project was briefly interrupted, but not forgotten.

Lucky Gail would continue living in our rented house in town where Dad was also keeping the office for his land surveying business. "I can look after myself," she told my parents. This arrangement would enable her to finish school at Homer High. Our parents trusted her. She was five years older than me—my role model, companion, and confidante. We loved sharing secrets, especially those about boyfriends. I had Jack Collie to talk about. He combed his hair in a ducktail like Elvis Presley, grinned at me, and horsed around to gain attention. Jack could leap up and touch his hands to his toes at the drop of a hat. Gail mentioned a few crushes. She showed me outfits that she put together to gain notice of one favored guy or another. Gail had received special glances from boys, held hands, and even kissed. I felt elated when she told me this. At age eleven I had no chance of remaining with her in town. How I would miss my older sister.

Just a few days later, having left Gail behind, we were bombing up the highway in a monstrosity of a green Ford sedan with long-finned taillights. Dad had rented it in Homer as our Chevy was being repaired. I thought we would make a showy and unusual entrance into Tustumena School, filled with pupils whose home-steading vehicles were most likely jeeps or pickup trucks. The school was set back from the road in thick forest. No houses or shops in sight. What would people think when we pulled up to the school?

I was focused on the grim reality ahead. At home Jerry and Brent had each other as playmates, and Mom and Dad worked side by side. Without Gail, I was now alone.

Worried about the classroom organization, I blurted out from the back seat,

"Going to a school with both fifth and sixth grades in a room is like moving backwards."

Dad, confident at the wheel of the enormous car, replied, "Chimney Rock one room schoolhouse in Boyceville, Wisconsin, gave me the best education of my life. Tustumena will be great."

"How can I concentrate studying a lesson while students in the other grade are discussing theirs?"

"You will learn," Dad insisted.

Jerry was entering second grade and voiced no opinion. Brent, at four, would still be at home. No one shared my concerns, my worries—no one to talk to who understood. I felt miserable.

We drove up to an empty school yard and parked. Everyone was already inside. That was a relief. Putting on a brave face, I walked with Mom, Dad, Brent, and Jerry into the modern four-room building. Eager Jerry was welcomed and whisked away by an elderly grey-haired teacher, Mrs. MacLane. The next door down the hall was my classroom. We knocked and pleasant, middle-aged, quiet spoken Mr. Lane introduced himself. Mom, Dad, and Brent made their goodbyes and departed leaving me to enter the room with the teacher.

I was late, apprehensive, and embarrassed. All heads turned to watch as I took my seat at the one empty desk remaining on the sixth grade side. My wavy hair fell around my shoulders, but all these girls had long hair pulled up in ponytails that bobbed up and down as they gave me shy smiles and their names. Linda stood out with large almond eyes, slightly darker skin, and dark hair. Dad had told me that the daughter of his surveying helper from a Kenai job would be in my class. We called all Alaskan natives *Eskimos*, although this family was of Aleut, Athabaskan, Norwegian, and Swedish heritage. The boys made their introductions and seemed rather subdued compared to the guys in Homer.

Lunchtime arrived, and I was the odd one out. The girls asked me to join them in a corner. I felt horror as they pulled out their sandwiches. All had commercially sliced white bread, fresh from the plastic bag, cut into matching triangles. I had Mom's home-made French baguette, sliced into thin misshaped rounds. With utmost care I left my humiliating sandwich inside the waxed paper wrapper so they would not see that it was home baked.

The chatter around their chewing was about "Rawhide," a popular television program. Linda giggled and asked,

"Mary, did you see Rowdy charge ahead of Wishbone's horse? Isn't he handsome? Oh, oh." Giggles from both girls. Then a more serious blonde, Susan, joined in, "Rowdy will always be the winner because of his looks. But I like Jim, Gil, Mushy, and even Wishbone. Last night…"

Homer did not receive a strong enough signal for TV reception. We certainly were not going to have a television in the tent at Porcupine Lake. I could not make comments about the characters in the story having never seen even one episode. On the other hand, munching my sandwich without filling my mouth with bits of torn wax paper took much concentration.

The girls' parting words were about meeting up in church on Sunday. I had attended Sunday school when younger with Gail, but not church, as my parents visited only at Easter and Christmas. As the new girl, I would have to be flexible and adapt to make friends at Tustumena. Was I up to the task? Most weekends we would be heading back to Homer to see Gail. I would catch up with my old town buddies then. Suddenly, more gloom descended. Would I now be an outsider amongst *them*? Going to a different school meant losing touch. Where did I fit in?

Mom's Lopsided Baguette
Makes Two Long Loaves

Not only was this recipe used for sandwiches, but Mom sliced a loaf without cutting through the bottom crust, and then brushed garlic butter between slices. She wrapped the prepared loaf in aluminum foil and heated it in the oven. We enjoyed it at most festive meals such as Thanksgiving and Christmas.

Sift into a large mixing bowl:

4 cups plain flour/550g

2 teaspoons salt

1 tablespoon sugar

Stir in 1 tablespoon dried yeast; make a well in the center of the ingredients and pour in 4 ounces skim milk and 8 ounces water. Stir thoroughly; cover with a slightly damp tea towel and let rise in a warm place for about 2 hours. Punch down the dough and divide into 2. Roll each piece into a long oblong on a lightly floured surface. Place each onto a greased baking sheet sprinkled with corn meal. Cover again with the tea towel and let rise until double—about 1 hour in a warm place.

Pre-heat oven to 400F/200C.

Place a pan filled with ½ inch water in the bottom of the oven. On a rack above, in about the middle of the oven place the risen loaves. Bake for 15 minutes and then reduce the heat to 350F/170C and bake another 30 minutes. Remove and cool on a wire rack.

Living In A Tent

Jerry and I climbed onto the school bus with others jostling for a seat. Mary Rusk and her two sisters smiled at me as they made their way to the back. Jerry pointed out a blonde girl and said she was Chlorine Kingsley, and in his class. She had a sister, and they would both be getting off at our stop. We drove through spruce and birch trees and over swamps. Only a few students got off the bus before our stop. One was a big guy in my class called Mike Rochan who lived in a trailer on a lake by the highway. He had large roving eyes.

At our stop the four of us descended from the bus and met Dad and Clovis Kingsley by their jeeps. Clovis had ventured in on foot when Gail and Dad were erecting the tent and introduced himself and welcomed us Johnsons as homesteaders. He had built the cabin his family lived in on their homestead. Most people had humble beginnings until more substantial houses could be built. Now Clovis was all smiles and said, "We'll have to do a rota when you get your trail more established, Henning." The dark haired older sister introduced herself shyly as Martha and said, "I'm in fourth grade."

Dad started our open-top jeep with the exhaust flowing out smelly and in spurts which embarrassed me. The Kingsley's covered bright blue jeep was pristine. They started off on the dirt track and soon were out of sight. We turned off at what we called the "Y" onto the blazed rough trail made by Gail and Dad. We bumped and rolled along for about twenty minutes before seeing our tent. It was a one and a half storey wooden frame twelve by twelve foot structure covered by Army Surplus canvas, built by Gail and Dad in only three days. It was impressive the first time I saw it when Mom and my brothers and I had hiked in, but now I would realize life living there. I climbed out of the passenger seat with my school books. Scamp was there to welcome us along with Brent. Dad leaped ahead and opened the tent flap for Jerry and me.

"Home sweet home," Dad said.

The downstairs seemed very compact. I could not imagine that we would live here very long without feeling on top of each other. I put on a glum face which was how I felt, especially as a result of the lack of privacy. The wood burning barrel stove opposite the tent flap was giving off heat. On the other side of it was a flat iron cook stove where Mom was hovering. There was a metal basin of water on an orange crate at the end of the cook stove sticking out into the room. I thought, my word, how easily one of us or Scamp could knock the crate and send water splashing out. A small half-metal barrel sink was not far from the stove with a plastic window above. Next to the wall facing the lake was an improvised table made from a piece of plywood set on two sawhorses. Metal folding chairs were arranged around the table. A Coleman lantern was hissing and giving off light from a hook in the ceiling in the middle of the room. Two army cots were shoved against the same wall as the door flap. There was a ladder beside the door flap and over the cots, going up to the loft.

Mom said, "Let me show you your rooms, kids." I was interested to see mine.

She climbed the ladder with Jerry, Brent, and me behind. The space had been divided into two with a cloth curtain. My space faced the lake and had a plastic window looking out to the water which was a relief to me because our lives were centered around the lake. An army cot was placed under the eave on one side and a rope for hanging clothes on the other side. The only standing room was in the middle of the space. I felt cramped standing there with Mom because we could easily knock into each other. Jerry's and Brent's side had one cot under the eaves and another sticking out alongside the opening where the ladder came up. The smokestack was in the eave. There was a plastic window above the top of the ladder.

"Change your clothes and come down to help," Mom said. "You can peel the potatoes and carrots, Judy."

"You boys can help me stack wood," said Dad.

Mom and Dad had clear ideas of male and female roles, but that never stopped me from driving a tractor and learning to hunt and fish.

I took off my school dress and hung it on the rope on a metal hanger and put my boots underneath. Next I pulled on jeans and a sweater that had been laid under the window. I put on tennis shoes. I was grateful to have my own space, but I felt discouraged about the five of us living in such a cramped fashion. Our rented house in Homer could have fit several of these tents into the square footage. Jerry and Brent were already outside with Dad and Scamp by the time I was back downstairs.

Mom said, "How was school?" as she pushed the potatoes, carrots, and onions over to me on the table with the peeler. "First wash your hands."

"It was ok," I mumbled not very enthused. I dipped my hands in the basin and gave them a good rinse. A towel hung over the heating barrel on a wire. I dried my hands and then began to work. As I pulled the peeler along each potato and carrot, I thought of Homer and my friends. How I missed them and what an easier life they all had. Here we hardly even had the basics.

"We've been working full out to settle in," she said. "Tomorrow we start building the outhouse."

I finished peeling the vegetables and gave them to her to add to the moose roast she had waiting. Then I started my homework at the table. Soon the smell of roast and onions pleasantly filled the tent. I finished reading and put my books down on the floor by the tent wall close to the end of the table. Plates, cutlery, and glasses were in the middle of the table; I set them opposite each chair. On a makeshift kitchen counter made from plywood and two by four boards, stood a large metal stainless steel bucket filled with lake water. There was a long handled dipper alongside. I knew that the water was pure, but it was also inconvenient to go down to the lake to fill the bucket. Hopefully, this would not be among my chores. I brought the glasses one by one over to the bucket, and filled each one with the clear cold water.

The flap opened and Scamp rushed in wagging his tail. Dad said, "Oh the good smell of roast." He showed Jerry and Brent the basin, and they each washed their hands. Then Dad brought the basin of water outside and threw it out away from the tent. I gasped thinking how barbaric. Then I saw that Mom was using the sink for washing up as she cooked. Dad placed the basin back on the orange crate and filled it with icy water from the bucket. Each of them dried their hands on the same towel I had used. Hygiene was not a high priority in the tent.

We gathered around the table and Mom lifted out the roast for Dad to carve. He heaped the food onto our plates. Mom said, "Eat up and then I have Betty Crocker chocolate cake for dessert."

After dinner it was up to me to wash the dishes. I took them to the barrel sink set in another wooden counter. Mom helped fill the sink with warm water from the reservoir in the cook stove as well as a bowl nearby for rinsing. She placed a dish rack on a towel in which to put the clean dishes. I squirted liquid soap into the water and started to wash. The warm water felt good on my hands.

Mom said, "There is enough roast left for sandwiches for your lunches tomorrow," and handed me the roast pan to wash. Mom always made sure there were plenty of leftovers for our lunches the next day. She then refilled the reservoir with water from the stainless steel bucket and handed Dad the bucket.

"Time for another, John," she said. Without a word as he would do for hundreds and hundreds of times, Dad took a flashlight from the bottom of the orange crate and went down to the lake.

I made the sandwiches and put them in small brown paper bags from the kitchen. I left the packed bags on the table. We had no refrigerator—no power.

Mom handed me a flashlight and said, "Now we can go up to your room, Judy." She climbed the ladder ahead of me holding carefully onto the ladder. She told me to put on the flashlight which I did. She sat down on my cot a minute and said that all the sleeping bags were very warm and even though it would be cold in the tent during the night, we would all stay warm. She left saying, "I hope that you will be happy here," and her expression was one of total honesty.

"Thank you," I mumbled. How was I to be happy living out in the boondocks so far away from my Homer friends? Then I remembered that I had not yet gone to the bathroom. That meant putting my boots and coat back on, grabbing the flashlight, and climbing down the ladder, opening the flap and walking a short distance from the tent. The moon was bright overhead and there seemed to be millions of stars. I squatted on the ground and my hot stream warmed me as I managed to keep my coat clear until I thought I heard something in the bushes. I jumped up! A moose? A bear? Or a wolf? I pulled up my panties and jeans and ran away from my bathroom spot in the cranberry bushes and moss. I was not sure that I would ever get used to this way of life. Nor did I want to.

Entering the tent, Dad called out, "Good night, Judy. Good night boys." Jerry and Brent were already tucked into their sleeping bags for the night. The light coming up from the open space with the ladder filled their side with a glow. I went over to my side of the loft and switched back on the flashlight. I removed my clothes, folded them, and put on a red flannel night gown that reached down to my feet. First I switched off the flashlight and laid it beside the cot, and then climbed into my sleeping bag. It took a while for my body heat to warm the space inside the army surplus sleeping bag. I felt discouraged living so remotely. We were totally isolated as the Kingsleys were over a mile away. Well, at least tomorrow we would have an outhouse.

Dad woke me up, while it was still dark and cold, with his "huba, huba, kids." This became our daily alarm and call to action. I remembered that I was no longer in Homer, but living in a tent on Porcupine Lake and needed to dress in the freezing cold quickly for Tustumena School. I slowly climbed out of my warm sleeping bag and stood up from the cot. It was still quite dark, but I could see first light faintly from the small plastic window. I reached for my dress hanging on the rope and for my underwear on the floor. I put my socks on first as my feet were cold on the plywood floor. I could hear Jerry dressing and coughing on the other side of the curtain. Brent did not yet need to get up.

Climbing down the ladder I saw Dad stirring hot cake batter in the corner kitchen area. The cook stove was giving off heat as well as the barrel wood burning stove by the flap. I put on my boots and opened the flap to go out to pee. The fresh air felt cold against my face. I quickly walked to about the same spot I used last night. Afterwards, I carefully made my way back to the tent.

"I've put warm water from the reservoir into the basin for you, Judy," Dad said.

"Thanks," I managed as I quickly washed my face and hands in the basin and dried myself with the family towel. I picked up the comb beside the basin and ran it through my hair.

Mom was still in her sleeping bag on her cot. The kerosene lamp hissed from the middle of the ceiling.

Jerry joined me at the table. The smell of hotcakes filled the tent as they cooked on the grill. We ate and took our plates and cutlery over to the small metal barrel sink in the kitchen. The plastic window by the table was just beginning to let in the morning light. Dad ate while I climbed back up the ladder and went to my side of the loft. My school shoes were ready to take in a cloth bag along with my school books. I climbed back down the ladder, picked up my lunch bag, and went outside with Jerry. The smelly exhaust was spurting from the jeep, and Dad was ready to transport us to the school bus for day two at Tustumena School.

Dad dressing out a moose

One September Morning

It was a bright crisp morning with glistening spots of frost on the low ground. I thought it was to be a normal school day, with a driving lesson thrown in, and had no idea it was also to be my first moose hunt. As I steered the open-top army surplus jeep along our blazed trail to the school bus, Dad instructed me on driving. Dad had instigated the driving lesson to please me, and it did make me happy and closer to him.

"Keep right around that large mound by the silver birch. Oh, ahead is that steep hill. Better step on the clutch and shift down. Slowly now." He had the 30.06 rifle beside him which banged against the metal door as we jerked along in my inexperienced eleven-year-old hands. September was both the start of school and moose hunting season. Dad took the rifle everywhere on the homestead in case the opportunity for hunting occurred. To Jerry in the back he said, "Keep looking. Conditions are perfect for moose."

Jerry coughed, shaking his short blond head, "Yuck...exhaust! I'm sick. This noisy jeep will scare moose...but ok."

We crossed the homestead border as I drove on through yellow falling leaves from the numerous birch, and around green needled spruce, reaching Swan Lake about three-quarters of a mile from our own lake. I feared that the loud engine would drown out any sound made by a moose stepping through brush. Driving with the cool fresh breeze whipping my hair as I mastered the gears and clutch, was a thrill and required most of my concentration. I held the steering wheel tightly and breathed in the autumn air. This is fun, I thought, but must keep my eyes on the bumpy path. I was unsure what could be lurking behind bushes and peering, but so far we had seen only forest.

Then up ahead, undisturbed by the sound of the jeep, was a moose standing erect to watch our loud, jostling emergence from the forest with head up and big ears raised. The majestic animal looked straight at us from open mossy ground not far from the water's edge.

Dad put up his hand for me to stop. "Do you see horns?"

"Why?" Jerry asked leaning forward from the back seat.

"Can only shoot bulls," Dad informed us.

He climbed out, raising the rifle to focus the sights precisely between the eyes. I held my breath and watched Dad take aim. Jerry and I sat watching as Dad slowly squeezed the trigger. Annual moose hunts had been part of his life in Alaska for nearly twenty years. From early teens he had hunted deer in Wisconsin. This was the first time Jerry and I witnessed a moose kill although we and the families around relied on moose for meat. There was a wood-pecker's persistent tapping, but all else was quiet except for the loud bang. The moose fell.

"No school today kids. We have work to do. Wait." He lum-bered over the spongy moss towards the fallen moose as he held the rifle in a ready-to-fire position. The animal could unexpectedly rise and charge. I sat on the edge of my seat watching Dad and was unable to breathe normally.

He sliced across the throat, and then returned to the jeep saying, "Keeps the meat fresh. Move over, Judy! We need Mom and Brent. There will be other chances for you to learn driving. Let's go. Humans aren't the only ones to enjoy a taste of moose. Animals...vultures...soon pick up the smell."

I climbed into the front passenger seat disappointed that my driving lesson and one of the first days of school had been interrupted. We were now homesteaders, and flexibility key. I had read *The Last of the Mohicans* and remembered the words: "to eat, 'tis necessary to get the game". It was the same for us.

Dad continued. "Along with the salmon and clams; lots of food in the freezer for winter."

Soon, we were returning with Mom and my youngest brother, Brent. She said, "You've no right using our new stainless steel water bucket for this, John."

"Perfect utensil. I know what I'm doing." Dad replied.

Mom stood her ground, "For God's sake, any plastic container would've..."

"Here we are!" Dad interrupted. The round trip had only taken thirty minutes. Thankfully, there was no evidence of interference. The moose would take up almost all the room in the jeep once dressed out and loaded. There would barely be room left for Dad to drive so the rest of us would return home on foot.

We gathered around the dead moose. Blood had flowed from the cut neck artery and was now mostly dark and congealed. Steam rose from the warm beast escaping into the frosty autumn morning. Poor moose thoughts came into my eleven-year-old head for a few moments, but were soon replaced with practicalities. Mom followed Dad's instructions, and seemed to work without emotion.

Her attitude would change a couple of years later when she pulled the trigger, killing a moose when Dad was away. Remorse overtook our mother then. She was raised in Chicago where her parents had purchased meat at the local butcher and brought it home in packages. "What have I done? What have I done?" Mom asked Jerry, Brent, and me shaking her head for days. I would be the one to comfort her. "The meat will be our food for the months ahead. With Dad away, you needed to be the person who killed it."

Dad sawed through the tough hide with a sharp knife, slitting the animal from stem to stern. Next he cut the intestines free with a few muscular swipes of the glistening blade. When done he said, "Ruth. Judy. Roll them out onto the ground. Don't want contamination. Could happen if my knife slips…"

The smell of fresh meat rose from the just killed beast as Mom and I bent down. My face warmed from the heat of the animal. Our hands slipped as we pushed the bulging guts into a roll. My nose twitched, but I rejected the urge to rub it. Revulsion started to rise within me, but stopped when Dad said, "Done! Come back."

"Further, John," Mom argued.

"Forget it!" Dad shouted.

"Yuck!" I said stepping away and back to the carcass.

Dad freed the liver, heart, and kidneys next. His skillful use of the knife made quick work of a job he had done many times. "The bucket, Jerry," Dad shouted. Jerry broke away from rolling on the moss carpeted ground with Brent and picked it up. He held it out by the handle as Dad dropped in each piece with bloody hands.

Jerry scrunched up his nose at the smell.

"Take it carefully to the jeep," Mom said.

Jerry coughed as he moved away with the smelly organs. His short legs sank down with each step planted in the spongy moss terraine. I watched as he wobbled, trying to hold the loaded bucket upright. Springing up and down without tipping out the contents slowed him down. The laborious short distance brought up heavy breathing, but he successfully placed the bucket into the jeep. Smiling back at us he said, "Did it!"

"You're a hero!" Dad said looking proudly at his six-year-old son.

Both Mom and Dad cut away the hide. "Ok, everybody grab and tug," Dad instructed. My arms ached and I grunted while pulling in unison with my family. With Dad leading, we dragged the hide to the jeep. He folded it into quarters, and we lifted it onto the metal floor.

Using a hand saw, Dad split the carcass in half from top to bottom along the backbone. The rest of us held the legs out of his way. Brent had one hand in his jacket pocket as he and Jerry made a half-hearted effort to help. They wanted to get back to their moss rolling. Each half was cut again making quarters.

Dad hoisted each hindquarter onto his shoulder, crouching and breathing heavily as he carried the meat across the moss to the jeep. He rested several minutes after each trip. This gave him a chance to catch his breath while admiring the small lake. Open ground surrounded the water at each end and birch and spruce forest on the hilly sides. Mom and I stood enjoying the same view.

The ground covered in blood and discarded guts, in contrast to the pure clean water of Swan Lake with birds swimming. Mom said, "Look! I think that there are two loons swimming at the far end. See... black and white beautiful birds."

Dad looked to where she pointed and said, "Yes, they are loons. Hear them call?" His voice was full of tenderness as he looked from the loons back to Mom. They were soul mates. I yearned for a special someone for myself, and felt it would happen when I married. Although my parents shared these moments of the beauty of nature, bickering between them usually erupted afterwards.

They stood enjoying the unspoiled scene, and Brent and Jerry laughed as they played. They rolled, leaped on the moss and erupted into laughter. Brent grabbed Jerry's bare arm with both of his hands, twisted the skin in opposite directions giving Jerry an *Indian burn*. Jerry howled and grabbed Brent to do the same to him. Loneliness swept over me. Gail, who had been my companion, was back in Homer attending high school. I was the extra.

Dad wiped his brow on the back of his red and black flannel shirtsleeve. Mom sniffed with a frown, saying, "Why do you do that? Use a handkerchief!"

"Forget it. The shirt will wash." Not that he will be the one washing it, I thought. He then sawed the front quarters into smaller pieces. Mom and I lifted and carried them together. The potent raw meat overpowered the smell of the damp moss.

With all the moose meat back at our cabin, the aging process followed. Using rope and pulley, Dad strung each quarter, covered with cheesecloth for protection, up on a pole supported by two spruce trees. He lit a small fire nearby to keep enough smoke curling up to ward off the flies. As we walked by, we breathed in a smoky pungent wild meat odor. Mom and Dad kept busy while the raw meat aged.

A use for nearly all parts of the moose was found. Dad soaked the hide in a big oil drum filled with lake water and ashes. A few days later, he and Mom scraped it with knives to free all the moose hair and load it into old pillowcases. Mom washed the cloth bags of hair in our Maytag, and hung them to dry on the clothesline near the cabin. She sewed up a bed-size case with our Singer from standard navy blue and white pillow ticking material. I stuffed the dried moose hairs into her stitched parallel sections in the case. This made a very warm comforter. The tent had no heat when the fire went out at night, but Mom and Dad were warm sleeping under this heavy cover.

A week later the meat was darker in color and ready for butchering into steaks, ribs, roasts, brisket, stew meat, and some left for grinding into hamburger. Mom, reared in Chicago, still had her *Every Day Foods* high school home economics book with pictures showing how to butcher. Following the open book, we worked.

Dad sawed and cut. He purchased raw pork at a grocery 20 miles away in Soldotna, to grind with the moose meat which was to end up as hamburger to make it juicier.

Mom said, "One and a half pound hamburger packages are right for our family, John. That allows one each and one extra." Later she said, "Make the roasts three pounds. Well…a few should be five pounds for when we have company. Judy, keep the wrapping paper tight. Allow one steak per person, except Brent."

"Give Brent his own steak. He is four but eats like a man!" Dad said.

We secured the packages with freezer tape and loaded them into a large upright freezer purchased from Mom's order to "Sears & Roebuck." Since it was our early days of homesteading, the freezer was housed in a tent. Months later the tent was replaced with an unheated shed and also housed our generator.

I sighed with relief when the moose was butchered and in the freezer. That hard work was behind us for a whole year. In the months ahead, the moose provided meat for the table, and gave me a feeling of wealth and security; we had a large choice of cuts to prepare our meals.

Immediately after dressing out the moose, Mom and Dad made dinner of its liver. They lightly sautéed sliced onions, and then fried the seasoned liver briefly, leaving the inside of each piece pink, succulent, and easy to cut and chew.

The moose gave up his life so ours could continue.

Mom and Dad's Tasty Fried Liver and Onions
Serves 4

Ingredients:
1 pound fresh liver, sliced (moose or beef)

½ teaspoon salt ¼ cup/4 tablespoons flour
½ teaspoon pepper Sprinkling of dried thyme
1 large onion or 2 small/ sliced 2 tablespoons olive oil

Heat 1 tablespoon oil in a large skillet; while waiting, shake salt, flour, pepper and thyme in a bag. Add sliced liver and shake to coat meat evenly. Place sliced onion in heated oil in skillet. Stir occasionally as onion softens; when thoroughly soft, transfer onion to a platter.

Add other tablespoon oil to heated skillet. Arrange sliced liver in the skillet, cooking briefly for about 30 seconds on each side.

Transfer cooked liver to platter with sautéed onions and serve with favorite green vegetable and mashed potatoes.

Dad with Kiisiki in cormorant parka

Dad as a young man

2222222222

From Tent to Cabin

The harsh winter of 1959 was approaching and the tent was never going to be warm enough for our family. By mid-October thin ice coated the washbasin each morning. We were wearing our winter jackets inside.

The day Dad came back in the dump truck with a load of sawdust and timber, I knew that my services would soon be needed. The following day Brent met Jerry and I returning from school as he had been keen to help with the work.

"What took you so long? I've been waiting for ages," four-year-old Brent yelled as he circled the drive trying to keep up with Scamp, who barked and wagged his tail, and leaped around.

Jerry and I stepped inside knowing that our help was required. The moose hunt had occurred in the third week of homesteading. Already it did not feel quite so strange to live in a tent as when we arrived.

Mom and Dad were converting the canvas dwelling into a wooden cabin. The outside boards had been nailed in place. They raced to complete the inside walls and insulate them because it was now October and dipping below freezing at night.

Mom wore blue jeans that I came to associate as her homesteading attire. She had purchased them from the Sears' catalog. Mom was stapling heavy aluminum paper to the inside wall, and said, "Hurry and change. Lots to do before dinner."

Jerry and I climbed the ladder to the loft where our bedrooms were situated and minutes later returned downstairs in jeans and sweatshirts. Mom handed me the staple gun. My hand dropped with the weight of it.

"We're using sawdust to insulate. From upstairs you'll pour it between the outside boards and the paper we staple to the studs. First the stapling." She motioned to the wall in front of us. I saw evenly spaced 2" x 4" wooden boards which I knew were called "studs" that were nailed vertically between the floor and the ceiling against the outside wall.

"Jerry, you hold this against the stud while Judy staples," Mom directed as she pulled up a cut piece of sturdy aluminum paper. "Watch fingers! I'll start the brisket."

"Ok," I said lacking enthusiasm, but curious about using the stapler.

Seven-year-old Jerry coughed as usual and held the paper up apprehensively. It flapped and crinkled around our heads. "Watch my hands," he said, nodding for me to begin.

Dad came through the canvas door flap. "Ok?"

"They're just starting," Mom said from the cook stove, studying *The Joy of Cooking*.

I held the loaded stapler on the paper against the stud. My wrist ached so I supported it with my other hand and pulled the trigger. The metal staple lodged into the soft wood as Jerry coughed again and moved his hands up higher, fingers spread to hold the paper for my next hit.

I turned to Dad. "Is that the way?"

"Yes. Go as high as you can. Then your mom and I will take over. We're saving lots of money by using sawdust. Rolls of insulation cost a Hell of a lot. Sawdust was free. The sawmill owner would've let it rot or—burned it."

"I don't know how we will manage without your surveying income," Mom grumbled as Scamp rubbed against her signaling that he was also ready to eat.

"We'll have to save everywhere we can. That's how." Dad countered. Cheap was good. Free even better. Dad had had to take time off from his business and his clients in Homer and now had to prepare us for the harsh winter soon to come.

Brent asked as he kicked one foot against the other, "What about me?"

"You start loading and carrying those plastic buckets upstairs," Dad said, pointing to the cardboard box of sawdust by the wood burning barrel heater.

Brent walked over to the box. He laughed as he scooped up sawdust and let it flow back down, leaving much clinging to his pullover. He covered his nose with his hands. Jerry and I glanced over and laughed.

"I love the smell! Hurry up…want to start," Brent said, filling buckets.

Jerry looked bored and asked, "Can I staple?"

"You can try lifting the staple gun…here."

He completed securing the paper as was reachable with his young arms. It seemed that they were more muscular than mine, as he worked faster than I. He may have been stronger since he stacked wood my parents sawed for the stoves and split kindling to light morning fires. Those logs and even the hatchet were heavy.

Mom broke away from cooking and yelled to Dad, "Come help, John! It's us now." He came in from sanding birch boards. They would be placed around the inside to cover the papered studs.

"It's looking good for a place that we'll live in for only a short time. In a couple of years we'll start our real house," Dad said.

Jerry and I climbed the ladder to upstairs and stood on the edge of the plywood floor to help Brent pour sawdust. The smell of fresh cut wood hung around our heads as we poured, refilled the buckets, and poured again. We made many trips up and down the ladder. Finally the four-inch space between the aluminum paper and the outside wall was filled.

The meaty-garlic scent of the moose brisket and root vegetables roasting eventually filled our nostrils, but not completely overpowering that of the potent smell of cut wood escaping from the floor, walls, and ceiling.

"Dinner!" Mom yelled.

We gathered around the makeshift table of a few boards on top of two wooden sawhorses. I plopped down on the fold-out metal army surplus chair and ate ravenously.

"Nice meal, Ruth. We earned it, by God!" He looked at me and caught my exasperated expression. Dad pursued, looking pleased, "This cabin will be our livable house."

"But it's tiny, and not even a bathtub," I objected.

He continued with enthusiasm, "It's all part of proving up—meeting the Federal requirements of building a house, clearing, and cultivating."

I knew that sponge bathing would get tedious on my side of the cloth curtain in the loft.

"It's temporary...I'll build a bigger one. First we'll clear the twenty acres required. But not this year. We've five years to prove up. Then the Federal inspector comes."

Mom had told us at length that today's requirements were the same ones that President Lincoln laid down. I was more interested in the metal pan holding a cake that she placed on the table.

"I baked this earlier. It's 'Betty Crocker's Chocolate Fudge' covered with 'Dream Whip.' Ready?"

I was pleased with the large pieces she cut and passed, but not at all with homesteading. Building a house was hard work that was being forced on me by my free-land seeking parents. I remembered raising concerns about the small house, outhouse, and lack of running water which were all ignored. Their euphoric outbursts and knowledge about Lincoln initiating homesteading annoyed me. I did not want to hear more and yet my Mom continued:

"Early settlers kept pushing west until all land was homesteaded clear to California and Washington State. Years later the offer was extended to Alaska. The weather put people off for some time."

"No wonder," I grumbled.

Dad reached for his second piece of cake. "We should be able to do another wall before bedtime. We'll be warmer tonight." He looked at Mom, caught her eye, and glowed. She smiled and then looked at me.

"Judy, you clear the table. I'll staple. Want to try holding the paper, Brent?" He jumped over to find the end of the cut aluminum sheet.

"Come. We'll sand," Dad drew back the canvas flap for Jerry.

I brought the plates and cutlery to the kitchen corner and put them in the barrel sink. It was a relief to get a longer break from the stapling and sawdust pouring so I took my time to finish the dishes. The domestic job was boring, but relaxing. My brothers were never asked to do dishes. My parents considered it part of the female role. But then Mom's role on the homestead broadened to include doing just about all there was to be done. At the time I did not think much about it, but now I see how far advanced she was as the modern day woman.

I finished and climbed the ladder slowly with a bucket of sawdust. Jerry and Brent joined me, and we eventually completed insulating the second wall. Late that night we crawled into our sleeping bags exhausted. Scamp nestled in close to the barrel heater. Over the next couple of weeks, Dad completed the downstairs with Mom while Jerry and I were at school.

"I handed nails and brought in wood for both stoves," Brent bragged. The bulging aluminum paper was covered with birch planks sanded to a high gloss.

It was a great day when we came through a real door before Halloween. We opened the door coming home from school and that wooden, door represented permanence. By Thanksgiving Dad and Mom had black tar paper protecting the outside of our cabin. The internal ladder was replaced with a steep staircase before Christmas.

Dad's interpretation of the Homestead Act put back our standard of living one hundred years in my opinion. Lincoln may have thought our 12'x12' cabin adequate for a family of five, but I soon felt embarrassed and frustrated living there. Most of the girls at school had flush toilets, and I knew they would visit. What would I say to them?

The toilet was an outhouse: a retrograde step for a town girl used to using a small indoor room in Homer. Running out there in daylight was bad enough, but on cold nights it was downright scary. Speed was foremost in my mind as I sat with my bare bottom on a cold rough board in the confined space of the damp draughty hut. Dad was always in a rush on projects; thus, he had not taken the time to sand the bench adequately. Mom eventually did more sanding to make it smoother. The foul dank smell permeated the air even in low temperatures. The hot urine escaping from me created a warm steamy stream. I felt guilty enjoying this comfort. I remember the first few weeks rushing back into the cabin at night and Dad asking, "Judy, how many ghosts were chasing you?"

I was frightened as I ran the short distance in the freezing air. We never saw hungry wolves or cunning coyotes, but we could hear them at night. I worried about them rushing me through the dark frosty nights between the outhouse and cabin. Jerry's and Brent's bolt back to the cabin spoke loudly of their similar fear. We dashed to leap ahead of wild animals with open mouths, fangs ready to sink into our tender flesh. Hurry! Hurry! Run!

After the first few weeks, we became accustomed to the routine. But it was always a jolt to leave the warm cabin and brace oneself to face the cold air.

Mom kept a night can downstairs, but I never used it. I preferred privacy when peeing. Brent and Jerry did use it occasionally, but did not always make it out of their beds. I saw them drop their heads with embarrassment as they removed wet sheets some mornings. The ammonia smell in the air drifted to my side of the curtain. It was not nice, and I felt sad for my younger brothers. Mom washed and froze her fingers hanging the sheets outside on the clothesline. My parents never harassed my brothers about bedwetting. Guess they understood that the problem would pass. It did.

The day started with either Dad or Mom making a fire in the cook stove with built-in water reservoir. The fire soon heated the water for washing and warmed the small house even upstairs where my brothers and I lay under thick covers. The cloth curtain across the room provided privacy for dressing; but I heard every cough, giggle, and whisper. With the heat came the slight smell of smoke drifting up through narrow openings around the stove as the logs were starting to light.

Dad's specialty was sour dough hotcakes. He kept the potent sour dough in a small crockpot on a beam overhead just reachable with a good stretch. Scooping out enough for breakfast, he then topped up the remainder with additional flour and water to maintain a ready supply. We would wake to the sweet aroma of the pancakes cooking on the cast iron griddle along with Dad's, "Hubba hubba, Kids." I spread mine with butter and poured on maple syrup which ran down the sides of the hotcakes. They were my favorite.

When Dad was away with his surveying business, Mom cooked oatmeal or Farina with the addition of an egg to give us extra nutrition. I added butter, a little brown sugar, and canned evaporated milk for taste. Food was important, but it was the door and the staircase that after two and a half months made it feel like a house; and I felt more like a homesteader. We would be protected from the harsh winter to come.

Slow-Cooked, Pot Roast with Winter Vegetables
Serves 5-6

3 to 5 lb, chuck, shoulder, top or bottom round, brisket, blade, or rump
Heat 2 tablespoons olive oil in a heavy Dutch oven; brown roast on all sides on high temperature.
Add to the pot:
3 to 4 carrots, washed, scrubbed, sliced into large pieces
3 ribs celery, sliced into large pieces, leaves included
1 turnip, peeled and quartered
4 potatoes, peeled and quartered
3 to 4 parsnips, scrubbed, and sliced into large pieces
1 to 2 onions, quartered
1½ cups beef stock, boiling (can use cubes, plus water)
½ cup red wine
1 bay leaf
Cover and bake in medium hot oven about 3 hours.

Sourdough Hotcakes
Serves about 4 people

The starter is easily made from yeast, flour, and water. We would prepare the pancakes using a small amount of the starter in the batter and then replenish the ingredients stored in a Crockpot. For those of you who have eaten sourdough hotcakes or bread, you know that they have their own unique tangy flavor.

For the starter:
Ingredients:
2½ teaspoons active dry yeast
½ cup/4 oz lukewarm water
Mix the above together and let stand for 4-5 minutes until yeast is dissolved, bubbly, and giving off a strong smell.
Then stir in:

1½ cups/12 oz milk, warmed to the touch

3 tablespoons unsalted butter, melted

2 cups/8 oz/250g plain flour

3 tablespoons white sugar

Cover the above mixture with plastic wrap or with a plate and set in a warm place for an hour. The mixture will become bubbly and increase in volume. Uncover and stir the sourdough starter down and then recover. Let the batter work overnight. When ready to prepare the hotcakes, remove the cover from the sourdough starter and mix. Transfer three-fourths of the batter into a mixing bowl. If you wish to keep the starter going, replenish with the above amounts of milk, butter, flour, and sugar; cover and let stand for another day or two.

To the batter withdrawn, add the following:

2 eggs

½ teaspoon salt

In a lightly oiled frying pan, heated, spoon in about 4 tablespoons of batter. The thin batter will spread into an irregular shape. Cook until many of the bubbles that appear have popped; turn and cook briefly on second side. Serve while hot with butter, your choice of fruit, and maple syrup.

Set net fishing with Mom, Jerry, and Brent

First Sunday at Kasilof Community Church

The girls in my class at Tustumena kept asking me to come to Sunday School and church so the first weekend that we were not going to visit Gail in Homer, I took them up on their invitation.

That meant walking out the two and a quarter mile homestead road to the Sterling Highway to catch a ride with Mary Rusk and her family. After several weeks of living out in the wilderness, I had become more brave about being by myself in the forest. I wove around spruce and birch trees and over hills in just under an hour. Birds and squirrels were plentiful, but I saw nothing bigger. It had not snowed yet, but the air was cool and hovering around freezing. My winter coat, fur-lined leather boots, and lined gloves kept me warm.

The Rusks arrived and Mary and her sister, Michelle, made room for me with them in the back seat. The Rusks had a luxurious sedan. Mr. Rusk was a successful commercial fisherman who operated a set net site on Clam Gulch beach. He had dark blue spots on his forehead which I was told were from the war. Mrs. Rusk was a heavy-set woman who had practiced as a nurse in the south '48. Mr. Rusk was jovial at the steering wheel; and Mrs. Rusk asked, "Judy, how are you and your family settling in on your homestead?"

"Fine," I said not mentioning that we kids helped convert the tent into a house. I was embarrassed and thought, 'Why does our house have to be so tiny with an outhouse?' Mary had told me enough about their house that I knew it had comforts of indoor plumbing and carpeting—and space.

We drove a couple of miles beyond Tustumena School up to Kasilof Community Church. It was a wooden frame building painted white. Linda Hermansen was already inside with her mother and sisters. She joined Mary and me in one corner in the back of the pews for Sunday School. Susan Mainwaring, daughter of the pastor, was already there with her mother who would teach our class. She warmly greeted me as did Susan Webb who was one year ahead of me in school. We sat in a circle on folding chairs, and Mrs. Mainwaring welcomed us all. She opened the class with a prayer and then started the lesson. This meant for Mrs. Mainwaring and each of us to take turns reading from the book of John in the New Testament. I had not brought a *Bible*, but Mary shared hers with me. I was not very interested, but kept smiling—at least I was with girls from Tustumena school who seemed interested in being friends. Mrs. Mainwaring closed the class with another prayer at the end saying, "If there is anyone here who hasn't taken the Lord Jesus as her personal savior, you are welcome to see me after class."

I opened my eyes feeling uncomfortable, but smiled at the other girls. Had I been singled out? If so, I chose to ignore it. We stood and chatted for a while and then made our way to the pews for the sermon.

Pastor Mainwaring stood at the pulpit, tall with a fresh haircut and severe demeanor. He said we would open the service by singing "Amazing Grace". I loved the hymn from the Sunday School in Homer I had attended, and belted out the words. Mary harmonized with her sister, Michelle, beside her. Afterwards, Mary whispered to me that it was Trudy Webb, Susan's mother, playing the piano, and Harlie Fellers, an old timer, on the violin. Pastor Mainwaring welcomed us all to church and made announcements which ended by asking anyone present for the first time to stand up. I felt flushed, but embarrassingly got to my feet. No one else was new that day. He thanked me for coming and said our next hymn would be "Onward Christian Soldiers". I also knew that one and strongly sang out the words. His sermon followed of which I do not remember much about because I was bored. My happiness was being with my fellow classmates. Pastor Mainwaring ended the service with a prayer; and I was self-conscious with his eyes roving across the congregation, when he said, "Anyone who does not know Jesus as their personal savior please come forward." I sat still and breathed deeply. It was not only about being singled out, it was about being a non-believer. I wondered how I could remain a non-believer in such an observant community. These people were entrenched in their beliefs from years of attending church. Pastor Mainwaring repeated the message several times and said there was no hurry, but not a better time to find your Savior. Finally, he finished the prayer, and we sang "The Old Rugged Cross" in closing.

We rose from the pews and we Tustumena girls spoke a bit. They all told me how happy they were that I had joined them at church. The adults were also happily visiting amongst themselves. Eventually, Mary and I said our goodbyes to the others and joined her family going back to the car.

Mary and I whispered in the back seat on the way to my stop. She asked me how I liked going to Tustumena School, and I replied fine except that I missed my Homer friends. "Of course. It is so good having you with us," she said as she hugged me. That made me feel accepted. Mr. Rusk pulled over at the homestead road, and I got out saying my goodbyes and thanking them for the ride.

The long walk was ahead of me. It gave me time to think about Sunday School and the service. I was glad that I had made the effort as it was the first time that I was with the Tustumena girls outside of school. Also it was nice to sing the hymns I had sung as a younger child. However, I still felt like an outsider from them because I was not a born again Christian, nor were my family or Homer friends.

I would become a regular at Sunday School and church and it did not change my lack of a personal relationship with God. The hymns, prayers, and socializing with my friends were a key part in my initiation into the community.

The Long Homestead Road

In the Kingsleys' jeep driving to the school bus we chatted. "Oh, they are sitting very close," Martha Kingsley said and caused Jerry's and Chlorine's cheeks to turn bright red. Martha and I smirked with success. Both our younger siblings were shy and about the same age.

We had wondered as a family in the months we had known the Kingsleys how Chlorine had been given such an unusual name. No explanation was given. I said, "I bet Pearl read it off a bottle while doing laundry." Mom laughed, shaking her head in agreement, acknowledging her belief that the Kingsley girls' mother was a trifle different. In Pearl's strict adherence to religion, she distanced herself from those who were not born again Christians.

A bus rota was established with the two neighboring families: the Kingsleys, and later the Jacksons who lived a mile and a half away on another lake, would drive us to the school bus. This worked well when the dirt road was frozen. In spring and autumn the road was too muddy to drive and we walked.

In summer and winter, road smoothness was maintained by each family's vehicle pulling a square flat frame made of metal bars called a drag which skimmed the dirt or snow in order to level out ruts.

Church was an important element in the lives of the Kingsley girls since their mother was an avid believer. They were made aware of all the good and none of the negative characteristics of the local church members. One winter day I shared a story with them about going home with Reverend Mainwaring's daughter, Susan, who was my age. Mrs. Mainwaring presented me with a pink and white decorated cake after dinner because it was my birthday. "Oh, thank you," I said, a bit embarrassed but also pleased. Susan led everyone in, singing "Happy Birthday." They finished and clapped. Pastor Mainwaring appeared disgruntled. Under his breath he muttered,

"This is probably going to make us late for my service. EAT UP!"

Martha and Chlorine looked amazed but kept quiet. Their father, Clovis Kingsley, laughed and laughed. He said, "The old grouch!" I soon learned that Clovis did not go along to church with the family. In fact, it became obvious that he and Pearl rarely went anywhere together.

Clovis allowed me to ride along to the Friday night square dances. He was the social one of the family. His wife would not attend, as her strict religion forbade it. Square dancing was brought to Alaska by westerners and mid-westerners staking their home-steading claims. A Quonset hut, a thick metal building with a curved roof from one side of the floor to the other, was the venue. Thousands of them were shipped to Alaska during World War II. They provided quick housing. This one was probably a relic from that era.

We entered the building ready to step rhythmically with a do-si-do and promenade to music from vinyl records. I even sewed my own square dancing skirt and matching top from red and black cotton material. The full ruffle on the bottom of my skirt and those of other girls' skirts, swished around as we danced. I loved keeping to the fast pace set by experienced dancers. There was usually only one guy at the dance from my class, David Osmar. He stood on the side. I would have accepted his request to be his partner, but he rarely asked. Perhaps he was shy. David's Norwegian/American family, with whom my father had immediate Scandinavian affinity, ran the local grocery with Post Office. We stopped in regularly for the mail and chatted, but did little shop-ping there because the larger stores twenty miles away, or in Homer, had lower prices. His parents were usually present on Friday nights and danced, drank a beer with others; and Mr. Osmar made a few trips outside for a cigarette with the smokers. I stayed inside dancing or talking with David and some of the students from Tustumena. Often the enthusiasm of the dancers made the flimsy floor bounce so much that the needle jumped off the spinning disc.

Riding with Clovis to the hall in his bright blue Willis jeep with heater on full blast was comfortable. Returning home was a different story. Clovis stayed dancing and socializing past my bedtime. This meant I had to get a ride back with others leaving earlier who dropped me off at the end of our long secluded road.

I walked the two and one-quarter miles home. Being out alone had become an accepted necessity sometimes during the day and at night. My need to be with people involved a long walk at the end of the evening as I trudged along in thickly lined leather boots and a heavy coat. In the dark, going through forest with the moon shining brightly down amongst thousands of stars, I came to know constellation patterns such as the "Big Dipper" and its rotating prominent "North Star." Sometimes northern lights (aurora borealis) overhead transfixed me. They were white and swirled in large funnel shapes. Even though alone, the dramatic heavens inspired me to sing the words to "How Great Thou Art".

O Lord my God, When I in awesome wonder,
Consider all the worlds Thy Hands have made;
I see the stars, I hear the rolling thunder,
Thy power throughout the universe displayed.
Then sings my soul, My Saviour God, to Thee,
How great Thou art, How great Thou art.
Then sings my soul, My Saviour God, to Thee,
How great Thou art, How great Thou art!

I thought, how does anyone not believe in God? The beauty of these nights was overpowering. It was not so much the rules and dictates of the local community church that drew me to religion. It was nature, something that has never left me. I was a believer even though I had not come forward in church to proclaim my feelings. These words written long ago by the Swedish preacher, Carl Boberg, flowed over and over in my head. They made me proud of my Swedish heritage as well as my belief in a supreme being.

Dad had bought me hand-sewn fur boots—mukluks, but I slid on the ice and snow with the sealskin soles. Instead, with wool socks and leather boots, my feet were warm and kept me upright.

It was eerie out in the virgin forest by myself at the ages of eleven and twelve. The primitive road took me across swamps and through woods, but I was determined to socialize as often as possible. As a pre-teen I was ready to mix with people. I prayed for God to keep me safe as I walked. I would have preferred Gail to talk to, but she was in Homer.

Moose congregated in the openings of the snow-laden swamps lit up by the moon. I could count up to forty moose by the time I reached the cabin door. They moved slowly, if at all. Mostly they stood around or lay resting—lethargic in groups of seven, eight, or more. During winter they rarely charged. Each looked like a large dark mound on the snow. Often a head would rise as I passed, but I do not remember one getting up and walking towards me. That would have ended my Friday night square dancing.

I continued to attend the square dances and Sunday School and church so that I could escape from the woods where only the company of Mom, Dad, Jerry and Brent was usual. Certainly I wanted friends at Tustumena School. I did not want a boyfriend in the rural community because I still had a crush on Jack Collie, who remained in Homer. I did not even think about him often as we did not see each other for months at a time.

As I walked, I realized the beauty of nature could not compensate for what I had left behind. So I formed a secret plan: I'd return to Homer for high school, following in Gail's footsteps. I'd also be a cheerleader as she was. Go to Ninilchik High School, twenty miles up the road? No way. There were only a handful of students in each class. The school was too small to play in the same basketball league as Homer. Tania Uminski, Mary Rearden, and Jack Collie were the friends I yearned to be with. At fourteen I would leave the moose behind and go to HOMER High School with them.

Mrs. Mainwaring's Birthday Cake
Makes a round 9-inch cake

Preheat oven to 180C/350F. Lightly oil and dust with flour, 3 cake tins.
Sift together:

   2⅔ cups cake flour

   2¼ teaspoons baking powder

   ½ teaspoon salt

Combine in a separate bowl:

   1 cup milk

   1 teaspoon vanilla and ½ teaspoon almond flavoring

In a large bowl, beat until creamy: 250g/8 ounces unsalted butter
Gradually add and mix into the butter:

   1½ cups white granulated sugar

Beat in: 4 egg yolks
Add the sifted dry ingredients in thirds, alternating with the milk. Beat until smooth.

In another large bowl, beat to soft peaks:

   4 egg whites

   ¼ teaspoon cream of tartar

Gradually add, beating on high speed, until stiff but not dry:

   ¼ cup white granulated sugar

Fold the stiff egg whites into the egg yolk batter. Divide between the three pans, spreading evenly. Bake about 25 minutes or until a toothpick inserted into the center comes out clean. Remove from oven and cool for 10 minutes on a wire rack before removing. Cool completely before icing.

Pink and White Icing
Makes about 2 cups

In a mixing bowl, blend together:

   4 cups powdered/icing sugar

   8 tablespoons unsalted butter, softened

Add and beat until smooth: Approximately 6 tablespoons of milk, add slowly and stop at a good spreading consistency.

Remove one-half of the frosting into a separate bowl; color with a few drops of red food coloring to achieve a pretty pink. Fill lightly between the cake layers with the white and also the cake top. Cover the sides with the pink. Hundreds and thousands as well as silver balls can be used to decorate.

Christmas Festivities on the Homestead

Dad came through the cabin door one morning when I was eleven, and announced, "I'm flooding an area for skating. It'll be ready this afternoon. Where are the outdoor Christmas lights, Ruth?"

This was early for Dad to make an ice rink on our lake. I had just finished my last bite of Thanksgiving turkey and slice of pumpkin pie.

Weather conditions provided perfect skating earlier that first year of homesteading in 1959. The ice froze thick enough to hold us. We each whirled around on bare ice up and down Porcupine Lake holding Dad's quickly made plastic sail. The sound of cracks ripping through the thick ice as I took a turn still rings in my ears. It was like a fighter jet racing for takeoff. After a couple of weeks, additional snow fell preventing skating on the virgin ice.

Skating was essential winter fun. Mom and Dad had met on an ice rink in Chicago in 1942. Their eagerness for us to enjoy the sport was based on the start of their lasting romance.

I hurried to finish the breakfast dishes, saying, "Let's tell the Kingsleys. They can have turns with our skates."

"Chlorine can wear mine," Jerry said as he tossed his monthly *Superman* comic upstairs.

Dad said, "Ok. Stuff them with a bit of dried grass while you're at it. Best insulator. Living on St Lawrence Island taught me that."

Brent came down the steep staircase backwards and held onto the sides so he would not fall. The boys pulled on heavy jackets and bounded out into the cold.

Dad barely finished hanging the multicolored Christmas lights on the spruce when darkness fell. The new rink was frozen solid, and lit by the floodlight high in the tree. We heard a jeep drive up, and the two girls from a neighboring homestead leaped out.

"Welcome!" Dad bellowed. "Come into the cabin."

Martha, one year younger than I, said, "Thank you, Mr. Johnson. I've never skated." She and her sister wore heavy jackets with hoods over thick sweaters and snow pants. They resembled astronauts traveling to the moon—with only the glass head bubble missing.

They put on skates, and we helped lace and tie them, and make double bows. Dad and I pulled both girls onto their feet. They stood with uncertainty, very unsteady. I held Martha by the elbow and Dad her younger sister, Chlorine. We carefully led them down to the lake, but I nearly fell once as Martha's stumbling dragged me around. They stepped on with the trepidation of beginners.

The fully illuminated rink was our own winter wonderland. Noise of our generator in the background reminded us that it was our own power plant in this secluded setting that gave us light. More dramatic and without any sound, aurora borealis swept slowly in brilliant white waves to light up the night sky along with the sliver of a moon and thousands of stars.

Wobbling, the Kingsley girls skated in jerky movements. Both fell on their bottoms trying to move with thin blades on bare ice, but got up eager to try again. We heard their laughter and Martha's cry of, "Oh no!"

"You'll get it," Dad said.

They remained upright longer with each attempt. Success brought smiles to their faces. Dad beamed with pride at having been able to pass on one of his skills. Martha went down but immediately bounced back up like the Pillsbury doughboy. She was obviously exhausted, but giddy with laughter as she struggled to balance on the skates wearing heavy layers. Most of us including me joined in—not laughing at her, but with her.

"Martha, Martha," Chlorine said, pleased with herself to have mastered balancing before her older sister. She breathed heavily, but her body slowly moved forward.

Finally, Brent, Jerry, Dad, and I had our turns. I felt comfortable figure skating quickly around the circumference of the rink. Then I changed gears. Leaning forward and gliding on one skate, I held the other foot up in back with my arms stretched out like a bird. I imagined I was flying. I gathered speed by making strong quick strides so I could repeat the bird act. Jerry and Brent raced, cutting across the rink in competitive bold strides. Dad skated around us with rhythmic ease, hands together, resting on his back.

Mom remained inside to bake the stollen she had mixed, kneaded, and shaped earlier. The cabin was filled with a welcoming sweet aroma as we clambered in to warm up and rest around the table.

She handed us each a cup of hot steaming cocoa with melting marshmallows floating on top. She had used the can of Hershey cocoa resting handily on the shelf above the sink. I removed my thick wool mittens and felt the warmth of the mug in my hand. The rich hot liquid, dipped from a pan on the flat iron cookstove, heated me through with each swallow.

Mom said, "Help yourselves," placing the hot stollen, glazed and decorated with almonds and maraschino cherries, onto the table. The cardamom scent sprang into the air as she cut the loaf. I quickly finished my first slice and grabbed another. Everyone else did the same.

As we munched, Dad picked up his mandolin. He had taught himself to play by ear any string instrument back in Chicago. The mandolin was kept in a cupboard under the stairs, and he brought it out each evening usually singing cowboy songs. Hearing him play would make me happy. Tonight he said, "Time for a carol. How about 'O Tannenbaum'?" He sang it in Swedish, a language I do not speak but always reminds me of him.

He sang and strummed the instrument, cradled on one thigh.

O julegran o julegran med barr sa troget grona
Ojulegran o julegran med barr sa troget grona
De ger oss gladje, frid och trost
Bad sommar, vinter, var och host
O julegran o julegran med barr sa troget grona

We joined in when he sang our favourite tune in Engish:

O Tannenbaum, O Tannenbaum,
How loyal are your needles!
You're green not only in the summertime,
No, also in winter when it snows.
O Tannenbaum, O Tannenbaum,
How loyal are your needles!"As the Kingsley girls were leaving,

snow began to fall. It was still coming down at bedtime.

We woke to several inches of fresh snow. Remembering stories Dad told about building snow tunnels with his older brothers in Wisconsin, I suggested following their example to Jerry and Brent.

"It's perfect for tunneling," I said while filling the reservoir on the side of the cookstove with cold lake water. I still had some tasks to do before I could play outside so I watched as the boys headed out into the yard in hooded jackets and snow pants. Mom and Dad busied themselves brushing snow off the Chevy and shoveling paths to the shed housing the generator and freezer and to the outhouse.

I tidied up the cabin waiting for the water to heat up in the reservoir. It would be a good time to wash my hair. Mom had already taken up and folded the sheets and comforter from the sofa bed. I lifted the back until it hinged, and then slid the sofa against the birch wall. Afterwards, I placed the small braided rug in front. Scamp moved from the wood-burning heater to the rug. Finding the shampoo, conditioner, and my hairbrush, I placed them by the barrel that served as the kitchen sink. With a glance out the window, I saw Jerry and Brent mounding snow into a row about waist high. I took down my towel from the wire above the stove and placed it by the sink. It was warm and soft. How peaceful the morning was inside the cabin by myself. Outside, grunting sounds from Mom and Dad working reminded me they were near. The only tracks were those of Jerry's and Brent's to the nearby tunneling spot.

I used a metal dipper to half fill the kitchen sink with warm water from the reservoir. Placing my head into the water and then lifting it out, I lathered with a generous portion of Clairol. I rinsed. Twisting my hair tightly, I squeezed out most of the water. As I grabbed the towel, I glanced out the window. The unbelievable scene before me made me stop. What looked like one of Jerry's arms extended out from the mound of snow up towards the sky. My God, I thought, overwhelmed with fright. My brothers' bodies were completely covered. They were pinned under the caved-in tunnel!

I ran out with my wet hair whipping around my shoulders and dampening my light blouse. Crystallization was almost instant, creating stiff strands of ice to beat against my cheeks and neck. In slippers I raced, yelling, "The boys!"

Mom and Dad came running. Frantically, we dug with our hands around Jerry's extended arm. My bare fingers were freezing cold, and I shivered as I worked alongside my parents to free Jerry and then Brent next to him. The boys looked grey-blue and lifeless. "My God! My God!" Mom cried. "Jerry! Brent!" No response.

Partially dragging, partially lifting, we got each boy into the cabin. Dad sat them on the hot water reservoir. They opened their eyes. Both were stunned. We removed their heavy jackets and vigorously rubbed their faces and arms.

Mom filled mugs with hot water from the whistling teakettle. She spooned in Nestles instant tea, a little sugar, and a shake from bottled lemon juice. After a stir, she handed the mugs to Dad and me to help Jerry and Brent drink. They sipped slowly as we held a mug to the mouth of each with one hand, and used our other arm to hold them. Steadily we worked, continuing to rub their limbs and faces and insisting they drink the steaming tea. Jerry's and Brent's coloring of pinkish beige gradually replaced the lifeless bluish grey. Finally they were able to sit on their own and then stand.

"What on earth?" Dad asked. Jerry and Brent looked around and then at me. I wept knowing what might have happened. They had tunneled at my suggestion.

"Ok," Dad said. "We will do safer things in the snow from now on. This close call ended well, thank God."

The next day we went out to scout for our Christmas tree. Gail had come from Homer High School to join the family and stay through Christmas. She and Mom immediately had heads together planning our festivities. I accepted background position knowing that my sister would later divulge their plans.

On our 160 acres of unspoiled land grew a deep green forest thicker than we could penetrate easily. Within this congested tangle, there were welcome openings now and again where we saw the bright white hoarfrost on large leafless birch limbs. It lighted like a beacon to guide us through.

We put on our skis and began a cross-country trek over the snow, with Dad pulling his handcrafted toboggan carrying the Swede saw and axe. Soon I felt overheated as I skied at a pace to keep up. I unzipped my thick jacket and let it flap. Scamp, excited to be with us, bounded around and barked at the chirping of chickadees and Canadian jays overhead in snow-laden spruce branches. As he leaped, he hit some of the lower tree limbs. I felt snow invade my neck and back and screamed, "Stop, Scamp. Stop, you dirty dog."

Gail, Jerry and Brent started throwing snowballs at me and each other, thrilled with my sudden plight. We laughed and skied further apart, dodging the streaming balls.

"Look carefully for a small symmetrical tree," Mom said, trying to get our concentration back.

"Try this one, it looks pretty good," I suggested, zipping up my jacket as I was chilled.

"The branches aren't as nice as the one over here," Gail said, pointing with her ski pole.

"How about this one?" Brent asked, skiing up to escape another of Jerry's snow missiles.

Dad opted to cut down all three. I took one end of the Swede saw to help and soon my shivering was replaced by warmth. We quickly loaded and tied them onto the toboggan and started back home. It would be Mom and Gail's decision as to which was best beside the sofa in the tiny house.

Back inside, we erected the tree Gail and Mom chose. Still Gail insisted on tying on a couple more branches to make a fuller shape before we decorated. The same colorful, bright baubles were used year after year; and the angel in light pink dress and honey blond hair adorned the top. Gail instructed me to move a few of my ornaments, and I did as I trusted that she had the more trained eye. Our black and white cat, Kitty, usually broke a couple of baubles with playful investigation. Gentle bubble lights of red, green, blue, and yellow were my favorite. I was enchanted by the colorful fluid with air bubbles moving endlessly through, and excited about the festively wrapped presents that accumulated under the low branch-es.

As usual, my Grandmother Dabbert's dark German fruitcake, rich in nuts, raisins, and candied fruit, arrived from Florida. The recipe had been passed down through the ages. She used comic strips from her city newspaper to protect the cake for mailing. Mom, Dad, Gail, Jerry, Brent, and I laughed as we read *Blondie*, *Dick Tracy*, *Little Abner*, and *Alley Oop* while unpacking her treat.

On Christmas day my parents prepared an apple/raisin bread stuffing to load into the fattest bird they could find in town. They laced it up with string and skewers before the long roasting. The project was done together like so many others, and all included disagreement and bickering. Christmas morning I heard Mom exclaim,

"John, are you blind? Your hands are in the way. I can't see where to wrap the string."

Dad responded, "I have to hold on or stuffing will come out, for Pete's sake. Go around, God damn it." The mid-western stuffing recipe and all the recipes came from *The Joy of Cooking*.

On they continued until placing the huge bird in the oven. Soon the smell of hot mouth-watering turkey brought up my appetite.

Mom also made a garlic baguette for this holiday and other family celebrations. Weeks in advance she prepared plum pudding so it would be fully mature by Christmas. Most spectacular was the bright red cranberry and apple gelatin ring garnished with mixed green leaves and placed in the center of the crowded table. Its sweet tanginess was a perfect accompaniment for the moist turkey Dad sliced and heaped onto our plates. Also on the table were giblet gravy, mashed sweet potatoes with marshmallow topping, and steamed broccoli. Other Christmases came and went, but that first one on the homestead in 1959 stays in my mind.

Stollen
Makes 3 medium size loaves

Ingredients:
1 package active dry fast-acting yeast
1 cup/240 ml/8 oz. skim milk
8 Tablespoons/100g/4 oz. butter or baking margarine
¼ cup/2½ oz./75 g white granulated sugar
1 teaspoon salt
¼ teaspoon ground cardamom
4½ cups/500g/l lb. 2 oz. plain flour
1 beaten egg
1¼ cups/ 190 g/7 oz. raisins
¼ cup/50g/2 oz. chopped, mixed candied fruits
¼ cup/50g/2 oz. flaked blanched almonds
zest from one orange, coarsely grated
zest from one lemon, coarsely grated
½ teaspoon almond extract
375g/14 oz. Marzipan (optional), if using, divide given amount into thirds

In a small glass bowl, heat milk and butter in the microwave for about one minute to melt the butter.

In another, large bowl, stir together the flour, sugar, yeast, salt, cardamom, raisins, candied fruits, almonds, and grated zest from orange and lemon. Stir in the yeast.

Whisk the egg into the slightly cooled milk and butter.

Add the almond extract. Add the liquid to the dry ingredients and stir.

On a lightly floured surface, knead the dough until elastic; about 5 minutes. Divide dough into 3.

Pat each piece into a 10x6 inch (25cm x 15cm) rectangle. Place a rope of Marzipan in the middle lengthwise if using. Fold the long side of the dough over to within 1 inch of the opposite side. Place on a baking sheet. Cover and let rise until double, about 1 hour.

Bake in a 375F/180C oven for 15 minutes, or lightly browned.

Remove from oven and brush with glaze.

Glaze: Combine 1 cup/100g icing sugar, 2 tablespoons hot water, and one teaspoon butter. Decorate with candied cherries or silver balls.

Roasted Turkey with Stuffing
One 12 lb/26.4 kilogram bird—feeds 8

Preparation:

Wipe the fresh bird with a damp paper towel; sprinkle and rub in 2 teaspoons salt. Stuff the bird (both cavities) with:

Mom's Midwestern stuffing:

In a skillet, sauté 2 peeled, chopped onions and 4 stalks, chopped celery in 6 ounces/150g butter.

In a large bowl, mix evenly:

  9 cups toast, torn into large pieces
  Contents of sautéed onions and celery from skillet
  3 tart apples, cored, and roughly chopped
  Handful of raisins
  2 teaspoons salt
  ¾ teaspoon black pepper
  1 teaspoon thyme
  1 heaping teaspoon sage

Insert skewers to close each cavity and secure with cotton string wrapped around and tied.

Place turkey in roasting pan at lower level of pre-heated oven: 325F/170C. Roast for 3 hours or until internal temperature (of breast) registers 165F on a meat thermometer.

NEVER STUFF THE TURKEY THE NIGHT BEFORE ROASTING as bacteria can build up to a dangerous level. The dry ingredients and seasonings of the dressing can be mixed beforehand and stored in the large mixing bowl; the onions and celery can be sautéed ahead and mixed together with the toast, apples, raisins and seasonings JUST before stuffing.

Remove cooked turkey to the kitchen counter and place on a serving platter (use oven gloves that can be washed for this heavy, hot job). Secure with aluminum foil across the top and onto the sides of the platter. Let the stuffed roasted bird rest for 20 minutes to an hour before slicing and serving.

Traditional Thanksgiving Pumpkin Pie
Makes one 9-inch single crust pie

First prepare enough short crust pastry to line pie plate. Flute edge and prick evenly with fork. Line with baking paper; load with ceramic baking marbles, and bake for 15 minutes at 425F/200C. Remove from oven onto wire rack to cool. Lift out paper with beads and set aside.

Using a large mixing bowl with whisk, or food processor and blend thoroughly:

> 2 cups roasted or canned pumpkin
>
> ½ pint evaporated milk
>
> ½ cup/6 ounces white sugar
>
> ½ teaspoon salt
>
> 1 teaspoon cinnamon
>
> ½ teaspoon ground ginger
>
> ¼ teaspoon nutmeg (optional)
>
> ¼ teaspoon cloves
>
> 2 eggs

Pour the mixture into the cooled pre-baked pie shell. Bake approximately 45 minutes at 350F/180C or until a knife inserted half way to the center comes out clean. Cool on a rack before cutting and serving with whipped cream.

Cranberry and Apple Gelatin Salad

Blend, in a food-processor:

> 1 lb./500g cranberries
>
> the zest from one orange
>
> ½ cup/4 oz./150 ml orange juice
>
> 3½ tablespoons lemon juice
>
> 1½ cups/10 oz./300g white sugar

Refrigerate overnight.

Soak, 1 tablespoon powdered gelatin in 2 tablespoons cold water for 5 minutes. Combine 1 cup boiling water with a 135g packet of lemon jelly; stir to help dissolve. Add softened plain powdered gelatin.

Add blended contents from food processor.

Pour into a one quart/1000 ml mold. Cool and then stir in 3 chopped tart apples. Allow to 'set' in refrigerator. Unmold onto desired plate.

The Homer Winter Carnival

Tania and I were sitting together in the Family Theatre where we sometimes met to watch a spaghetti western. The building was made of cement blocks and in the center of town, and a gathering point for the local community. Tonight we were not there for a film, but the beauty pageant sponsored by the Homer Winter Carnival.

Tania said, "Gail was in. Mom helped her choose a pink strapless chiffon. Skirt stands out full with cancans underneath...falls just below the knee. Have you seen it?"

"Oh, yes. She looks kinda baby doll-like in it," I replied and looked around as more people took their seats. There were only a few remaining, but not for long, I thought.

Gail was one of the contestants. Dad, Mom, Jerry, and Brent sat close by. The auditorium was filling as this was one of the most popular events during Carnival. Not just because it was indoors, when February weather was well below zero, but because everyone was fascinated with who would be crowned queen. Each girl's talent played an important part of the judges' final decision. That meant relentless practice by the contestants before the big night.

Gail had stunned Dad and Mom in the kitchen when she announced that she and Lois were entering the beauty pageant. Dad dropped a piece of coal into the cook stove and hesitated, replacing the fire lid. "I'll teach you a Swedish song," he said. "She already knows the hula," Mom countered as she poured cake batter into tins. "Let her do that."

"No! Time for her to learn Swedish, by God!" Dad replied with determination. I grabbed the cake batter bowl and spatula and began to lick greedily.

Gail excitedly said, "I might win this with the hula." Gail had entertained students in schools up and down the Kenai Peninsula since age eleven with her hula dances involving many variations on the basic steps. Her initial performance before the Homer School student body soon became known, and she was invited to entertain at schools further afield. She was known for her gracefulness in a grass skirt. Neither Gail, nor any of the rest of us, spoke Swedish.

"I hate you selling those carnival tickets, Gail!" Mom moaned.

"Mrs. Heath will have them in the shop." Mrs. Heath was a heavy set, short woman who had a good business mind. "Some will sell there," Gail said. She worked weekends at Mrs. Heath's "Alaska Wild Berry Products," a local budding industry in a log construction which cleaned berries picked by the locals, and made them into jams and jellies to sell to the public.

"Lois and I will hit the streets after school. The tickets will sell. I can give a few books to you guys to take up to Clam Gulch…"

"Oh God, is there no escape?" Mom uttered as she continued to prepare dinner, pushing the carrots towards Gail to peel.

Dad began teaching my seventeen-year-old sister a Swedish song that his mother had taught him back in Wisconsin. It was a risky decision.

"It is so good to have Carnival and the pageant tonight, Judy. You can't believe what's been going on," Tania grabbed my arm and looked straight at me.

"What's been going on?" I asked, feeling my best Homer friend was frustrated.

"Kids in our class have been stealing. They were doing it in groups…taking stuff from Myhill's new drug store. Stuff they didn't need…couldn't use. Crazy…" Tania said shaking her head.

"Nuts…for twelve-year-olds," I said, annoyed that the two seats in front of us were now taken.

I remembered taking the candy from Myhill's old drug store at age nine. I did not tell her of my own thieving as we waited for the pageant to start. I felt older when I heard about my former classmates shoplifting. I had long outgrown such behavior. Since leaving Homer in September, I had helped build our homesteading house, dress out and butcher a moose, and saved my brothers from suffocating in a collapsed snow tunnel. Plus, I had made new friends at Tustumena School. My old buddies had nothing better to do than steal?

We stopped talking as the Master of Ceremonies walked onto the stage looking dignified in his dark suit and red tie. He smiled broadly at the audience from under a blond crew cut, and crossed the stage confidently. Mrs. Wiltrout, the contestants' coordinator, looked briefly at him and quickly ended her chitchat with the local judges, and took a seat in the front row.

"Welcome, Homer," The MC shouted into the microphone. "We'll begin with a few announcements, proceed to the talent contest, and end with each girl modeling her ball gown. Our judges' final decision will result in the crowning of the 1960 queen of the Homer Winter Carnival." He kept smiling as he walked to the front of the raised platform and looked at us.

"Let me tell you about the weekend events: Saturday night will be the Ball at the Elk's Club with live music. Tonight's crowned queen will reign. Sunday the jalopy car races on Beluga Lake! Volunteers with snowploughs on their pickups have cleared a racecourse. Ladies' powder puff race is the last competition and always fun. Thanks to all who participated in the parade this morning…and for the many of you who worked tirelessly building the floats. What a lot of tissue paper stuffed into wire mesh! Great community spirit, Homer! And didn't all the contestants look beautiful on the leading float? Last year's winner wore the fur parka made by Mrs. Bea Watson which will be a gift for the lucky lady crowned tonight! Plus there are gifts from every store in town for our 1960 queen. Ladies and gentlemen, it's talent time!"

Gail's best friend, who was cousin to Gail's boyfriend Jack, stepped up to the microphone wearing a long black slinky skirt and form-fitting turtleneck. Lois with her chin up and bright red lips clearly visible across the auditorium, recited a poem. She eyed the audience confidently behind black-framed glasses. Every word was familiar to the audience:

Sam McGee
There are strange things done in the midnight sun
　　By the men who moil for gold;
The Arctic trails have their secret tales
　　That would make your blood run cold;

The Northern Lights have seen queer sights,
But the queerest they ever did see
Was that night on the marge of Lake Lebarge
I cremated Sam McGee.

Lois was rewarded with thunderous clapping. Some stood up.

I remembered the four of us in Gail's bedroom several weeks earlier. Lois and Gail had tossed out talent ideas. I was fascinated, and knew then that I, too, would run for queen when older. Tania sat by me on the floor listening closely to the older girls.

Gail sat on the bed with her chin resting on a hand and shook her head. "I don't know...the hula? Dad is still keen on a Swedish song. I haven't made up my mind. I really want to win."

"You know the hula through and through," I said.

Lois replied, "*Sixteen Tons* was sung a couple of years ago by the girl who won. Got to have something Alaskans like...Gail, are you going to change your hair?"

Tania leaned over to me, pulling at her wool socks, and said, "Lois is right."

My thoughts returned to the present as Gail walked on stage. She was wearing what Dad remembered as Swedish country dress. It was homespun looking instead of the sexiness of Lois's black number. Gail sang the folksy tune in rhythm to the mandolin. I saw Dad flinch at one point and wondered why. Gail stepped off, and then the others performed. None were better than Lois.

After about twenty minutes, each girl modeled her gown. Gail was very pretty and graciously stepped and turned on the stage. Her short, brown hair curled around her face. She had applied enough make-up to make her cheeks rosy and her eyes prominent, but it was not caked on. Mom had made sure of that. The contestants paraded and stopped in a line facing the judges.

The roar of a drumbeat held us in suspense for a few moments. It stopped as one judge stood up and handed an envelope to the MC. The auditorium fell silent except for the ripping open of the sealed document. Holding it out, the MC bellowed: "The winner of the Homer...Winter...Carnival...beauty pageant for 1960 is...Miss Lois Reynolds!" Lois stepped forward confidently smiling. Last year's queen secured the rhinestone crown onto Lois's head. Gail and the other contestants smiled and clapped with all of us in the audience gazing at the lucky winner.

Tania and I stood, and then made our way to the front exit behind many people ahead of us. I thought maybe Gail could have won with a hula, but remembered what Gail had said in the weeks beforehand. "Lois is favored by our teacher—the bag, Mrs. Wiltrout—so she will win." At twelve, it brought home to me that who you know might be as important as talent, looks, or delivery.

I walked out feeling the cold air bite at my face, but was warm inside my long fake-fur white coat lined with red velvet. I had paid for it with my own money earned from Alaska Wild Berry Products. There were plenty of wild cranberries to pick around Porcupine Lake when we could free ourselves from homesteading projects.

We walked home, leaving Gail with friends chatting and watching Lois open her gifts. I said goodbye to Tania when we came to her house behind the store.

Once we arrived back at the rental house, Mom removed her coat and put the kettle on. She and Dad liked a cup of tea before turning in. I ran upstairs to bed just behind Jerry and Brent. My brothers' murmuring stopped as soon as they hit their beds.

Mom and Dad's voices traveled up from downstairs in the quiet house. "I heard in the post office this afternoon that the powder puff race was great fun. Virgo Anderson had just been there," Dad said.

"God, I would never stand in the freezing cold to watch women competing in an old car race. The postmistress wins every year anyway. I've heard that she circles the ice like a bat out of Hell," Mom laughed.

Dad laughed along and then said, "Yes, those were Virgo's words. He asked us to drop in to see him, Margaret, and Fred tomorrow afternoon."

"Hmm…maybe, but lots to do before we drive back to the homestead," Mom said.

I lay in my metal army surplus bed nodding off when I heard the back door open. Gail entered and stomped the snow off her boots. "Gail...it's you. How pretty you looked tonight!" Dad said.

"Yes, and so grown up," Mom added.

"The song was good, but you mispronounced a few Swedish words..." Dad informed her more quietly.

Gail almost shouted, "Who cared? No one else there spoke Swedish besides you."

Gail was right. As I drifted off to sleep I decided that when I ran for queen, I was not going to let Dad choose my talent number. No way.

Henning & Ruths house in Chugiak
About 1952

Probably J O Y 2 G I L in windows

Log house in Chugiak, 1952

Two Tustumena Friends

As we were so isolated on the homestead, it was a special moment when Mary Rusk invited me to return home with her from church and stay the night. She was pretty, the cleverest in the class, and the most popular. Her father had built their ranch style log house which even had indoor plumbing. Mrs. Rusk was comforting and on the heavy side of plump. She showed me the house. One unusual feature was an extra foot width of the halls for easier passage. A red strip of carpet, not laid down for me, ran the length and was welcoming and soft under my feet. Mary and her two sisters each had their own bedroom.

Mrs. Rusk pulled us to the dining table; and as we sat down, her dad said grace: "Dear Lord, we thank you for the friends with us today to share this food. We ask you, God, to help non-believers in the community find the way to be saved. In Jesus Christ's name we pray. Amen." Was this a direct reference to my family? I wiggled in my solid wooden chair—hopefully inconspicuous. Mom and Dad only attended Christmas and Easter services, and probably would not have been thought to be "born-again" Christians.

During my visit, Mary and I did not play outside because her family had a black and white television that was a luxury to me. It meant a life-style completely at odds to me and my family. After lunch we watched First Lady Jacqueline Kennedy give a tour of the White House. She had redecorated. The Blue Room was no longer painted blue. This was confusing, and I found out later that many Americans felt the same, including President John F. Kennedy!

Soon afterwards I invited Mary to come home with me after school on Friday. She was to stay for the weekend. I worried about her reaction to our small rustic cabin after seeing her house; but thought, oh well, we are friends.

I knew she would be uncomfortable inside so I suggested a few outdoor activities. "Mary, would you like to try skiing?"

"No, thank you."

"Skating? Dad's flooded a rink."

"Oh, no. I would fall and…"

"Walking around…seeing more of the lake?"

"It's pretty cold now. Maybe later."

In the cramped house she did not say much, but kept a brave smile as she looked around. Furniture and the two stoves utilized almost every inch of space. Mom insisted on order and cleanliness, so we had that.

She seemed bewildered watching me make us an after school snack. I laid a couple of slices of white bread directly on top of the flat iron stove griddle, quickly turned them over to avoid burning, and placed them on a plate with margarine. She followed me to the table as I used a knife to cover mine with margarine, and sprinkled it lightly with a spoon of cinnamon sugar. Mom had taught her childhood favorite to my brothers and me. Mary brightened briefly after a couple of bites. Thank heavens I had not burned the toast which sometimes happened, and required scraping with a knife, leaving a lingering pungent smell. The smell of such a mishap might have been more than my visitor could have handled.

Mom left us to visit upstairs on my side of the curtain while she prepared dinner. We sat on the bed under the sloping roof, and Mary took in my private space. There was barely room for two to stand between the bed, chest of drawers, and clothes hanging behind a curtain. She got up to the window and looked out at the lake covered with snow. "Do you see moose out there?"

"Sometimes," I shrugged. "More often just tracks."

"I'd be frightened if one appeared while we were walking," she said.

From the hi-fi downstairs came music, loud and clear. I smiled at Mom's much loved record. Mary looked up,

"What's THAT?"

The "Bolero."

"Oh, never heard it before. Different from our gospel records."

"She plays others—'The Merry Widow'; 'A Christmas Carol'. These are favorites that her parents played in their home in Chicago."

Mary raised her eyebrows as she cocked her head to one side and opened her mouth. I waited for her to say something. She looked like she was about to. Instead she scrunched up her nose, shook her head, and looked away.

"I love the sound of you and your younger sisters singing special numbers at church, Mary. Beautiful harmonizing."

"Oh, thanks. We love singing for the Lord."

Mom yelled, "Dinner!" We quickly stepped down, as did Jerry and Brent from the other side, and the four of us gathered around the table with Dad. I sat erect—tense. My stomach knotted. We never said grace before eating. What would Mary think of us? Oh, God, please have Dad make an exception this time and say a blessing, I prayed.

Mom placed the round steak roast with onions, carrots, potatoes, and gravy on the table. She sat down with a smile, but wrinkled brow. Mom was uncomfortable in our tiny cabin, especially when visitors came. She and I were forever locating a house plan to show and discuss with Dad. We all yearned for a bigger place, but no additional construction had been started. Looking at him, Mom asked, "Shall we begin?"

I glanced down and saw that Mom had folded paper napkins into triangles and placed one under each fork. We usually made do with paper towels.

"Yes, yes, let's eat," Dad said as he began carving the roast. "Do you like your slices thick or thin, Mary?" he asked with his usual twinkle.

"Thin please, Mr. Johnson," she said politely, but her ponytail remained glued to her neck. She kept her eyes on Dad's slicing.

Oh, dear God, I thought. What kind of impression are we making? Jerry and Brent chatted about a *Superman* comic. I knew they couldn't care less about saying a prayer. Was she thinking we were Antichrist? Mary, her head slightly bowed and hands folded, appeared to be expecting grace.

Mom asked as Dad put a couple of pieces of roast on her plate, "Will your father be fishing this summer?"

"Oh yes," Mary replied. "Mother, too. Our family lives on the beach during fishing—except for attending church every Sunday and, if we can, on Wednesdays."

"How nice!" Mom said as she spooned carrots, onions, and potatoes onto each of our plates.

"Oh, no onion, please," Mary said, shaking her head emphatically so that the ponytail swung reinforcing her request.

Mom spooned some that had dropped onto Mary's plate back onto the platter.

Dad interjected, "Great roast, Ruth," and forked a piece into his mouth followed by plenty of onion.

Obviously, there would be no grace. I noticed Jerry and Brent studying my friend as she closed her eyes and mouthed, "God bless this food. Amen." They then looked at each other, shrugged, and began cutting sizeable bites.

I closed my eyes so that I would not have to look at my guest. Why just this once had Dad not offered to say it? Strained, I picked up my fork and slowly started to eat. Mary did the same as Mom and Dad talked about going to Homer the following weekend. The meat and vegetables were well seasoned and tasty. Mary kept smiling while chewing, and I tried to do the same. She finished all but the pieces of roasted onion that had managed to creep under the carrots and potatoes onto her plate. I ate everything. She and I did not talk much, but listened to Jerry and Brent laugh and go on about the powers of *Superman*.

Mary and I did the dishes and talked quietly. "We have a new car. You'll see it the next Sunday when you come to church, Judy."

"Sounds nice," I said as I handed her the last plate to rinse. "What color?" I did not hear her answer as Dad started playing "Amazing Grace" loudly on the mandolin.

We retired to the sofa where he sat entertaining. There was only Mom's small handmade rag rug on the plywood floor under our feet. Mary looked amazed when I said, "My parents sleep here by folding this out into a bed." It was just a few feet from the kitchen table. Scamp lay curled up on the end of the rug by Dad's tapping foot.

Mary smiled and we sat listening. I was pleased that she looked happy after being quiet during the meal.

"Nice, Mr. Johnson," she said getting up. "I love that hymn.

"Another one, Dad?" I suggested.

"How about one of my cowboy songs?" "Little Joe"?

Mary was already up. Dad looked, trying to get her eye, but failed. "What about *Puff, The Magic Dragon*? I just know it from listening to the radio."

She was climbing the stairs. I felt disappointed that Dad had not been able to win her over with more of his music. She seemed to enjoy the hymn, but...Scamp yawned and moved closer to Dad. He was not wagging his tail as usual. Mary and I went upstairs and sat on my bed. She looked around taking in the stack of *Nancy Drew* books stacked by my *Bible* on the chest of drawers. I said, "Are you taken up with *Nancy Drew's* detective mysteries, Mary? Mom keeps orders of books coming from the state library in Juneau."

"Not *Nancy Drew*, Judy. You are still reading the *Bible* each day?"

"Yes," I replied.

Mary went on, "That's good. Learning God's Word is important. I hope to be a missionary in a foreign field one day."

"Oh, me, too," I said. Mary is like me I thought in that she plans to travel and see more of the world.

We each quietly read a chapter in "Exodus" aloud. I found reading about Moses out in the desert beside a burning bush with the angel of the Lord speaking to him without being consumed, bewildering. She said, "Such a good passage."

"Yes," I said, folding back the thick covers so we could get into my double bed. She nestled her head into her pillow and said, "Michael looks at you with bulging eyes and smiles."

"I know—creepy. Can't stand him. Fat. Yuck. David's nice. I'm glad his desk is in front of mine. He picks up my pencil and also Virginia's if they drop...shares math answers. I often talk to him at the square dances. Do you like him, Mary?"

"Oh yes. He's kind, but not a born again Christian. We should pray for David. Who is your best friend in Tustumena, Judy?"

"I like all the girls, but...you best, Mary."

"Thank you, Judy. I hope that I don't have to get up before morning. It's cold out! Good night."

Making it to the outhouse was a nuisance, but I went with Mary.

In the morning she asked to be taken home. The reality of the moment nearly extinguished my positive twelve-year-old spirit. The girl who I wanted to be best friends with would not be coming for another visit. I looked around the tiny downstairs. If only we had more space...had said GRACE...and had—a TV.

Monday, at school, she thanked me for the stay and said, "My leaving early had nothing to do with your small house, Judy." Hurt, I only smiled and said, "I know, Mary." We continued to have a good relationship at school because I was one of Mary's admirers. I wanted friendship, but Mary needed an entourage of religious followers. I worked hard to be one, and continued walking to the end of the road each Sunday for a lift to church with her family.

Previously Gail and I had gone to Sunday school and church together in Homer, but on the homestead I was on my own. I missed her as I hiked in the quiet forest. Spruce hens flapped their wings and came down from the trees in October and November, pecking hungrily on cranberries growing plentiful along my way. Woodpeckers hammered. I prayed to God silently to protect me if a moose or bear crossed my path. During my solitary walks I missed Gail: I could have confided my upset state caused by Mary's abbreviated visit. That would have been comforting. I did not speak a word about it to my parents or brothers, nor they to me. I thought how lucky Gail was to be in Homer in the bigger rental house with plenty of room for our family and for friends.

I was disappointed that Mary, who I still befriended did not feel comfortable on our homestead. I needed a friend to share secrets with at home.

Later that year, on instinct, I invited Virginia Tri for the weekend—a girl in my class who I had rarely talked to before. She was from a large Minnesota Catholic family. Virginia was game for everything: skiing, building a snowman, and baking. She raced back and forth to the outhouse in easy strides. I do not remember us going to church.

Saturday afternoon we came in from skiing and I said, "Let's make brown sugar bars!"

"I'm ready." Virginia looked up. "Who's singing? Think I know the voice..."

"Oh, Dad's put on his favorite record…Jussi Bjorling."

"I know that tenor. We're from Red Wing, Minnesota. Everyone there knows Bjorling's 'O Holy Night.' Brown sugar bars… pass me the mixing bowl."

I pulled down *The Joy* from the overhead beam and opened to the recipe. "Cream the margarine first, and I'll get the rest of the ingredients."

"Gotcha." Virginia used the wooden spoon to attack the solid block of margarine. I measured the flour and other dry ingredients into the sifter. "I'll cream the brown sugar into the margarine. Can you sift?"

"Sure," she said turning the handle to the rhythm of Scamp's tail beating the floor. We laughed. Scamp increased the tempo and likewise, Virginia sifting. This caused some of the flour mixture to spray out and dust the floor.

"Oh, silly me. No, it was Scamp's fault." She laughed. "Where's the broom?"

"Just outside the door."

"A good straw one like ours." She quickly swept the floor clean. We got the mixture into the baking pan and onto a rack in the hot oven.

Thirty minutes later I yelled, "Anybody who wants hot brown sugar bars, come." Jerry and Brent rushed down the steep stairs and Mom and Dad came in from the porch.

"Smells good!" Dad said.

Mom tore a paper towel from the kitchen roll and handed one to each of us. "Let's not dirty dishes."

Jerry and Brent each grabbed a bar and started munching.

Virginia said, "If they are too moist, it's Scamp's fault. His wagging tail made me turn some of the ingredients right out of the sifter."

"Scamp? You bad doggie." Mom said and laughed.

"Ha," Dad chuckled as he reached for another. "I think these are perfect," He said as he devoured the second.

Virginia and I laughed and looked at Scamp. He came over to investigate with his head up and tail wagging.

I was excited when Virginia invited me to their large wooden two-storey house that was unfinished—black tar paper on the outside. While Virginia and I set the table, her older sister, Dawn, brought in a large bowl of spaghetti while her brother, Guy, carried in the steaming meat sauce. I liked Dawn and thought how lucky Virginia was to live with her older sister. Dawn said with a comforting smile, "So glad Virginia brought you home, Judy!"

Mrs. Tri heaped the food onto each plate, and we dived in. "There is plenty more, Judy."

Guy said, "Ok, Judy first after me. Ha!"

Dawn frowned and said, "Mind your manners, Guy!" I laughed and looked over at Mr. Tri. "Where did you get your family's moose?"

"Oh, just like your dad, Judy, not far from the house."

"Makes good sauce," I replied as I finished my last bite.

Mr. Tri had only one arm, but flew a bush plane besides getting the annual moose! Years later, my own brothers made friends with the Tri boys who were as active and ready for anything as Virginia.

In the future Jerry and Dad would survey their homestead to divide it into lots for the family to sell. Virginia had settled into married life in Minnesota, but returned to be involved in her siblings' decisions regarding the sale of the family homestead. Mom said, "Virginia was the same fun, kind person. It was wonderful when she came to the office. We laughed and talked about old times."

I spoke to Mary once on the phone when home for a visit after living out of state for many years. I was over forty and living in the U.K. She could not see me because of a painful back which was the result of a car accident. We chatted about Solid Rock Bible Camp. It was still managed by the same pastor and his wife. The Mainwarings had moved to California. She ended by saying, "I've become a born again Christian, Judy."

"Mary, I'm confused. You were a born again Christian when we were girls at Tustumena."

"Not really, Judy. But now I am really a Christian. My husband and I are leaving for Mexico soon. We will be missionaries."

That Christmas I received a Christmas card with a religious tract from Mary. There was a message about her teaching in the evangelical church in Mexico with her husband. All along I felt Mary never needed a friend as her religion was enough. Looking back, I'm glad Dad did not say grace at the table.

Oven baked Round Steak (roast)
Serves 5 to 6

Pre-heat oven to 350F/180C
 One eye-round roast (beef or moose) about 1½-inch
 thick, cut.
 1 to 2 white or yellow onions, peeled and sliced
 1 to 2 cloves garlic, peeled and sliced
 1 tablespoon oil
 Ground black pepper
 1 can condensed cream of mushroom soup

Over medium heat, lightly sauté the onion and garlic in the oil, using a heavy skillet with lid, or Dutch oven; push to one side of the pan and brown both sides of the steak. Sprinkle with pepper.
Pour over the cream of mushroom soup, cover, and place in the oven for about 45 minutes to one hour, or until cooked to your taste for doneness. We preferred the meat slightly pink for tenderness.
Serve with steamed potatoes or rice, and a green vegetable

Cinnamon/Sugar Toast

This quickly made snack is more easily prepared with a toaster than a flat-iron cook stove griddle as we used on the homestead. Less chance of burning too! Butter the toast and sprinkle lightly with a mixture of white granulated sugar and cinnamon.

Brown Sugar Bars
Makes 16 squares

Pre-heat oven to 350F/170C
Melt in a saucepan:
 ¼ cup/100g butter
Stir in until dissolved:
 1 cup/7 oz. brown sugar
Cool these ingredients and then beat in:

1 egg

1 teaspoon vanilla

Sift together and then stir into the above mixture:

½ cup/3 oz. plain flour

1 teaspoon baking powder

½ teaspoon salt

Add ½ cup chopped nuts or grated coconut if desired.

Pour the batter into a greased 9 x 9-inch pan. Bake 20 to 25 minutes. Cut into squares when cool.

Meat Sauce (Like the Tri's)
Serves 4-6

Ingredients:

4 tablespoons olive oil	1 large onion, chopped
2 garlic cloves, peeled and sliced	4 to 6 slices bacon, chopped
2 carrots, roughly shredded	4 celery sticks, finely sliced

500g/1 pound, ground, moose, caribou, or beef

150 ml/½ cup red wine   ½ pint whole milk

Dash or two of ground nutmeg

1 x 425g/14 oz. can chopped tomatoes

2 teaspoons granulated sugar

1 heaping teaspoon dried oregano

Salt and ground black pepper to taste

500g/1 lb dried spaghetti or any pasta of choice

Parmesan cheese, grated (to sprinkle on top by each person at the table)

Heat the oil in a large heavy pan (Dutch Oven is best) on medium heat. Add onion, carrots, celery, and garlic and sauté until soft. Add the ground meat and let brown, while stirring to evenly mix in the vegetables.

Pour in the red wine and bring up to simmer. Add all the spices.

Pour in the milk, and bring back to simmer. Add the tomatoes and sugar. Turn heat down so that the meat sauce is barely bubbling. Cook slowly with the occasional stir for about 2 hours or until thick. Taste to adjust seasonings. Serve on top of hot boiled pasta. Pass Parmesan.

Two Sisters On the Lake

I always looked forward to summer with plenty of fresh vegetables and berries, but weeding and hoeing were tedious and dreaded. The summer of 1960 was especially exciting because after the year of living on her own in Homer, Gail was spending a month with us on the homestead. I was so happy she was coming back even though she might be leaving again soon.

I remember the day she drove up the homestead road to the cabin. She looked like an adult after the months living on her own in Homer in the rental house. She walked in and blurted out, "The wheel came off on the drive to Clam Gulch. The Heaths came to fix it when I called them from a gas station." The Heaths ran Alaskan Wild Berry Products where Gail worked part-time.

Gail had completed high school in three years rather than four, and was late to apply at the University of Wisconsin. She may have preferred California, but Dad was adamant that his home state was to be her destination. California was full of long-haired no goods in his opinion. He was determined that she attend college and distance herself from Jack, but he hated losing her from Alaska and out of our lives. We liked Jack, but he was eight years older than Gail and a Homer man without further education. Mom and Dad preferred she date others before marrying her first serious boyfriend.

Dad jumped in the car each morning to check the mail box for Gail's university acceptance letter. Disappointment built up with his return saying, "Nothing today." I was glad she was attempting to live out of state and hoped that she would succeed setting off to the U. of W. as that would lay the ground work for me to do the same when I received my high school diploma.

Apparently another out-building was essential if we were to emulate Abraham Lincoln's lifestyle. The whole family was erecting spruce logs vertically against the terracotta earth in a space dug out in a hill beside the lake. This would be a cool room to store harvested potatoes and carrots in bins; cabbages from the ceiling; and keep Mason jars of homemade jams, marmalade, and salmon.

Breathing heavily, Dad put down the chain saw and yelled, "Gail, I'm glad that you're helping build the root cellar before leaving for college. Grab onto this log."

"Go to Hell, John. If you'd have let her work out this month at Alaska Wild Berry Products, she'd have more money for college. Stupid," Mom cried out with disgust. Gail had been employed at the family run business in Homer after school, Saturdays, and summers through her teens.

"Yeah, now I'll have to work and go to class," Gail said.

"For Pete's sake," Dad replied, "You completed high school in three years. Part-time work at the University of Wisconsin will be a good way to meet people—from Wisconsin." Having disposed of the possibility of Gail's last month's Wild Berry salary, Dad was determined to gloss over the loss of earnings and her spare time at college.

Dad's focus returned to his construction: "Hey, we're ready to put up the slabs. Jerry, Brent, start bringing them over. They're light and will keep the soil from creeping in between the logs."

"I prefer cooking jams and jellies and shipping them around the world," Gail said assuredly. "Selling them in the shop is more fun than tugging around logs."

"You won't regret helping your family," Dad replied. We knew once the roof had been put on, Dad was planning a root cellar vestibule.

"Say John, how about a vestibule for the cabin?" Mom said. "A cold draft rushes in every time you come with a pail of water or someone runs to the outhouse."

"The new house," Dad replied, "will have everything."

I did my share of holding logs into position for Dad or Gail to secure. Finally one week before college commenced, Gail's acceptance letter arrived. My sister confided in me as we were tucked up in my double bed that night,

"Dad thinks he's done enough by buying my airline ticket and the three piece Samsonite luggage set. I do love it—all white. Plus the wool suits and dresses were fun to choose, but I could have earned enough for them and more at Wild Berry. The Heaths like me. Dad just wants me to be a part of this damn homestead."

"I know, Gail. Think of me without you to talk to weekends. We'll be making fewer trips to Homer with you away. I dread the weeks ahead. Freezing and canning to store the garden harvest." I was quiet a few moments.

I planned to leave the homestead as soon as possible. Before college I was determined to go to high school in Homer—as Gail, and also be a cheerleader and run for Miss Homer. She interrupted my thoughts.

"Well, Judy, stay busy. Your clothes look professional so keep sewing."

"Ok," I said. I was glad she had noticed my skill.

"Read. Write to me," she paused and then continued, "I'm excited about university life. I'll miss Jack, but meeting new people will be wonderful. Gosh…Who'd a thought…Let's brave the cold with a swim tomorrow. Think you can make it across the lake with me? Just straight over from the cabin."

"Yes. I'll be right behind you," I said. The next morning was piercing cold, but we stepped out through the lily pads surrounding the lake. I dog paddled as fast as I could to keep up with her because she could swim. The water was pure, and I felt as one with Gail in the ten minute swim across the lake. These were moments that would last forever in my memory. The loons were landing, and the spruce and birch trees reflected onto the water.

The day she left was difficult for me, but I saw how happy Gail was to embark on college life. Over our sourdough hotcakes at breakfast, I did not say much, but she went on about the new adventure before her. "Wonder what these students will be like? The letter from the dormitory said my roommate's a girl as it houses only females. Many students are bound to be from Wisconsin, but other states, too; and maybe other countries. Probably not one other person will be from Alaska. Ha."

Mom and Dad beamed and nodded. Dad added, "There will be plenty of Swedish Americans—like us."

Gail looked slim and confident dressed in the new tailored pea green wool suit as she climbed into her boyfriend's Ford. Jack was driving her the six-hour journey to the airport in Anchorage. Their last hurrah for some time, I thought; and as I watched the dust from Jack's car settle on the road, I wondered how my life would unfold without her.

The rest of us finished shoveling dirt onto the log roof of the root cellar. We filled it with our garden harvest. There was no refrigerator in the cabin in 1960 as we only had oil lamps plus our own generator running part time, but this walk-in room built into the hill held enough to fill numerous home refrigerators.

Cold weather came with autumn, but inside warmth was maintained in the root cellar with the addition of a kerosene lamp to keep the temperature just above freezing. We would enter by closing the outside door quickly after us, walking the few feet to the inner door, and collecting jars of food and vegetables for the day. And so day after day passed with our homestead routine before Gail's first letter arrived from thousands of miles away. I rushed upstairs to sit on my bed to read it in privacy.

> Dear Judy,
>
> It is beautiful in Madison with the autumn red, orange, and yellow leaves falling outside my window. I'm on the top floor in an elderly couple's home. There was another Gail Marie Johnson enrolled who got into the dorm room that I thought was mine. Big confusion that resulted in me fainting on the spot. Two girls, settled into their room, let me stay for a couple nights. I still often go to films and meals with them. They both have boyfriends, and one is talking about marriage.
>
> The University is like a city within Madison. It is bigger than any place in Alaska outside of Anchorage.
>
> The Art Department is full of beatniks. The girls wear tight stretch pants that look like leotards, and loose baggy sweaters. The suits that Mom insisted on buying would make me stand out like a freak.
>
> How are you? What have you sewn? Are you still square dancing, or is it mostly church?
>
> Jack says he is coming for Christmas and wants to get

married. I haven't told mom and dad yet. Mum's the word, Judy. My money will be running out. I've no real friends in art classes. Those kids are too far out for me. Everyone in Homer likes Jack. He did leave Alaska for the army. But, I don't know. Probably he and I will visit Grandma and Grandpa in Florida over the holidays.

Love,
Gail

The rhythm of this month with Gail had been enriching in some ways, opening my mind to future possibilities, and choices I might be able to make. Yet the stillness of the lake was a constant reminder of her absence.

Gail's Cranberry Marmalade

Ingredients:
3½ pounds oranges
1½ cups water
3 cups granulated white sugar
12 ounces fresh cranberries

Remove the rind from half of the oranges, using vegetable peeler; slice into thin strips. Pell remaining oranges and cut into sections. Combine rind strips, sections, 1½ cups water, and 1 cup sugar in a large saucepan; bring to a boil and reduce to simmering for 15 minutes, while stirring occasionally. Add remaining sugar and cranberries. Simmer one hour and 30 minutes or until thick, stirring occasionally. Remove from heat, and pour into sterilized small Mason jars and seal with lids and rings.

Gail's Blueberry Jam

Clean and pick over blueberries and put them in a large heavy pan. Crush the bottom layer and add ½ cup water. Simmer over medium heat until almost tender. Add for each cup of blueberries: ¾ cup white granulated sugar. Stir while cooking over low heat until a tablespoon of the mixture dropped onto a small plate will stay in place. Pour into hot sterilized jars. Place lids on top and secure with jar metal rings.

Canned Salmon

Clean a salmon; do not remove any bones. Cut into chunks the size of pint size Mason jars. In each jar add ½ teaspoon salt and salmon to fill. Wipe rim with a damp cloth and cover with a lid secured with a ring. Put all filled jars in a large pan with a heat protector in the bottom of the pan, and fill pan with water to almost top of jars. Bring up to a heat to simmer for 4 hours. Remove jars when water has cooled and store. Rings are removed and stored.

Jerry and I beside freshly picked strawberries in Homer

Cabin Fever

Gail studying at the University of Wisconsin meant Mom and Dad giving up the rental house in Homer and us spending almost all our time including weekends on the homestead. School, Friday night square dancing, Sunday school, and church were my only diversions. Gail wrote to say that Jack did meet her in Madison and that they would be going to Grandma and Grandpa Dabberts' in Florida for Christmas. Her letter which Mom read aloud downstairs, came after the holidays:

December 27, 1960
Dear Mom, Dad, Judy, Jerry, and Brent,

We had a good Christmas lunch with Grandma and Grandpa, Uncle Roy, Aunt Betty, and their kids. One hiccup was Grandpa shouting at me for leaving the iron on all night, saying I was wasting money. I won't forget again.

My wedding dress will be Grandpa's and Grandma's Christmas gift. I found a short lace one with long sleeves and a full skirt with a princess waist. Jack will wear the wool jacket and tie he brought on the trip. We've set Valentine's Day as the date for our wedding.

It will be in the local Lutheran Church with Uncle Roy as Best Man and Aunt Betty as Maid of Honor. The kids will carry flowers. We will go out for a nice lunch with all the family afterwards.

The day after the wedding Jack and I will head for Reno, Nevada, where we will honeymoon and stay until May. We'll both look for jobs. Jack hopes to win enough gambling to buy a car to drive back to Alaska.

I said "yes" to Jack as soon as we reunited in Madison, but as the wedding date approaches, I do have a few butterflies in my stomach. I wish that you guys could come, but know there is no money for it.

I hope you are all well.
Love,
Gail

"My word, they are going for honeymoon where many go for divorce," Mom exclaimed after reading the letter aloud.

"I'm pleased their wedding is in a Lutheran Church, but she is not marrying a moneybag," Dad interjected.

"Who has?" Mom shouted and then added, "My father can be rough going. I'm going to reply right away to give her reassurance that both he and mother are pleased that she is including them in her wedding. After all, I eloped."

I climbed the stairs and went to my side of the cloth curtain. Gail was so lucky to be marrying the man she loved even though she had to quit college. Mom and Dad signed a bill for gasoline and groceries at the Clam Gulch Store, and they owed other people besides. Dad would settle accounts after a good surveying check came in. Cash was usually scarce so I knew there was no way Gail's college fees would be paid by Dad. But, who cared how much money the newlyweds had. They might win at the poker tables or roulette wheel. I, too, wanted to go to college and hoped I could save more than Gail to stay longer before marrying. Part-time work would definitely be on the cards for me.

I spent endless hours in the cabin that winter, and one day was almost too much for me. We had finished Saturday breakfast, and I was laying a pattern onto material spread smoothly on the kitchen table. This would be a new school dress. Using the measuring tape, I placed each tissue piece correctly. The dress had to be cut out before lunch and time was short.

Mom was sponge bathing while Dad, Jerry, and Brent were out getting wood. I screamed when Scamp came up vigorously wagging his tail, and the tissue patterns flew onto the floor.

"I had measured them all on straight of grain," I moaned.

Mom was naked, but quickly wrapped herself with a towel and opened the door for Scamp. "Go now," she said. February air rushed in as Scamp obediently went out.

I relaid the pattern pieces and yearned for a bigger place. For

God's sake, I lamented to myself. I sewed ferociously. It was fun and interesting not only to create my own clothes, but also to be recognized as accomplished by friends. At school, Mary Rusk said, "Your dress definitely looks store bought." "I wish that I could sew like that," Virginia Tri echoed. These comments made me feel stylish and clever. Gail had learned to sew on the Singer before me. Remembering Mom and Dad praising her for professional garments inspired me, along with Mom's encouragement to sew now.

Mom put on blue jeans and a turtle neck sweater. She opened the hi-fi which sat on my parents' dresser squeezed between the table and sofa, and put on *A Christmas Carol*. Hearing the story told dramatically by actors made me forget my sewing frustration. In my mind the miser, Ebenezer Scrooge, was wearing a rumpled black suit, bent over, fumbling with his key to unlock the door. His lips were tight and scrunched up into his nose where wire rimmed glasses dropped down. He turned with a jolt when Marley's ghost approached him—a white gown fluttering around. "I am the ghost of Christmas past," he said. It was frightening and left me waiting on tenterhooks for Scrooge's reply. As I glued my ears to Mom's record, I preferred my created images rather than those provided in books.

Dad came through the door with Scamp and stomped the snow off his boots. "For God's sake, leave him out, John. He has caused trouble this morning."

"How am I to know? The boys and I have been sawing and loading wood. What trouble?"

"It's not Scamp…it's this miserable house. No bigger than a postage stamp. Can't do a God damn thing. No privacy. Nothing," Mom yelled.

"Well, Hell. It's the best I can do for now. Be patient. Bigger will come. I'm hungry as are the boys."

"You'll have to wait until Judy clears the table of her sewing and helps me get lunch. I can only do…"

The atmosphere in the cabin got to me, no space—no one my age to talk to, and the bickering between Mom and Dad—too much. I ran outside for space in the cold. My brothers were chatting on their way back from the root cellar.

I yelled, "Chasing," and they dropped the potatoes and jars of canned salmon to run in opposite directions. In a burst of energy, I caught up with slower Brent. I grabbed his hair in my fingers of one hand and made a clenched fist and shook him.

"Judy. Ouch. What are you doing?" he said with a laugh and looked up at me. I let go and backed off.

Jerry yelled, "Can't get me."

I do not remember what I said, but I was embarrassed that I took out my frustrations on Brent. This was not the last time I forced this game on poor Jerry and Brent.

We ate lunch, and I went upstairs to my side of the curtain to read one of my brother's *Hardy Boys* books. I had finished all the *Nancy Drew*'s sent from the Juneau library. The books provided escapism and were about teenagers sleuthing.

Dad had taken over the table to draft a plat for a client. He was running behind schedule, and would have to finish it in the next few hours. No chance for me to sew.

Later that day after dinner, Mom and I sat on the built-in bench under the window facing the lake. It was covered with soft orange vinyl—hand tacked by Mom. She opened the *Lindal Cedar Homes* catalogue. Many other times we had looked at other catalogues. In *Sears & Roebuck* and *Montgomery Ward* we shopped for material, shoes, boots, jeans, and even the large upright freezer on this bench. Catalogue browsing and dreaming were part of our lives.

I hated the cigarette in her mouth, in her hand, and in the ashtray nearby. Thankfully, she was not a chain smoker. The cabin filled with the repulsive smell. Dad also lit up cigarettes in the early days of homesteading. The air reeked of smoke—coming from the two stoves and cigarettes.

Dad sat on the sofa playing his guitar and singing "Puff, The Magic Dragon." Mum and I hummed along as we searched for the right house. We pictured a spacious one to replace the tiny cabin. The hissing Coleman lantern sitting on the table was loud and constant, but did not distract us from Dad's music. We turned the pages and looked at the pictures and plans.

"I want an open plan kitchen, dining, and living room," Mom said. "Space for a sofa and a couple of comfortable chairs...deck projecting towards the lake. Oh, look at this: celestial windows plus floor-to-ceiling windows at the front. Mid-day winter sun would stream in. It would warm us…almost like on the beach in Hawaii or Florida."

"A fireplace downstairs," I said. "Scamp could curl up there. Plenty of room for a games table to play Scrabble, Monopoly, and work our jigsaws. Maybe even a piano. I could learn to play like Tania."

Dad put down the guitar and picked up a *National Geographic* and seemed to be listening to us as I glanced at him. I thought the burden of responsibility weighed heavily on Dad.

Mom and I sipped our hot tea, and knew that in such a house we would be comfy in spite of the cold outdoors where snow swept up in drifts across our yard and road. We lay in our beds night after night in the cabin listening to the wind whistling a tune through the branches of trees surrounding us. Only the howling wolves, yipping coyotes, and hooting owls with thick coats could survive in these harsh conditions.

Dad laid his magazine aside, tossed a log in the stove, and joined us with his mug. "Upstairs has to have four bedrooms plus a bathroom. I like the toilet separate."

Mom added, "Yes. We need a workroom for the Singer and table to lay out patterns. And storage…lots. It is a nightmare here." She took in a deep breath and blurted out, "I can't stand being cramped up much longer. I need space. Space." She lit another cigarette and looked away.

Dad lit one for himself, and slowly sucked in as he put an arm around Mom. "We will build a bigger house." He blew the smoke upwards and looked at her with conviction and tenderness.

Both Dad and Mom quit smoking during our "proving up years." Mom had smoked since age 14. It took her three years to quit—inspired by Jerry, Brent, and me sharing the gross health effects shown in films at Tustumena Elementary. More motivation for her to kick the habit was Gail expecting her first grandchild the following year. Dad dropped his cigarette accidently onto a surveying plat he had stayed up all night drafting. The plat was ruined, and Dad stopped smoking.

But the smell I remember from that evening came from something else. Dad popped corn in a black cast iron skillet on the flat-iron cook stove. He slid the heavy pan back and forth rhythmically to avoid burning the kernels. There was the hissing, the sliding, and then the welcome popping. These sounds linger now nostalgically in my mind. I can still smell the fresh hot kernels, and long for the taste of them with melted butter and a sprinkling of salt.

My parents made their dream home shortly after that evening. It was done in miniature scale using card and my father's drafting skills. Their model dream home was displayed on the Singer sewing table in the middle of the downstairs for weeks after completion. That meant no sewing and all of us skirting around the dream construction with groceries, laying the table for meals, using the hi-fi, and folding up clean clothes. From the date Dad and Gail had blazed a trail into Porcupine Lake, twenty-eight years would pass before the new family house was built.

For me, the expansiveness of the homestead would always be at odds with the smoky claustrophobia of the small cabin.

The Newlyweds

Jerry and I stepped from the school bus one day the last of May, 1961, to find a dust-coated four-door sedan parked at the beginning of the muddy homestead road. It was my sister Gail's and her husband Jack's: only driving through Canada on the Alcan Highway did cars end up so dirty that you could not detect paint color. We walked home and rushed into the cabin to find them sitting close on the sofa visiting with Mom, occupied in the kitchen corner. They leaped from the couch and greeted us with hugs. I sensed a reviving of a sisterly relationship with Gail; but although she was back, I was losing her to Jack.

"You both look great," Gail said looking skinny in snug purple trousers. Jack's dark hair was cut short, and he looked tidy in a long sleeve plaid shirt and blue jeans.

"And you both look very thin," I honestly replied. Obviously their new married life had not had large amounts of food to supplement love.

"I'm going to fatten them up with salmon croquettes," Mom said from the kitchen corner. "Change your clothes, and we will eat as they need to drive on to Homer today." She looked at Dad at the table, "John, I need the light plant on so I can use the deep fat fryer."

Dad rose with a big smile, and said, "Tell Judy and Jerry your news, Gail."

"Dad and Mom have given us two and a half acres with the old missionary cabin," Gail exclaimed.

"After we settle in to stay with my folks, we want to get up to have a look at the cabin," Jack added. "We'll fix it up and move in as soon as possible."

Dad and Mom beamed. They were cash poor, but land rich due to Dad sometimes taking land as payment for a survey. Gail's fellow high school classmates were getting dish sets and household goods from their parents, and she was receiving property with a first marital home, which only needed cleaning and decorating.

"Great," I said and thought, not a bad wedding present. I knew there was still an adjacent piece of land next to their gift, and hoped it would be mine when I married. A dream house looking out at Cook Inlet, mountains, and glaciers would not be a bad way to live. Plus, town was only a couple of miles below. I could picture my house next door to Jack and Gail's, with the modern conveniences that the homestead cabin lacked. "I'll get changed and help set the table," I offered and noticed that Gail had risen to do the same as Dad left to start the generator.

Jack was talking with Brent and Jerry. "The Ford I bought in Reno with a bit of luck at the poker tables is actually two-tone pink and white. Needs a good wash and vacuum when we get to Homer." They had not found jobs in Reno. As Gail and I set the table just as we had as children, it was like going back in time.

Jerry petted Scamp and said, "Saw it at the end of the road caked with dust. Pink and white you say?"

I looked at the happy couple wondering about their skinniness and their adventures. A new phase of our lives was about to begin.

Salmon Croquettes

Mix:
  2 cups flaked canned salmon
  2 cups mashed potatoes
  1½ teaspoons salt
  Good shake of coarsely ground black pepper
  1 beaten egg
  1 tablespoon minced parsley
  1 teaspoon Worcestershire sauce
Chill, shape, and bread, dry and fry the croquettes in deep fat. Drain on paper toweling before serving.

Solid Rock Bible Camp

"You have to promise me that if one of you 'gets saved,' the other will throw the 'saved' one into the lake," Mary's mom said as she handed us the $10 for Mary to accompany me to Solid Rock Bible Camp, the summer of 1961.

Mary Rearden with her family had moved from California to Homer. Like mine, they were not a church going family. Her father was a hunting guide and head of the area state Fish and Game Department. They lived in a large tent on their town property while Mr. Rearden built a huge log house alongside. Mary and I had attended Homer Elementary School together before my move onto the homestead. On weekends I visited her upon returning to Homer.

Dad did a complimentary surveying job for the Solid Rock preachers, and they offered **his** kids a week's stay on the house. Jerry, Brent, and I would go different weeks because of our ages. I was eager, thinking joining other kids at the camp would bring excitement into my life. It also meant I would miss hoeing potatoes and vegetables.

My parents drove Mary and me to Solid Rock, twenty miles away in Soldotna, with our camping clothes and sleeping bags. Soldotna was a small growing community with strong Christian roots. Solid Rock Bible Camp was new and unique on the Kenai Peninsula. Its catchment area was from surrounding communities. Half a century later Solid Rock Bible Camp is still there. The new wooden buildings were nestled amongst mature birch and spruce trees close to a lake. Wild pink fireweed spears, blue geraniums, and lupines grew between the trees and dirt paths connecting the buildings.

We settled quickly into the girls' dorm, and I introduced Mary to my girlfriends from Tustumena School. They each had a personal *Bible* beside their bed. Mary Rearden had not brought a *Bible*.

"Here's another Mary—Mary Rusk. Her family fish commercially. She is talented—sings with her two sisters at church. And this is Susan. She is the daughter of our minister. And Linda is the daughter of an old surveying buddy of Dad's and also lives on a homestead. She's always cheerful. Her family fish." They grinned during our exchange of hellos, but made no real attempt to chat, preferring to keep to themselves. I felt that they were uncomfortable with my Homer friend, Mary Rearden, who had only pleasantly said "hello." It would have made the Tustumena girls more comfortable if she had brought a *Bible*, or uttered, "Praise God," after a couple of the introductions, but she remained quietly smiling by my side. We slept upstairs in the large wooden building on canvas army cots lined up in rows.

Mary and I were amazed at the modesty of the girls. We were the only ones who changed into our pajamas beside our camp beds. The others got into theirs contorting inside zipped up sleeping bags. "Gosh. Are we brazen hussies?" I asked, shaking my head at Mary. She laughed, grabbing her toothbrush and paste. I noticed that my Tustumena school friends flushed pink as they looked over at us. "Oh, well," I said under my breath. I was growing up in a two-roomed cabin without central heating. Speed rather than modesty was the priority when dressing or undressing at home, and my parents had not brought me up with nineteenth century values about nakedness being next to Godlessness.

Camp wake-up call came early. It was already light. But then it had never gotten very dark because it was summer, and we were close to the Arctic Circle. It was a brilliant clear light. I quickly washed, changed, and headed to the main hall with Mary. Stacks of thick pancakes were being placed on the tables along with margarine and syrup by church volunteers, including Linda Hermensen's mother. We were ready to eat, but I knew that first grace would be said. Mary Rearden picked up her fork to take a bite and then set it back down as she sensed we were all waiting. I saw Mary Rusk look embarrassed at the mistake. Pastor Bert, the manager, said grace: "Bless this food to our bodies, dear Lord, and keep all one hundred campers safe as they enjoy this beautiful day at Solid Rock." I noticed everyone ate with enthusiasm as they chatted about their chosen activities. These ranged from archery, hiking, badminton, to water skiing. We remained for a short prayer service after breakfast.

In the afternoon, many of us lined up on the dock for water skiing. "You first," Linda told Susan, laughing and running to the end of the line. "No way," said Susan escaping. A game of dodging the position of head of the line ensued. Mary Rearden sat on the dock, dangling her feet in the water. When it was actually time to go, I was the only one willing to put on the skis and grab the rope. Off I went, unsure of myself at this first attempt. My experience on snow skis was so different.

It was a thrill to confront the challenge of remaining upright while skimming the water at an angle behind the boat. My mind was free without worry about Mary Rearden's lack of acceptance by the Tustumena friends and her lack of interest in them. Then I moved into the surf. The muscles in my thighs ached, as I bumped roughly along. I was determined to keep going. My arms felt strained as I gripped the plastic rope handles. The boat speeded up. Fatigued, I fell. The lake water felt warm and embracing in contrast to being chilled to my bones in the cold wind that swept over my exposed body while on the surface. The driver circled back with the boat for me. After a couple of attempts, I was back up skiing. I was wet and cold but felt invigorated as I saw we were headed back to shore. As we approached, I heard my friends clap and yell, "Yay!"

Unfortunately the novice driver had brought me in too close to the dock. I did not realize this until he slowed down, and the narrow wooden platform loomed directly in front of me. Suddenly I saw trouble and panicked. I could not turn the skis, but leaned away in terror as momentum continued to carry me forward. As I sank into the water, my speed slowed down but not enough to prevent my right leg scraping the rough boards as I glided in. "Yikes," I screamed. "Ouch." It hurt. From the corner of my eye I saw my friends cover their faces as they gasped out, "Judy." Looking down, I saw blood oozing from torn skin as I shakily climbed up onto the dock.

The preacher standing nearby screamed, "Stupid fool. Were you looking? Never, NEVER bring anyone in that close."

Humbled, the university student said, "So sorry, Judy. I'll be more careful next time."

"Let's get you to first aid, Judy." Holding onto my elbow, the preacher marched me off to the camp nurse—an R.N. volunteering her time. She had a look at my wound and reached for metal tweezers. "Nothing too bad," she said. With alcohol on cotton balls, she sterilized the pinchers and my scrape saying, "This may sting a little." It did and I winced with pain and shed a few tears even with her caring hands. Mary Rearden, who had followed me to the first aid station, walked back to the dorm with me. "You're braver than me," she said sincerely.

I was not deterred by my sore leg, and enjoyed more days of water skiing. Inspired, I decided I would ask Dad to rig up skiing on Porcupine Lake. We did not have a dock, but could take off and land in the water. Safer. I knew Jerry and Brent would be keen.

After dinner each evening, there was a service, and we sang well-known hymns. My favorites were, "How Great Thou Art", "The Old Rugged Cross", and "Amazing Grace". I joined in with gusto but then felt intimidated when the evangelist stood up. He was slim with dark complexion and slicked back black hair towering before us. He looked about forty and striking in white sports jacket and blue tie. He started with pounding-the-*Bible* preaching, ending with the invitation to come forward to "be saved." His voice reverberated around the room as he proclaimed, "The book of Revelation tells us over and over again that it is Hell and damnation to all who do not believe in the Lord Jesus Christ as their personal Savior."

The first couple of nights, sitting with Mary and my new homesteading friends, I was moved by the music; and listened to the sermon, but remained in my chair as the message to come forward was given. A few young teenagers did go up. Glued to my seat, I remembered what Mary's mom had said.

The third night, I sat between my new school friends, Mary Rusk and Susan Mainwaring. Their parents were "saved," and that had been instrumental in both girls making the commitment to be "born again Christians" years before. This was the root of their closer relationship than that with me. I longed to be included. Though I knew that I was generally liked, I still felt I was an outsider. I had eighth grade to complete at Tustumena before I would be returning to Homer for high school and rejoining Mary Rearden, Tania Uminski, Jack Collie, and other friends there.

Mom was not bothered by religion. My dad had been raised a Lutheran in Wisconsin by Swedish immigrant parents. There was no such church near us. With Sherry's death, he fell back on his childhood religion for a Christian burial. Since then, he had not attended church services. I always regretted my parents' decision.

The music from the small pump organ filled the hall as we sang, "Just As I Am".

> Just as I am, without one plea,
> But that Thy blood was shed for me,
> And that Thou bid'st me come to Thee,
> O Lamb of God, I come. I come.

The evangelist lifted his *Bible* and asked, "Do you hear God speaking? Can you admit you are a sinner? If so, walk this way. Christians are praying that you will wait no longer…have no more excuses to put off what you need to do RIGHT NOW. Come forward. Be cleansed. Follow your heart. Come…" He looked right at me with piercing blue eyes and pleading outstretched hands. I looked down.

I glanced to each side and saw my new school friends praying. Their eyes were closed and hands together as they mouthed the words to the hymn. I thought that they were praying for me to accept Christ personally as they had. The second stanza began…the organ music softer than before…

> Just as I am, and waiting not
> to rid my soul of one dark blot,
> to thee whose blood can cleanse each spot,
> O Lamb of God, I come, I come.

Should I go up? My hands became clammy as I held them together. I struggled listening to the invitation. I looked at Mary Rearden who appeared bored. The evangelist repeated the invitation, closing his eyes in prayer. I did believe in God and his son Jesus Christ. Should I make it public? Now? To be accepted in Tustumena I knew I must.

Others were walking forward in response to the persuasive words. Some were weeping. The organ music continued with the third verse of the hymn...

Just as I am, though tossed about
With many a conflict, many a doubt,
fightings and fears within, without,
O Lamb of God, I come, I come.

Overwhelmed by the atmosphere in the room, I felt tears well up. I slowly got out of my seat.

The evangelist said, "God is here...I feel his presence." He stood with open *Bible* in one outstretched hand, and motioned us to come with the other.

On reaching the front, I was received by born again Christians, both male and female, who were about my age. They ushered me into the back where I sat down with the wife of Pastor Bert. She was comforting with a soft voice saying, "Make a simple prayer asking Jesus Christ to forgive you of your sins. Thank him for dying on Calvary for you, and ask him to be your personal Savior." I made the prayer, speaking quietly. That was it. Done. I was pleased, but mostly relieved.

As I returned to the hall, everyone was walking out. My friends from Tustumena school had waited. They each gave me a hug. Susan said, "Congratulations, Judy." Mary Rusk, "God bless you, Judy." Linda smiled and took my arm. Mary Rearden came up chuckling, "Judy, is now the time for me to throw you into the lake?" I felt embarrassed but smiled, shaking my head. We left...I, and the new school friends, followed by Mary lingering behind.

At the time I did not think about Mary's feelings. Or being true to my own background and beliefs. Finally being accepted by the Tustumena group trumped any other consideration.

Presentation of Awards on the final day of camp provided a nice surprise for me. I was chosen "best camper" and given another free week the next summer. On my return home, Mom and Dad found this ironic as they claimed I was the messiest of all the Johnsons. They had a good laugh. I did not tell them that I had been "born again."

Camp Perok

A Russian meat dish made by Dorothy Hermensen, Linda's mother. It is served with cranberry relish and creamed corn or creamed spinach. This recipe requires a 9 x 13 inch baking pan and serves approximately 12.

Ingredients:
2 pounds/1000g lean moose or beef, ground
2 cups/300g white rice cooked el danté
2 chopped onions
1 chopped clove garlic
Salt and Pepper to taste

Mix all the above and place evenly in oblong pan. Prepare and roll out short crust pasty to cover. Bake at 400F/190C for one hour. Serve hot.

Short Crust Pastry

Combine in a large mixing bowl with a pastry cutter:
2 cups flour, dash of salt, and 1 cup unsalted butter.
Roll out on floured surface to a rectangle to cover 13 x 9 inch pan.

Cranberry Relish

Combine in a large pan:
1 pound/500g cranberries
2 cups/400g granulated sugar
½ cup/100 ml water
juice and zest of one orange

Cook, uncovered, over medium heat until most of the berries pop open or about 10 minutes. Let cool before serving. Keeps one day in the refrigerator.

Homestead Hospitality

Our cabin was in the midst of nowhere in Alaska. The "private drive" was two and a quarter miles long, and our nearest neighbor far too distant for a trumpet call or even a canon shot. But my parents were hospitable by nature and wanted their children to have friends stay. Instead of the single night sleepover favored by U.S. urban parents, I very occasionally had friends stay for a week at a time because of the long journey. These friends had to be selected with care: not all my classmates would welcome sharing my bed in a two roomed cabin where my younger brothers slept a few feet away separated only by a curtain. Not all my contemporaries felt relaxed about meeting a moose at night if they needed to visit our only lavatory—outside. But I knew that my fearless friend Tania, who left a homestead herself at age six, and lived behind her parents' Homer store, would relish the chance to rough it in our cabin. There was something that I did not know about her.

Tania arrived with her sleeping bag, change of clothes, and swimming suit fresh off the rack from their store. She was eager to swim even in the cold water of Porcupine Lake.

Gung ho Tania, Jerry, Brent, and I stepped out the door and raced to take the plunge. There was a light breeze creating very small waves on the lake, and the temperature was barely above 60F. The top few inches of the water were less cold than the depths below.

My brothers jumped in dog paddling close to shore. I waded out to just above my waist with Tania, our feet moving up and down quickly in the cold water. Mom arrived and stayed on shore longer, dipping in one foot and taking it out again as she psyched herself up for submerging. I decided to go in with the breaststroke. Tania was not going to be left behind.

She tried to move in the same way as I, and did fine for a couple of moments, then panicked. In her frightened state, she managed to grab onto me, locking her arms tightly around mine so that I could not move. It was a stranglehold. "Get off," I screamed, gasping for air. Her weight was pulling me under. I remembered what my dad had said a person experiences just before drowning. "A thousand thoughts race before your eyes." I could only think of how I wanted out of Tania's tight grasp. Tania only held on tighter. She was determined even in normal times.

I saw Mom start to move as my head and Tania's bobbed up and down in the water, and we gulped for air. I felt helpless. Could I escape? Tania had no intention of releasing me. Suddenly, there was a Styrofoam surfboard pushed close to us that Mom was holding onto and kicking ferociously from the back. I decided to leap for it; and in the process, felt the heavenly sandy bottom of the lake under my feet. I started walking, and Tania realized that we were safe and let go.

Oh God, Judy," Tania cried.

"My God, my God," I replied, exhausted.

We were shaken but relieved as we slowly staggered to shore.

Mom shook her head and said, "My lands, Tania, I thought you could swim."

Tania muttered a tearful, "Sorry." Her head was down, and I figured that she was embarrassed; but from her chattering teeth, I knew she was cold.

"Don't worry," Mom said. "You will learn. Now get up to the house and warm yourself by the stove."

After that near disaster, Tania joined right in with hoeing the garden; boating and fishing in Porcupine Lake; and conversing over a cup of tea with Mom and me at the kitchen table. She visited in the early days of homesteading when the mosquitoes were so ferocious we covered our heads with nets when fishing trout from the lake. Being game for anything, she fit right into homesteading life.

My parents' hospitality could extend to groups. Again they needed to be carefully chosen so that my guests did not return to school and make me sound unsophisticated or a freak. I continued to feel misplaced since being yanked from town at age 11 to homestead out in the sticks.

The second summer that we were on the homestead, I was keen to invite former classmates from Homer to come stay. But who would fit into homesteading life and get along in the group?

My first selection was Jack Collie, the boy I had a crush on since we were in fourth grade. He had remained the most popular boy in the class as he was handsome, friendly, and talented at sports—especially basketball. Who could resist a good looking, smiling extrovert? Second was Steve Walli, who was the grandson of our family friend who owned the main grocery store. Steve was a comfortable outdoorsman. His parents were divorced, and he lived with his paternal grandmother in the back of the Homer Cash Store. His father visited and trained him to hunt and fish. I knew that he was friendly with Jack and would love to fish in the lake. Third, I asked Mary Rearden who was not overly keen to rough it, but had experienced aspects with her own family in Homer while their large log house was constructed. She had attended Solid Rock Bible Camp where there was limited privacy and plenty of outdoor living. Dad drove them to the homestead in our Chevy sedan one Friday evening along with their sleeping bags, a couple pair of blue jeans, t-shirts, and fresh underwear.

I had been tense before their arrival. The outside of our cabin was ghastly. Dad's attempt to split wooden shingles to cover the black tar paper on all sides was quickly abandoned because of the call for more pressing homesteading tasks and his land surveying business. The two-storey cabin was very small with the toilet an outhouse. What would my friends think? Unlike Tania, none of them had lived on a homestead. They were used to comfort—not roughing it. I prayed that they would accept me since I would be returning to Homer to attend high school in a year. Mary Rusk had asked to be taken home after one night and was still a painful memory. I had so wanted her to be my best Tustumena friend. As the engine of the car stopped and they came in, I held my breath and clenched my hands together over a knotted stomach. I searched their faces for telltale signs. Disgust? Pity? Revulsion? Jack said with his big smile,

"Hi, Judy. Great to see you. Hi, everybody."

"Welcome," Mom said smiling. "Come in."

Mary slept with me in my side of the upstairs of the cabin, and the boys in a tent nearby.

The next morning we were on the lake in the rowboat for the first time and amongst the thick lily pads. We rocked the boat from side to side in water deep enough to drown. It was such fun to horse around in our small row boat on Porcupine Lake without any adults hovering. We wore life jackets because Mom had made it standard practice from day one of homesteading.

Steve said, "Fish. Quiet now."

The guys were good at pulling in pan-size rainbow trout. Mary and I ignored Steve's quiet request, and sang while dipping our fishing poles up and down and swishing them in time to the lyrics we belted out.

"Ten Bottles of Beer on the Wall" was a silly one that kept us going for long spells. This ditty was broken up by exclamations from the guys on bringing in fish they were proud of. "Look at this beauty," Steve said. "But how about mine? Look. It wins the trophy," Jack replied, laughing. All four of us belted out Allan Sherman's hit, "Hello Muddah Hello Faddah Here I am in Camp Grenada".

Scamp barked and chased around the edge of the lake trying to get our attention. Steve was as adept at cleaning the fish as catching them. Mary, shaking her short ash blond hair while pushing up her glasses, said, "I want nothing to do with smelly fish." "Me neither," I said, not because I minded but wanting to agree. Jack delved right in. The stainless steel blade flashed as he popped it out of his Swiss army knife.

"Watch me," Steve said as he showed him what to do. "Got it," Jack said, winking at me. "Hey, Judy, you and Mary grab buckets." I thought I was close enough to Jack with mine, but Mary pushed in front with her bucket. I was left to smile up at Steve. A contest developed as they used the knives skillfully to remove "the evil bits" from the trout. I watched Mary's nose wrinkle as Jack tossed in fish.

"Come on, come on," I cheered.

Finishing, Steve held up my hand and shouted, "We won. We won. More in our bucket. Hardy-har."

Jack, "You lucky guy, Steve. Wait until tomorrow. I'll show you."

Mom fried the trout as Mary, Jack, Steve, and I picked fresh tomatoes, cucumbers, and lettuce from the greenhouse for salad. Dad dug new potatoes from the garden. As these boiled, Mary and I set the table. The aroma of seasoned, floured fish frying filled the cabin. I felt hungry but also very happy as I took my place with the others.

After the meal and dish washing, Dad entertained us by singing cowboy songs, and encouraged us to join in a chorus or two as he strummed the mandolin. He finished with, "Little Joe the Wrangler", which was made famous by Marty Robbins. Even though Little Joe dies tragically under his fallen horse, Dad sang the catchy tune with confidence and feeling. We sat, swaying in rhythm. Scamp lay beside Dad with his tail going up and down to the beat. I was a bit embarrassed thinking they would judge him on his old songs, but my feelings changed a moment later.

Jack, "Judy, this is great. Your dad is good."

Mary, smiling, "Yes, Jack, I like it, too."

Steve, "It's ok…yes…good Henning."

The next day Steve and Jack went out in the boat by themselves to see who could catch the biggest fish. Steve won.

Just before the group departed, Jack and Steve took one last turn out in the boat. Mom, Mary, and I stayed inside the cabin collecting clothes that had been drying on a line over the stove. We folded and stacked them ready for packing-up. As Jack rowed the boat only a few yards away, he yelled, "Judy Johnson, I love you."

I thought, WOW, Jack does have special feelings for me.

Mary looked away. It was obvious from her downcast eyes and frown that she had also developed a serious crush on wonderful Jack.

Pan-fried Trout with New Potatoes and Button Mushrooms
Serves 2

Ingredients:
1 medium fresh water trout, cleaned, washed, and blotted dry
2 tablespoons plain flour
½ teaspoon salt
½ teaspoon black pepper
1 teaspoon dried thyme plus
     extra shake over frying potatoes and mushrooms
2 tablespoons olive oil
5 to 6 small new potatoes, each cut in half
1 packet (200g) button mushrooms
½ cup/4 oz. white wine
2 Tablespoons toasted flaked almonds

Put the flour, salt, pepper, and thyme in a bag with the trout and shake to coat. Remove trout from bag.

Par-boil the potatoes for 10 minutes. Drain. Heat oil in a large heavy skillet to medium. Add the potatoes and mushrooms; sprinkle with a bit of dried thyme; cook for about 5 minutes, turning occasionally.

Add the floured seasoned trout to the middle of the skillet, making way between the potatoes and mushrooms. Cook for 5 to 6 minutes continuing to turn over the potatoes and mushrooms occasionally during the cooking. Turn over the trout. Add the white wine and cook for 2 minutes. Cover and cook for 5 minutes more.

Divide trout into 2 fillets, removing the back-bone in the process. Sprinkle each with a tablespoon of toasted flaked almonds. Serve hot with fresh lemon, new potatoes, mushrooms, and your favorite greens and vegetables to make a salad.

Jack's Letter

Jack Collie's two-page letter arrived within days of his visit. My dad brought the letter from the mailbox at the end of the homestead road. Dad looking knowingly at me as Jack's return address was on the envelope, said, "Judy this is for you." I took the letter upstairs to read it in privacy. Pleasure rushed over me as I read his words. "Sleeping outside in a tent had been great, trout fishing superb." He asked me to thank my parents for him. But it was his next sentence that jumped out from the page. "Will you be my girl when you return to Homer for high school?"

An immediate flush of excitement warmed me. For three days I reread the letter in my private confined space upstairs, sitting on my double bed, gleefully thinking of Jack, wonderful Jack. I had liked him since fourth grade—age nine.

I carried on dreaming of Jack while doing my usual cooking, garden harvesting, and sewing. It was during these daily chores that I began to remember the teachings of the local church. They crept into my thoughts and interrupted the joy of Jack's steady girl proposal.

Without discussing the decision with my family or friends, I wrote back earnestly from my side of the cloth curtain:

Dear Jack,

It was so nice to get your letter. My parents, brothers, and I loved having you and the others here. Did we ever stop laughing?

The request to be your girl overwhelmed me with pleasure. It was so unexpected. After pondering and thinking about it, I realize that I have an inner conflict. I became a born-again Christian at Solid Rock Bible Camp this summer. This means I must say "no." The community church I attend discourages born again believers entering into a relationship with anyone not of the same conviction. I know that you and your family attend the Homer Methodist Church, and it teaches that a person is a Christian without being born-again.

I sadly decline your offer although you have a special place in my heart. I've always admired your entertaining personality, basketball skills, and adore your company. However, I feel my decision is the right thing to do.

I hope we can remain very good friends.

Love,

Judy

Tania and I with trout caught in Porcupine Lake

Anniversary Spring

It was 1962, and nearly a year since Gail and Jack had returned as newlyweds. They had sanded the inside logs of the missionary cabin, added plumbing from a natural pure spring on the property, and moved in. Now they were adding on to the original small structure to make two bedrooms and a bathroom. We saw them only occasionally. In fact, I had become much closer to Jerry and Brent and felt my sense of responsibilities towards them.

Spring Break-up came and the road froze at night and thawed during the day. One day Clovis Kingsley was driving us in his Jeep at a good clip while Brent entertained us by singing Johnny Horton's popular and much played hit, *Sink the Bismarck,* a song he knew by heart.

The British guns were aimed and the shells were comin' fast
The first shell hit the Bismarck, they knew she couldn't last

As Brent blared out the second line, Clovis confidently drove onto the ice of a massive puddle. There was a crunching, cracking sound and then Clovis' "hold on." We were stunned when the Jeep broke through the ice, the wheels sinking low into the water.

Clovis said, "We're in deep. I will have to get something to pull us out."

"I sunk the Bismarck," Brent said joyfully.

The Kingsley and Jackson children, Jerry, and I laughed. "Yes, you did," we chorused.

We walked the rest of the way to the bus. Our moods soured by the unexpected trek, but we made it in time. Clovis owned a road grader—sourced from a State auction—and used it to pull the jeep out of the hole. Quick circulation of this story meant Dad kept his distance around the treacherous spot for his afternoon collection of us. He was not going to let the new Land Rover, we had only taken ownership weeks before, become another Bismarck.

Walking through the cabin door after school that day, Jerry,

Brent, and I changed and ran down to devour Mom's hot Spanish rice casserole. Her one-dish dinners were a perfect choice for these afternoons when we wanted to get outside. Gulping down the last bite, we threw on our jackets, grabbed thick gloves, and dashed out for skiing. Hopefully, there would be an hour left before darkness fell.

The icy crust scrunched and crackled under my rhythmic strides. Afternoon sun had melted the top of the snow earlier, but it had refrozen. I was careful to avoid losing control by skidding off the icy path as I skied. Once, even though slowing down, I completely lost balance and fell, but climbed back up. A favorite hill above "the little lagoon" was not far from the cabin. There we could whizz down, and laboriously climb back up as we were hundreds of miles from the kind of swanky ski resorts that had lifts to take the effort out of going uphill on skis. We huffed and puffed hauling ourselves up using our poles. Even in temperatures below freezing, I was sweating when I reached the top. I unzipped my ski jacket and caught my breath, savoring the scent of spruce in the air.

I loved the wind biting my face as I raced down hill, knees bent, and poles tucked under my arms. Days before, Jerry and Brent had built a ski jump by mounding heaps of snow near the bottom of the steep slope. Hitting this at full speed propelled me into the air for a few glorious moments. I flew like an eagle. With the rush of adrenalin came the fear of the next few moments. A successful landing meant gliding onto the white blanket that covered the lake, glistening in the low sun. Pure joy. When unsuccessful? Well, lots of laughs from Mom and my brothers as I ploughed deep into snow and felt the Alaskan winter invade my body.

As the sun set, we skied back home. I looked forward to a hot mug of cocoa. I thought of Gail. Back in Homer, we had prepared cocoa together many times and I could not help going through the process again and again in my mind; stirring a heaping spoonful of dark red powder from the Hershey container; adding sugar, water, and milk in a pan on the stove; and the addition of marshmallows dropped on top of our full cups to add to the sweetness. Sitting by Gail at the table, sipping, had been a time of sharing.

If she had been with me skiing, it would have been more fun; and we would have talked afterwards. However, now she was married to Jack, and they talked about starting a family. Gail had less time to ski when she came to visit as she and Mom spent the time talking about pregnancy and childcare. I listened and missed the one to one conversations that we used to have as sisters. I was pleased that she was happily married, but had inner conflicts. Jack was her confident now; and although I felt somewhat left out, he was quiet and nice, and we all liked him. Times like today I wanted the sister back who confided in me and wanted to hear my hardships and joys.

Every couple of weeks, my parents walked out into the surrounding forest with both the Swede saw and the chain saw to get a supply of wood for heating and cooking. Dad used the chain saw for felling a tree. The Swede saw had a half-moon handle over the blade for two people to operate by one standing at each end and alternating the sawing motion in rhythm. The ease of their repetitive back and forth motion was relaxing to watch. Dad, as a Swedish American, considered anything Swedish superior including this saw. Since he needed Mom as a constant companion of the sawing, he was happy. They hauled the cut logs back home in our handcrafted toboggan for Jerry and Brent to stack neatly against the cabin. Mom and Dad cut through the forest with conservation of nature always at the forefront of their minds. They selected dead standing or fallen trees for firewood.

Although pioneers in spirit, my parents had traditionally defined roles for most of our family responsibilities. I worried about them when they were late returning. Had there been an accident with the saw hitting an unexpected knot and slipping from the hand of one of my parents, any resulting injury would have been life-threatening. The nearest hospital was sixty miles away. First, the able adult would have needed to stop the bleeding, pulled her or him onto the toboggan and skied out of the forest, and then, driven to the hospital. If Mom had been the injured one, Dad would have had to rely on me to take on the domestic responsibilities; and I and my brothers would have been required to assist him outside. If it was Dad who was injured, Mom and we kids would be burdened with his duties except for surveying which provided the family income. This anniversary of Gail's return brought home to me the many responsibilities I would soon have to bear.

Mom's Spanish Casserole
A one-dish meal that serves 6

Pre-heat oven to 350F/170C
First steam 2/3 cup rice.
Chop 1 cup celery, and 1 bell pepper (any color, seeds and membrane removed). Melt in a large skillet, 2 tablespoons butter. Add 1 chopped onion, celery and bell pepper; sauté over medium heat until soft. Add 1 pound/500g ground lean beef (or moose.) and mix and season with scant teaspoon of salt and ½ teaspoon paprika. Cook until pink and then stir in the prepared rice. Transfer to a baking dish (with a lid). Pour over 1 can condensed tomato soup (10.5 oz.) and cover. Bake for 30 minutes and serve.

Hot Cocoa

Use a double boiler or a pan over direct but low heat. Combine in the pan:
    1 cup boiling water
    4 tablespoons cocoa
    Dash salt
    2 tablespoons sugar
When the above ingredients are simmering, add 3 cups hot milk and stir. Serve with two marshmallows on top of each mug. Enhance flavor with sprinkle of cinnamon, cloves, or nutmeg.

Becoming an Adult

Jerry and Brent raced ahead as they engaged in banter. They confidently dodged the wet and muddy places, wearing jeans selected from the *Sears and Roebuck* catalogue, laughed, and shouted out comic book episodes. Jerry loved *Superman*, and said, "Brent, did you read the one where *Superman*..."

I lost what he said as they leaped around the bend under young May green leaves of silver birch and Sitka spruce. My teacher's end-of-the-day announcement had left me thrilled, and I was eager to tell Mom and Dad the news. I lifted my feet—mud crept up my boots and onto my bare legs under the cotton dress I had recently buzzed up on the Singer.

The two of them muttered as they planted tomatoes and cucumbers in the greenhouse when I reached the cabin. I went straight up the steep staircase and changed into jeans and sweat-shirt behind the heavy cloth curtain. Putting my dress on a hanger on a rail under the eaves, I glanced at it and was relieved it was not muddy.

Back downstairs I read Mom's note: "Judy, please start peeling the potatoes and carrots for the pot roast. Your dad and I will be in for dinner around 6 p.m." Why did she always say "start" like she would be coming to help. That did not happen. This note meant for me to make the dinner she had planned. All her notes were the same, but today I was especially peeved...I had exciting news to share. I grabbed the peeler and commenced venting my disappointment on the carrots.

Jerry and Brent were outside laughing beside the cabin. They stacked wood cut by Mom and Dad earlier. Jerry's chuckling was interrupted by his usual cough now and then. He had had the cough ever since I could remember. Mom had taken him to the doctor to have it checked, but no cause had been found. Mom and Dad had previously smoked, but not us kids. Jerry's cough never seemed to materialize into anything serious; it was just part of Jerry.

I placed the peeled vegetables into the pot alongside the moose rump roast, added a couple of onions, salt and pepper, and placed it in the oven of the wood-burning cook stove. Prying open one of the burners, I saw wood was needed so I added a couple of logs. Banging each one with the iron poker, I arranged them to fit. Each hit helped release my disgruntled feelings, but smoke stung my eyes. It quietly floated to the upstairs, and I began setting the table for five as I had done countless times. The aroma of the roast cooking was comforting.

Sitting at the kitchen table, I penciled a few thoughts on a notepad that could be used in my speech. I only had two weeks to get it written. I jotted, erased, jotted, and then…

Mom and Dad came through the door. "Judy," Dad exclaimed. "What a smell. Dinner must be ready."

Mom said, "Thanks, Judy. We've been busy planting, and the greenhouse is well under way."

As they removed work gloves and light jackets, washed their hands, and looked ready to sit down for my meal, I felt like an adult.

"I'm Valedictorian of the class," I blurted out.

"Valedictorian…well done. An honor to be top student," Dad said with a big smile.

Mom reiterated what Dad had said and added, "Nice, Judy. Did Mary Rusk place?"

"She is Salutatorian," I replied. "She will make her speech before mine at graduation."

Brent and Jerry had come in, washed their hands for dinner, and slid into usual places at the table.

Jerry coughed and with a smile, asked disbelievingly, "You have the top grades in your graduating class?"

"Yes. I beat Mary to the punch once again." Valedictorian was the top honor, and Salutatorian was the runner-up.

"You beat her before. I remember…" Brent said

Mary and I had been friends at Tustumena, but with a limitation in the friendship. The teachers favored Mary. She was from a more affluent family who were regular community church attendees. Her dad was a commercial salmon set net fisherman on Clam Gulch Beach. Her mom was a nurse, but I do not remember her working in a hospital. Instead, she was a helper/partner to her husband on the beach fish site.

In the winter Mary and I, with other girls and boys, had competed to represent Tustumena at the state spelling bee. We were the last two, and she was given a word and stalled for time. "FAMILIAR," our eighth grade teacher repeated for her. "FAMILIAR," Mary said, and used an index finger to trace the spelling onto her palm. She smiled and shifted from one foot to the other, trying to work out the correct spelling. Our teacher hesitated. Did he want Mary to win? While we waited, he said, "Many people have trouble with this word. I know exactly what you are going through..." She finally spelled the word as she thought it to be: "F A M I L A R."

"Sorry, Mary," the teacher said shaking his head as Mary stepped slowly to her desk.

He looked at me, "FAMILIAR."

"FAMILIAR," I said. "F A M I L I A R."

"Correct. Judy you will represent Tustumena in Anchorage."

Feeling happy, I looked at Mary. She was staring down, but had a brave smile as the teacher said to her, "Rotten luck."

Mom and Dad primed me at home by calling out words from the *State Spelling Booklet*. The words were monsters such as *deification, Feldenkrais*, and *avoirdupois*. To me they were like Swedish ones which combined an entire English sentence equivalent. Dad wanted to teach us a few because that language was his mother tongue. Gail, I, Jerry, and Brent tried, but after a few days could only remember *Karleksstigen* which means Lovers' Lane, and Mama and Papa. I got many more wrong than right from the *Spelling Booklet*, and both my parents became disenchanted and fed up. I knew that correctly spelling the word, arithmetic, was only possible for me by learning the rhyme, "A Red Indian thinks he may eat turkey in church". "These words are beyond you," Dad said shaking his head. Mom met his eyes and nodded in agreement.

Dad had driven me and the younger runner-up to Anchorage for the State competition. I had easily past the first couple of words, but had failed on the third round and had been forced to step down. Tustumena School would soon forget that I had represented them. I kept the identification badge that had been pinned on me in the spelling lineup for my scrapbook. It would be a reminder of what was important to me as a contender.

That day in Anchorage had been fun, and I had beaten Mary to get there. Dad had treated us to a restaurant meal before we had headed back home: burger, French fries, and a chocolate milkshake, my standard on the rare occasions of eating out. I had felt happy as we had driven the five hours back to the homestead. Ha, ha, Mary, I remember thinking.

Sitting at the table this May evening with Mom, Dad, Jerry, and Brent, I felt elated. The taste of the moose and vegetables was satisfying, but I was overcome with happiness with my Valedictorian announcement.

Dad said, "Judy, I want to help you with your speech. It is an important time in Alaska with the major gas discoveries in Cook Inlet. We will get those thoughts in…after dinner…"

Mom and I cleared the table, and I sat down with Dad. He held my notebook and started to write sentences that came to his mind. I sat and waited for him to finish my speech. It was irritating that he did not ask me for input. I wanted to talk about my friends, not Alaskan politics. Mom's initiating our move from Homer into the woods at Porcupine Lake to homestead removed Dad from political involvement on the PUD board in Homer, and he missed being a small town politician. My speech was his chance for a comeback. I said nothing as I fiddled with my pencil.

He finished and read the five-minute speech to me. "See, Judy, we need to tell about the imminent change in Alaska with the discovery of major gas fields. We live close to Nikiski and North Kenai where the refineries will be located. If our politicians get it right, tankers will be shipping Liquid Natural Gas from there to Japan."

"OK, Dad," I said. I knew at this point it was hopeless for my own thoughts to be added.

The next day all of us drove to Soldotna to do the usual grocery shopping, plus an extra stop for me. Dad, Jerry, and Brent waited in the car while Mom and I went into the log cabin that was the

Ladies' Clothing Store. From the dozen choices, I selected one for my graduation dress. It was light blue chiffon with white embroidered petals on the cummerbund. The owner of the shop had become a friend of Mom's. She was middle-aged and motherly and had helped years of graduates. When she saw my selection, she said, "Oh, gorgeous. Yes, it falls just below the knee. That is perfect. You must have nylon stockings. Here, let me show you how to put them on…" She gathered one up in her hands to the toe and then handed it to me. I pulled both on.

"She listens much better to you," Mom said to the shop owner, looking embarrassed. "I've also shown her how to put on stockings," and shook her head as she handed me a pair of shoes with a slight high heel.

"Oh, thanks," I said. "I love them with the dress." I looked down thinking that Mom had never shown me how to put on stockings, but I was not going to cause more embarrassment with the truth. She probably felt that it was her responsibility as my mother to have taught me how to put on stockings. Or, perhaps Mom wanted to make it clear to the shop owner that we were not hicks from the sticks. In Chicago, she had certainly worn nylon stockings as a teenager.

"I'm calling your father in to have a look," Mom said as she went out and brought him back.

"Splendid," Dad said. "Is this our Judy? You look lovely."

With my package under my arm, we left the shop and headed home.

The evening of graduation I tramped out the dirt road in my knee boots and jeans, and carried my graduation dress and shoes in a plastic bag so as not to muddy them. I changed into the billowy blue dress behind willows at the end of the homestead road. The fifty yard stiff net "can can" to be worn underneath caught on a couple of twigs, but I managed to get it and the dress on. Mom zipped me up as we wobbled standing on moss and cranberry bushes. The stiffness underneath made the dress stand out fashionably. Thank heavens I had put the nylon stockings on in the cabin. Better yet, I had not made runs standing on the rough terrain. With my new heels in hand, I climbed into the Land Rover with the family. We drove and parked at Tustumena school in about fifteen minutes.

"Now, speak slowly, and look up at us often as you read," Dad coached.

We entered the double classroom with the plastic accordion partition pushed back. All twelve graduates sat in the two front rows, and families and friends of about fifty behind. Mary looked lovely as she smiled at me and the others. Her flowered dress was more conservative than mine with a higher neckline. Mine had a scoop neck. It did not reveal anything, but was definitely more of a party look.

She spoke first, but I could not concentrate as I was becoming tense and anxious. I was not used to speaking before an audience. Mary sat down to lots of clapping. Her parents and their many church friends gave her full support.

I stood and walked carefully up the two steps to the stage after my teacher's introduction. Heels felt different from my usual flats, but I was proud wearing them even though more cautious with my steps.

Looking down at Dad's speech, and then out at the audience, I started with the welcome. Placing my clammy hands on the podium, I looked at Mom, Dad, Jerry, and Brent. I felt nervous and skipped over much of the gas discovery and how good it would be for our economy. I did not meet Dad's gaze as I knew that he would be upset with the omission. Looking at Mary, Virginia, Bruce, Dorothy, Susan, and the other class members, I zeroed in with a personal tribute. Grateful for my three years at Tustumena, and how being a pupil there had meant new friendships after my move from Homer at the age of eleven. I would be leaving these friends to attend Homer High School and would miss them.

The speech was concluded much sooner than Dad planned. "Returning to Homer means I will live with my older sister, Gail, and her family during the school week. I look forward to spending more time with her for my high school years. Dad will drive me to the homestead many weekends to be with Mom, him, Jerry, and Brent. I hope that will mean meeting up with Tustumena friends, too."

People clapped. I folded Dad's speech and walked back to my seat. Mary squeezed my hand as I sat down. I looked at Dad—he was frowning. I knew he was disappointed that I had not stayed with his written words. When his eyes met mine, he smiled slightly and nodded. Maybe it was the blue dress that helped him change his expression to that of a proud father.

My mother as a young woman in Chicago

An Opportunity Opens

One sunny day in April, Jerry, Brent and I walked in the mud from the school bus to the cabin. Clovis Kingsley was visiting with Mom and Dad at the kitchen table.

"I'm sure that you and Judy can do it," Clovis said, nodding his blond crewcut and looking at me with determined blue eyes as I removed my muddy knee boots.

"Do what?" I asked, already wary of plans made in my absence.

"Fish below on the old Libby McNeil & Libby trap site," Dad said.

"We can claim the site by setting out a buoy keg with my initials. You kids can start earning your college money," Mom announced.

"I was against statehood, but it closed down fish trap operations. For that, I'm now pleased," Dad added.

"What are fish traps?" Brent asked.

"They were horrible wire mesh cages along the shore that bled the ocean of sea life," Mom said.

"That's right," confirmed Clovis.

Clovis was a commercial salmon fisherman and was abreast of the changes in fishing opportunities. I knew that Mary Rusk's family and Linda Hermansen's, fished on the beach and both girls helped operate nets. Many others in Tustumena School fished. The opportunity to identify with Mary and Linda, and earn college funds, appealed to me.

"Great," I replied, putting down my school books and pulling up to the table.

"I would get that buoy keg out there tomorrow. Fishing season opens in only a couple of months," Clovis said.

"Ruth and I will get a keg painted and tied to one of the old iron fish trap bars on one of tomorrow's low tides," Dad said. "Let's go over the fishing gear, Clovis."

Our First Summer of Salmon Fishing, 1962

That first summer of commercial salmon fishing, we grossed $1,200. This was by fishing one net donated by a friend, an old-timer Alaskan.

The first day, Mom, my two brothers, and I woke at 4 a.m. to the cold on the homestead even though it was the 8th of June.

"Wow. It froze last night. Ice in the bottom of the boat," I said.

Jerry, nine years old, proceeded to chip the ice with an oar. I was exasperated with Mom for getting us up at this early hour. She was determined that we begin earning money towards university educations by fishing. I groaned thinking of the physical work required on top of homesteading chores and whether this had been a good idea after all.

She moved her sturdy frame onto the passenger bench of our 10-foot boat, her ears protected from the wind by a handkerchief scarf.

"Come on, Brent," she said and patted the space beside her with a work-glove hand.

Brent, his blond hair covered by the hood of his sweatshirt, rubbed his sleepy eyes and said, "Ok, ok."

Jerry and I carefully pushed the boat from shore. We moved through the thick lily pads, and jumped onto the boarded bow at just the right time to keep our knee boots free from the ice-cold water of Porcupine Lake.

"I'll row," I announced as I climbed into position. Jerry straddled the bow sitting with hands in his sweatshirt pockets, happy to take it easy. Engaging the oars, I started across the lake. Scamp was left barking in frustration as he was made to run along the shore. Dad was not along; his work as a land surveyor around Alaska took him away most summer days.

In ten minutes we reached the other side, pulling up to a beavers' house made of branches caked in mud. Two beavers emerged before we docked. Their white front teeth protruded from slicked back brown, fur heads as they skimmed the surface and paddled proficiently underneath. Scamp caught up and began fiercely barking and leaping beside the water.

"There he goes," Jerry laughed. The beavers teased the dog by swimming up close. Scamp jumped ready to attack. Simultaneously the beavers lifted and whacked their tails, making a loud splash before diving under. Poor Scamp was left whimpering.

"Maybe he'll get one next time," Brent said. Scamp gave up the chase and returned to shore. He stood for a few moments to shake off and then ran to us.

"Silly dog," Jerry said as Scamp took the lead. The rest of us chuckled as we started to climb the hill.

We were still drowsy from the early rise, and made little conversation walking the quarter of a mile to the beach through the Sitka spruce, silver birch forest, and open swampy area. Our boots sunk into the spongy ground. The slurping of water as we pulled our feet up and down in the bog was the only sound other than Scamp rustling through low tree limbs, watermelon berry plants, and tall grass as he pressed ahead. No torch was required to guide the way even though it was 5 a.m. Alaska is the land of the "midnight sun."

On reaching the bluff, we surveyed the scene 200 feet below. The smell of the fresh cold sea air was invigorating, and we began to waken. The grey blue waters of Cook Inlet were receding in the outgoing tide. Blue mountains with patches of snow rose up from the Pacific Ocean on the other side of Cook Inlet. Mount Redoubt, most majestic and often an active volcano, was in the forefront. Seagulls squawked along the water hoping to feast on sea life, particularly salmon and bald eagles, our National bird—really vultures—who glided along the cliff enjoying a free ride on the updraft. Any salmon exposed on the sand were soon devoured.

"Last one down is a rotten egg," Brent shouted as he rushed carelessly out of view. Jerry was close on his heels.

"It won't be me," he yelled.

Scamp leaped down in long strides. He reached the bottom and immediately chased seagulls off the beach up into the air as he barked and looked in command.

Mom and I gingerly made our way down the steep bluff by carefully stepping in the wet, heavy clay on the uppermost part; and then along sandstone, and finally loose sand. Jerry and Brent bounded in leaping strides down together, with me trailing and Mom bringing up the rear.

A two hundred and ten foot gill net was draped neatly on the log rack from our previous efforts to prepare for this day. I hopped onto the seat of our farm tractor and waited for Mom to crank start. She got it running; and I drove along the bluff with a strong brown hemp rope attached to the net, but also threaded through wooden pulleys. The net eased into the seawater.

Mom, Jerry, and Brent held up their hands and yelled, "Stop," when the outside end, designated with a red and white buoy keg, reached the outside pulley. The cork line held one edge of the net on the surface, and the lead line sunk to its depth of three fathoms.

"Help tie to the post," Mom said.

"Ok," I replied, jumping down. The wet, rough textured rope clung to my cloth work gloves leaving them soggy. Still my hands burned from pulling the rope tight to secure the net. Jerry and Brent stood watching to see if we were catching anything.

The cork line shook creating white froth as the salmon hit. "Yay," Mom shouted. "Money."

The fish swam into the mesh and could not back out—secured by their gills. In the outgoing tide, we caught seventeen. We picked them from the net and sold the fish to Kenai Packers who paid per salmon, no matter the weight. They were a Seattle based company thirty miles away that collected fish from surrounding beaches.

We always picked the salmon from the net as it was exposed in the receding tide, and by doing so, beat the seagulls to them. The bright silver scales glistened in the morning sun. Mom could work them free wearing gloves, but not me. I lost all my long fingernails for the duration of the summer removing fish tangled in the mesh. Seagulls hovered and squawked, ready to pounce with open beaks if we turned our back on the catch.

Mom and I could carry a couple of salmon in each hand by threading gloved fingers through the gills. Brent and Jerry dragged the salmon across the sand and gravel to the pile above the reach of the tide. I covered the fish ready for collection with another burlap to protect them from flies and seagulls. Surprisingly, there was little smell from the fresh fish.

The cannery truck from Kenai Packer's came. "Red," the driver, had a sharp stick with a metal point on the end. He jumped down from the driver's seat and said, "Hello. Look at all these fish you have. I love this cool Alaskan weather. Today I won't take off my jacket. Not hot like Arizona where I live."

He speared each fish and tossed it onto the truck as he clicked a counter. At completion he handed us a ticket with the recorded catch of sixteen fish.

We left the net to be submerged in the incoming tide and made our way back up the steep bluff, retracing our steps home. Mom and I took turns carrying the heavy salmon for a Teriyaki dinner made from a recipe in *The Joy* and one of our favorites.

Scamp ran ahead and was waiting for us at the boat. I sat down ready to get home. The breeze had picked up making bigger waves on the lake than when I had rowed in earlier. Still, they were much smaller than the ones on Cook Inlet where we had our gill net. A feeling of pride and accomplishment ran up my commercial fisher girl's body as I pulled the oars through the water.

"It was a good first day," Mom said gazing out onto the lake. "Tell you what...we'll have a restaurant meal at the end of fishing season when the Kenai Packers' check comes. Today's catch will cover the bill."

"Sounds good," I replied, looking across the strong ripples of blue water to the cabin. Elvis Presley's song, "Return to Sender", came into mind. I sang the words, and Mom hummed and swayed to the catchy beat.

Jerry's and Brent's pockets bulged with rocks they had collected from the beach.

"Which restaurant?" Brent asked.

Jerry said, "Let's go to Royal Parkers. Have a beef steak."

They ignored our singing as they threw rocks out skimming the water, and enjoyed a contest of who could throw the farthest. Plunk, plunk, plunk.

"I won," shouted Brent and bounced around on the board seat

beside Mom. "Ha, ha."

"No you didn't," Jerry said, quite sure of himself. "I threw one or two way beyond yours. Here we are anyway."

I ran the bow through the lily pads and onto the swampy ground of shore. Scamp came bounding around the shore and waited at our docking spot. Jerry jumped off and pulled us up. We all climbed out and walked slowly to the cabin.

Mom and I decided on a hearty meal for a late breakfast. She started the generator and came back in with a bit of oil from the loud engine on her face, but looked in the small mirror over the wash basin, and wiped herself spotless. She then stepped outside to clean the salmon for later while I mixed waffle batter from a recipe in the *Better Homes and Gardens Cookbook*. I loved them with blueberries we had picked last September in the big swamp— about a mile from the house. We had many packages in our freezer. An additional topping was homemade from brown sugar syrup flavored with vanilla. There was a permeating scent of sweetness in the air as the waffles baked in the electric Sunbeam waffle iron. The radio played "I Left my Heart in San Francisco" and "Speedy Gonzales" while we ate. Then the news: The Albany Protest Movement was still continuing in Georgia. Demonstrators were non-violent, but had been met by mass arrests.

"Oh dear, those poor people," Mom said, putting down her fork. "They can't drink from the same water fountain as whites…have to give up their seat on the bus for a white person. Even Nat King Cole probably can't enter a restaurant in the South through the front door." We all often sang "Ramblin' Rose", his famous song. The radio began playing Bobby Vinton singing, "Only Love can Break a Heart". I had finished eating and sang along, glad that we did not live in the South '48 where many people were not treated right just because of the color of their skin.

Other days, we stayed on the beach waiting for the net to go dry so we could pick out the fish before the seagulls attacked and greedily devoured them. We spent our time digging hand-size razor clams from the cold wet sand smelling of the salty sea.

One day, Brent, Jerry, and I walked in our rubber knee boots to a sandy area along the water in search of clams. They are evident by small dimples, or holes, in the surface caused by the clams breathing through their gills. The advance of the incoming tide seemed to stimulate the dimples. This day was usual for Alaskan summers with mostly overcast sky and cool. Our long sleeved sweatshirts and jeans felt good. I carried our only clam shovel.

We stopped at a hole. I yelled against the pounding waves, "Stand back and I'll go in first with the shovel."

After my quickly scooping up three loads of sand, Brent said, "Stop and let Jerry and me get him out with our hands. You'll break his shell with the shovel."

The clam was squirting and digging down quickly, but Jerry and Brent were faster, tearing down into the sand with rolled up sleeves and crouching over the spot where the clam was trying to escape.

"Got him," Jerry said placing the clam in the bucket.

"Nice one," I said, admiring the large golden gray shell with the clam's neck still protruding and squirting seawater.

We quickly found another dimple, another and another, soon filling the bucket with them. Just as we knew that it was time to retreat as the water was reaching us, yet euphoric because of our success, I said, "Hurry, we have time for one more."

I dug the shovel in vigorously and drew out sand. Brent went in with his hands to retrieve the clam, but in my excitement and rush to beat the water coming towards us, I continued with the shovel. "Ouch. Good God," Brent yelled in bewilderment as I hit one of his hands with the blade.

Mortified, I threw down the shovel and wrapped my arms around him, pulling him close, while rocking us from side to side. He broke loose and grasped his bleeding hand by the other and hopped around crying out in pain, "My hand. My hand."

Jerry grabbed the heaped up bucket of clams, and we raced up the beach to Mom. She consoled Brent with, "Dear oh dear, It will be ok."

I watched her tenderly bandage his wound and then hug her youngest child. I felt guilty about hurting Brent, and that afternoon as I climbed up the bluff, I thought of the mishap. I was glad his hand had not been cut worse. Danger lurked with our fishing work and free time activities like digging clams.

Brent had a good excuse for refusing to help Jerry, Mom, and me clean the wet clams, oozing seawater through pulsating necks protruding from partially opened shells. It was also some time before he trusted me near him with the clam shovel.

Scouting the beach for fish, which sometimes came loose from neighbors' nets in strong tide and washed up on shore, was another pastime. My brothers and I gleefully returned to our site with them, and laid the ready "cash from Heaven" on top of our hard earned pile. Mom was always delighted with the extra fish, and knew very well how we got them. The neighbors whose nets lost these fish never complained, but did give us curious looks. Once one drove us back to our site on his tractor with salmon lost from his nets. I guess this was his way of letting us know that he saw what we were up to. Indeed, Brent, Jerry, and I were beach scavengers. In this instance I felt embarrassed, but was not long deterred.

Fishing days that summer were Mondays and Fridays, 6 a.m. to 6 a.m., two twenty-four hour periods per week to conserve fish stocks. That meant two trips to the beach each 24-hour period. There were those days we became stressed out, afraid that we would fail to get the net out of the water by the closing deadline because of the old tractor not responding to mom's cranking, or the net getting caught on iron bars embedded in the sand from the days our site was a fish trap. By some miracle we always made it in time, and were never fined or marched off to jail.

Once while we were setting the net on an in-coming tide, much of the net was submerged in the loud pounding surf when Mom yelled, "Judy, the inside end is loose. Look."

I ran to grab the free end as it was dragged along the sand. I got it, and Mom joined me to pull. No luck. Even with the two of us tugging with all our might, it was impossible to bring the rope back to the post to right the net. Mom and I were left gasping for breath.

She cried, "We won't catch a thing. Won't make a dollar. Oh my sainted aunt, our net. It'll tangle and tear around rocks and those damned iron bars. My God."

Quickly we changed tactics. We waded into the icy water with our rubber boots. The sand shifted around my feet in the current. I dug in my heels to remain standing. Mom took hold of the cork line, and I took the lead line. Tugging with the full weight of our bodies, and crouching low, we slowly pulled much of the net onto dry beach. Fortunately, the tide was nearly high and not running as strong as before. We strained ourselves, but eventually realigned the net.

I yelled, "We've reached the post."

"Thank God," Mom yelled back, wrapping the rope around once and then tying a secure knot. We looked at each other, shaking our heads in exhaustion. I removed my drenched gloves, and slowly trudged up the beach to climb the bluff and make my way home with Mom, Jerry, and Brent. The net was fully submerged with the cork line floating, and pulled by the tide in a crescent, secured on each end. I was relieved, but nearly losing the net in the rough current ran through my thoughts. Would we always be so lucky? As I lifted my feet, and I thought about the hard work of fishing and this near disaster to earn college money. I felt it was worth it as I meant to attend university and become a teacher—an easier life than Mother's.

Back at the cabin we were ready for brunch. Mom switched on the radio, and ran out to start the generator so that we could use the waffle iron. I got down *The Better Homes and Garden Cookbook* and opened to Waffles Supreme. Jerry and Brent sat at the table with comic books as Mom and I pulled out the ingredients, and I mixed a full bowl of batter.

"Sit down, I'll bake them," Mom said and then added, "Quiet."

The radio newscaster announced that Marilyn Monroe had been found dead at 36 years of age. Barbiturates were found at her bedside. So sad. She was pretty, and I remembered her pictured in the paper singing "Happy Birthday" to President Kennedy. I had also enjoyed the film, *Some Like it Hot*, and had imagined that stars like her had a good life. Even in my exhausted state, after realigning the loose net, I was amazed and thought…Marilyn's life must not have been all that good.

Days later I told my friend, Mary Rearden, in Homer about nearly losing the net. She replied, "Judy, I know it's hard work, but you're lucky. You have something to do while earning money. In town we only have babysitting now and again. Much of the time we're bored." This came as a surprise, and made me feel lucky and even proud.

We continued to row across the lake and climb up and go down the bluff to fish two days a week. There were always salmon and sometimes other surprises.

Once a dead Beluga whale washed up on our small site. We had always known there were whales in Cook Inlet, but I had never seen one. It looked to weigh about half a ton as it was the size of the back of a pick-up truck. Luckily it stayed clear of the fish net as the waves brought it in. The putrid stench of that decaying mammal was horrific. Our only relief was the wind changing directions with the turn of the tide and carrying the stench away. I lay in bed nights afterwards thinking how fortunate we were that the whale did not get tangled in the net. We would have had to cut it free with the result of damaging the mesh.

My brothers, who spent the majority of their time building sand castles and loading sweatshirt pockets with unusual rocks, opened small savings accounts. Each of us kids made one dream purchase out of our takings. Brent's was a chemistry set; Jerry's, a small Styrofoam surfboard with sail for the lake. Mine, blue and yellow plaid fabric along with a "Simplicity" pattern to sew a dress for my first day at Homer High School.

At the end of the summer, we looked back proudly on busy days full of structure, purpose, and nest eggs. Mom and I, with some help from Jerry and Brent, had worked as a family team, sometimes against rough ocean currents and inclement weather. I finished the season with confidence knowing that I was in command of the work and had become a fisherman. I had $300 in the bank.

I would continue to fish on the site with Mother and my brothers for four more seasons. Mom sold the site to a beach neighbor after fishing five additional seasons.

Below I share my sister-in-law, Judy's, recipe for good clam chowder.

Clam chowder
Serves about twelve

Ingredients:
1 pound clams, shelled, cleaned, and chopped
1 pound bacon, chopped
3 onions, peeled and chopped
1 head celery, sliced fine
1 can evaporated milk
1 large can whole kernel corn
4 pounds potatoes, peeled and sliced

Put all of the above into a large pot. Add between 2 and 3 quarts (3000ml) water. Bring to simmer and allow to cook until the potatoes and celery are tender. Season with salt and white pepper to taste. Amount of water varies according to your preference for thickness.

Baking powder biscuits are great with the clam chowder. The recipe is in the Fourth of July chapter. Omit the sugar when making the biscuits to accompany a savory dish.

Teriyaki Salmon
To serve approximately five

ingredients:
One side of wild Alaskan salmon, filleted
⅓ cup Saki
⅓ cup Soy Sauce
⅓ cup Mirin

Put all the ingredients in a large plastic bag and tightly close; turn over several times to mix and refrigerate for at least 2 hours.

To grill/broil, remove the salmon from the bag and place on an oiled foil covered grill rack, skin side up facing the heat. Grill for about 3 to 4 minutes (until skin is brown) under a pre-heated grill and then turn. Grill for another 1 to 2 minutes or until just cooked. Remove from the heat and place on a serving platter. Garnish with Samphire or parsley and freshly cut lemon.

I Return to Homer

I stepped off the school bus at Homer High School the first day of classes in September, 1962, and made my way through the doors, the same as 122 other students. I was fourteen. Dad had asked me months before,

"Don't you want to be with your family and go to high school in Ninilchik?"

"No, I'm going to Homer to be a cheerleader like Gail and return to my friends," I replied without hesitation. I did not say that I still had a soft spot for Jack Collie, but he was on my mind. Mom nodded in agreement. She had been aware of my committed decision almost since the day we arrived at Porcupine Lake three years earlier.

My thoughts of Jack as I walked down the hall and hung a light jacket in my new locker were uppermost in my mind. Would he already be sitting in homeroom where attendance was taken? What did he think of me now? What would I say when I saw him? Yesterday on the drive with Dad through the woods from the homestead, and the hour and a half on the two-way gravel highway, I had pictured him getting off another school bus, sinking shots on the basketball practice court, and walking towards me with his sly smile and twinkling blue eyes. But after receiving my letter a year ago saying I could not be his girl because he was not a born-again Christian, would he walk away after a brief greeting and glance? Or, did he, too, have thoughts of us getting back together?

I was living with Gail and her husband, Jack Sibson. Gail was a bank teller, and Jack drove a taxi and was building on the house after a summer of commercial salmon fishing on a drift boat. In the evenings and weekends, Gail assisted Jack adding onto the old missionary cabin. Five and a half acres surrounded it on the Homer hillside—my parents' wedding gift. Jack and Gail had no time or interest for church.

Neither did Tania, Mary, Steve, and other friends; but they and the students in Homer High regarded themselves as Christians. So I did not go to services either even though I felt a personal relationship with God. While walking the half-mile up Mission Road from Gail's to the school bus, or while vacuuming, or dusting, I often prayed silently. I had done the same hiking in and out of the private road through the woods to Porcupine Lake. Speaking to God at these times was a replacement for not having a companion. Plus God was all-powerful and would protect me from harm.

The church in the Clam Gulch community instructed all Christians to proselytize as born-again believers. I wanted to do so, but was embarrassed. I decided to go bravely ahead and asked Gail if she believed in God. She replied, "Guess Jack is my God. I do everything for him. Besides, I used to go to church—remember? I think they are all a bunch of hypocrites and talk a load of bull."

Shocked and disappointed with her reply, I knew that my sister was committed to her opinion from past experiences with the fundamentalist church in Homer. Her rejection of these Christians made me realize that to pursue the conversation further would only bring on an argument. That would be unpleasant. Furthermore, Jack looked away and left the room when I brought up God one time with him.

The weekends I went back to the homestead I would help with family projects, ski, or skate. The girlfriends from Tustumena School were attending Kenai or Ninilchik schools. They would all be making new friends and spend weekends with them rather than attending our old church. I did go a couple of times, and met with Mary Rusk and her sisters. I felt removed from the commitment of being born again, and realized that they and their parents still lived and breathed it. Mary became more and more polite on such occasions and less interested in pursuing our old friendship.

My life had changed with the move away from rural life back to town. Regret for writing the letter filled me as I looked around for Jack. Yes, I was born again, but who cared at Homer High? I felt I was a Christian, and so did my friends and fellow students who had not walked forward publicly to accept the Lord as Savior.

Tania had saved a desk next to her in home-room, and I slid in. Her smile was warm as usual.

"Like your blue plaid shirtwaist, Judy. Brings out the tan from your summer on the fish site."

"Thanks. The material is from your store—and the Simplicity pattern," I said, and smiled and nodded to her and old friends. Jack was in the rear of the room talking to another basketball player. They both looked up long enough to nod pleasantly before the roll call was made.

The head teacher penned in a check by each of our names after the answer of "present." She clipped the report slip to the outside of the door, which showed the number present and that no one was absent. School funding was deducted for absent pupils. All of us long-term Alaskans knew the importance of school attendance. Our parents' pride and concern for our education demanded that we go.

The bell rang and we filed out. Jack made no attempt to catch me then, or when we were in English and later in Biology. His avoidance hurt, but I knew that my written words had brought it on. Over the next months, I asked myself a thousand times, "Would he ever forgive me?"

I became a member of the student council and varsity cheerleaders. Half the student body and I joined the Spanish club. The teacher heading it up said, "Let's wash cars, make Spanish food to sell, and take a bus to Mexico." The trip never materialized— parents regarded the idea as ridiculous. A lot of money was made from our enthusiastic fund-raising which ended up in the General Fund.

Then I kept running into Jackie Alexander, a new boy to me who came into my life—a basketball player, popular, with a car. Even with his many attributes, he never had the same effect on me as Jack Collie. Despite this, when he asked me out on a double date I accepted. It would be my first date, and I was eager for that and for diversion from constantly thinking of a guy who ignored me. The other couple was fun, and I knew they were both from old Alaskan families like mine. Mike and Jackie played on the starting-five varsity basketball team. Jackie's car was a new Morris Minor—

a present from his parents for passing the driving test at sixteen years of age. The four of us would laugh at almost every turn in the road as Jackie drove us around town and up to the hillside to park. The two in the back and Jackie and I in the front necked. Jackie left the radio on while we steamed up the windows with our petting to songs played over and over in 1962: "Twist and Shout" and "Loco Motion". Soon bored, I was mostly relieved when, after about six weeks, the relationship of the other couple and of Jack and me fizzled.

During that time, I never stopped yearning and pining for Jack Collie. He had a way of looking around with his pencil behind one ear against dark hair slicked into place with Brylcreem, seemingly taking everyone and everything in effortlessly. Tania and Mary waved when seeing me in Jackie Alexander's car; and Jack Collie must have heard we were dating, but he did not seem the least bit jealous. I was aware of his entrance into every classroom, his step down the hall, and his winning ability at basketball games. I figured Mary Rearden also became a cheerleader with the hope that she would get some attention by shouting his name during basketball play. Neither of us had much success. He remained aloof.

My time with Gail and her family ended before planned that year. She called me aside privately before I left for the school bus one morning.

"Judy, Jack and I feel having you stay with us is too much of an invasion of our privacy in this small cabin. Plus, he finds your spooning peanut butter directly out of the jar disgusting. God, Judy…"

It was a sad moment for I idolized my sister, but I was also concerned with the lack of privacy. Hearing bits of their pillow talk and intimate moments through the thin wall separating the two bedrooms embarrassed me.

Dad acted quickly when Gail told him that I must leave. He talked to our old friends, Margaret and Fred Anderson. Margaret phoned me immediately.

"Judy, you are welcome to come stay with us. Ricky and Maron think it will be swell having you," she said with earnest enthusiasm.

"Thank you. I'll pack and have Dad drive me down," I said,

relieved.

Dad and Margaret were old buddies from when he served on the PUD board and she was its President of this governing body for Homer.

Ricky was the same age as Jerry, and he had a large room with built in bunks, cupboards, and shelves all painted red, white, and blue. Fred had built the room to resemble a boat as he and his brother Virgo fished salmon and king crabs commercially on their own *Tasmania*. I could sleep in the bottom bunk. Preschool Maren knew me as I had helped Margaret with her a couple of summers before we moved to Porcupine Lake.

The new lodging worked out well. I was treated like family; when I became sick with ovarian cysts, Margaret nursed me with hot broth, temperature checks, and called in the doctor.

Simple Hot Broth

Place 1 beef, chicken, or vegetable Bullion cube in a mug and fill with boiling water.

Cheerleading

Shaking pompoms while screaming boys' names got their attention. Every athlete gave the cheerleaders approving glances. In the 1960s in Homer, girls sought popularity and admiration from boys by getting on the cheerleading team. Likewise, the boys sought adulation by participating in school athletics. Track, cross-country, skiing, and especially basketball provided the high school boys with opportunities for recognition from the opposite sex. A guy on the starting five basketball team was assured of being a school idol. We girls were all dying for these boys to notice us. Jack Collie was often in detention for lack of completed homework and brought into the principal's office for a paddling; but these disciplinary actions made him even more of a hero because he was tops at darting through opponents and getting the ball through the hoop time and again.

To become a cheerleader, I and other girls performed an individual routine in the gym in front of the entire student body of one hundred and thirty. Selection of six was made by popular vote. I was anxious before the "try-outs" because I feared that I was not popular enough. I had never had a "steady" boyfriend. My looks were good and gave me confidence, but I was often shot down with eruptions of acne. Mom and I tried every "cure" available, but none did the job. Neither was I able to master flips or cartwheels. A mediocre backbend and painful splits were my repertoire in the stunt category. These and my routines were achieved after hours of exercise and practice with other girls on the cheerleading team. Cheerleading brought not only popularity, but status.

First tryout in my Freshman year had me in the gym in front of all the high school students dressed in a black Homer sweatshirt and black, white, and yellow striped peddle pushers sewn by Mom and a hand-me-down from Gail. I flashed the knee side laces as I screamed and moved my hands and feet in coordination to the popular cheer, "Go Back Into the Woods":

Go back, go back
Go back into the woods,
You haven't, you haven't,
You haven't got the goods,
You haven't got the rhythm
And you haven't got the jazz
And you haven't got the team that Homer has.

My proud ending was a much practiced back bend. Less than elegantly I found my balance and raced off the floor to learn later that this first attempt had won me a varsity position. I did continue to survive the torture of tryouts and was a varsity cheerleader all four high school years.

Mom and Brent in front of round green house

Change

I returned home to salmon fish in the summer. No Jack visited this time. Tania came and we had our usual good talks in the cabin, boating on the lake, and walking on the beach. She still could not swim, but at least did not try to drown me as she had that summer when she panicked and got me in a stranglehold.

September, 1963, I was a sophomore at Homer High and eagerly hoped for a breakthrough with Jack. What magic could I use to bring him back into my life? My daydreaming went on and on. A favorite was him suddenly catching me up in the school hall, falling into step with me, and putting his arm around my waist as he leaned close to ask me out. I could sense his touch, and with every breath, the scent of his clean body after his morning shower. This dream stirred me, all conjured up from constant thinking and endless glances at my first love.

This fantasy was shattered by a redheaded California girl. She was dating Jack, and then wearing his ring on a chain around her neck as "his steady." It was upsetting to see them hand in hand in the hall. Cattily I told Tania, "She is freckle faced and plump."

She and I did not become well acquainted as we were not in any of the same clubs, nor had she become a cheerleader. Tania, Mary, and I often saw her leaving the principal's office following lunch in the cafeteria. She was stepping into the hall after dropping in her parents' note to excuse her morning absence. Jack's girl usually arrived only for afternoon classes. We joked saying that she must be suffering from morning sickness.

I lived with an elderly religious widow my sophomore year. Helen Edens contacted Dad through one of her adult sons with a request for me to stay. Her house was below Gail and Jack on the East Hill so it would be handy for me to visit them. Best news was that I would have my own bedroom with a door. I agreed even though I knew that I would miss the Andersons.

As an avid believer, Mrs. Edens attended a church similar to the one in the Clam Gulch community. She assumed that I would accompany her on Sundays. There were no other teenagers there. For many services I was asked to sing a solo as a special number. I chose hymns like "The Old Rugged Cross" and "Amazing Grace" which were my favorites. At first I was flattered when the pastor's wife asked me, but it became a blatant assurance of my attendance. Embarrassed and reluctant, I finally found the courage to say, "No, I probably will be away visiting my mother and family in Clam Gulch."

There was no peer pressure at Homer High as there had been at Tustumena to be a born-again Christian. In fact, my friends at Homer High mocked the born-again business.

I often thought of Jack and hoped to bump into him in the hall or that he would chat to me in a class. That never happened. One day, to get his attention, I teased my below shoulder length hair until I resembled a grizzly bear, smoothed it over and pinned it up into a towering French knot. A heavy dose of hair spray lacquered it into place. I sat in front of the English class knowing most eyes were taking in my skyscraper hairdo.

The teacher assigned us an essay to write in twenty minutes, and then for a few to read aloud. I do not remember mine, but I do Jack's. He jumped at the chance, and had written about outlandish hairdos:

"Some are rat-combed and brushed into towering heights—just like beehives," he read, chuckling. He ended with: "My question is how does the girl scratch her scalp when an itch develops?"

Everyone laughed including me.

For a minute I thought we had reconnected. A spurt of hope along with pleasure rose inside me. I remained in high spirits as we filed out of class.

Soon the morning sickness joke between Tania, Mary, and me was not funny. Jack's steady was rumored to be pregnant. It must have been true because his parents moved to Anchorage with them to live. They probably thought that Jack could better pursue a flourishing basketball career in the state's largest city, and that she could attend classes and have the baby away from the small town

of Homer where gossip thrived.
Goodbye, Jack Collie.

Lost Lover Cinnamon Rolls

Ingredients
450g/l lb/4 cups plain flour
100g/4 oz./½ cup white sugar
1 teaspoon salt
1 package fast action yeast
225 ml/8 fl. oz./1 cup skim milk, warm
75g/3 oz./⅓ cup melted butter or margarine
2 eggs

In a large mixing bowl stir together flour, sugar and salt. Add yeast and stir until blended. Add milk, butter and eggs, stirring until mixed; knead on floured surface until smooth and elastic. Roll out to a ¼ inch rectangle; clover with filling below.

Filling:
225g/7 oz./l cup brown sugar
2½ tablespoons cinnamon
75g/3 oz./⅓ cup softened margarine or butter
100g/4 oz/½ cup chopped pecans, optional

Roll up in jelly roll fashion and cut 2½ cm./1 inch slices for cinnamon rolls. Place cut side down next to each other in baking pan. Cover with tea towel and place each baking tray over a bowl of boiling water. Let rise about 30 minutes until double. Bake approximately 20 minutes in 180C/350F pre-heated oven or until done.

Ice while still warm with mixture below:

Icing:
175g/6 oz./1½ cups icing sugar
75g/3 oz./¼ cup cream cheese
½ teaspoon vanilla
pinch salt

Vietnam

We all remember where we were, I was rustling around in my hall locker for the World History textbook, while swaying and humming bits of Frankie Valli and the Four Seasons' 1963 hit, "Walk Like a Man".

The book...the book. I found it under many others and several cheerleading magazines. I pulled it out from the pile, and slammed the metal door shut singing the words more clearly.

Ray Martin, one of the starting five basketball players and a junior, one year older than me, came by giving the thumbs up when hearing the tune as he bopped along in his basketball sneakers. I had sensed by the way he looked at Margie, a sophomore student, that he regarded her special. How I longed for someone special to look at me that way. She caught up with him at the classroom door, and they gave one another a sheepish, lingering grin.

Suddenly, a loud announcement came over the PA system. It was the Principal. Everyone stopped in the crowded hall.

"John Fitzgerald Kennedy, the 35th President of the United States, is dead at the age of forty-six. He was shot by an assassin while being driven through the streets of Dallas, Texas, at 12:30 p.m., CST today."

Stupefied by the news, I looked around and saw stunned faces on fellow students. Tania had covered her mouth with a hand as we fell into a slow step towards class. Mary had her mouth open, unable to speak. Others were holding their heads in their hands.

"Gosh. Can you believe it?" Tania gasped, shaking her head.

"In Dallas. Unreal. Where were his bodyguards...the police?" I asked, walking with my best friend into World History.

My usual desk was free so I slid in with my text and notebook. We whispered bits of the announcement to one another. All of us were shaken.

Mr. Pease, our teacher, strode to the front, head lowered, and stood beside his desk. He was a firm, formal type, never very friendly; yet, he was a good teacher. His reconstructed harelip, the subject of many silly comments among the students, soon faded into the background as we became engrossed with his knowledge and love of history.

"All of you have heard the news of the death of our President by an assassin a short time ago. It will be transmitted around the world. People will be sad, like you, but reassured because the United States of America is a country with a constitution enabling continuity of leadership without the turmoil of war. Kennedy is the fourth U.S. President to be assassinated." Mr. Pease paused a minute and looked out at the trees lightly covered with snow. I could not help feeling one hundred years of our national history passing through him. He looked back at us and continued.

"As we shake our heads and ponder our President's death, Air Force One is carrying Mrs. Kennedy and the body of her husband back to Washington D.C. Vice President Lyndon B. Johnson will be sworn in as the thirty-sixth President of the United States of America on board the plane." He stopped to walk slowly to the back of the room, and then said, "Lincoln's assassination most people remember because he freed the slaves. His death took place in 1865 in a theatre not long after the War Between the States. John Wilkes Booth, a famous actor, was the assassin. We also know that Lincoln signed the Homestead Act at the end of the Civil War. That brought pioneers to settle in the west and finally in Alaska. Many of you are sons and daughters of these pioneers."

I felt a warm glow of pride rise in my chest knowing that my parents were among these Alaskans. After living on Porcupine Lake and working to meet Lincoln's homesteading requirements there, I regarded myself a pioneer. My teacher's words now connected me to our broader American history.

Mr. Pease, remained standing and was quiet for a minute looking at each of us. He was usually able to stimulate class discussion, and today was no exception.

"Thanksgiving is in a few days…Jackie, little John-John, and Caroline will have the large Kennedy family to comfort them, but I don't imagine they'll have the appetite to enjoy much turkey.

Lying in state, and the funeral will take place first. All of them will feel the void and the loss, much more than us."

I felt sad and looked down, but then looked up as junior guys started firing questions. As star basketball players, they all had the confidence to speak, but the questions they asked were on my mind, too.

Mike, with reddish hair styled in a crew cut and on the starting five, raised his hand and got the nod from Mr. Pease to speak.

"After Kennedy is buried, and Thanksgiving, we will be ready to get on...like you say, the American way." He hesitated. His matter of fact way belied a deeper concern. "I don't see our commitment to Vietnam lessening. Won't Johnson just carry on Kennedy's intentions?" Impending war was on the minds of Homer High students. The U.S. draft meant the boys could be sent to fight.

"I think we can expect President Johnson to carry on Kennedy's wishes," Mr. Pease replied. "We'll soon find out."

Ray lifted his hand, and his usual grin was replaced by concern. Mr. Pease gestured with a rise of his hand for him to speak.

"So what about the domino theory? What if Vietnam goes Communist along with all its neighbors? They are all talking about the need to protect South Vietnam, aren't they?"

Mr. Pease was, again, short and to the point, "I would imagine so. Continuity is the key. We'll have to wait and see."

Brad, with dark crew cut hair and a freckled face, was another talented basketball player and anxious to add his concern: "We could all be drafted and eat our Thanksgiving turkey over there if Johnson moves in with ground troops..."

Mr. Pease said, "You're all thinking too far ahead with the possibility of combat. Though that is a possibility in this situation, I'm afraid. The Government is committed to stopping the spread of communism. That has been evident for some time. Yes, of course we will listen and keep up with the news of our new President's plans. But if continuity is the American way, then Thanksgiving is part of that; and we will eat our turkey, cornbread, sweet potatoes, and pumpkin pie.

The points raised about President Johnson escalating the U.S.

involvement in South Vietnam worried me. President Kennedy had been assassinated and that was deeply unsettling. Soon, we could be led into war. Oh, God, I thought. I had no reason to hate people who lived far away and about whom I had little knowledge. I would have to search to find the country on the globe. It did not seem fair for my fellow students to worry about being drafted to fight thousands of miles away when they were nineteen.

The bell rang and we filed out one after another. None of us engaged in our usual banter. Life had become very serious.

Thanksgiving Corn Bread

Ingredients:
1½ cups/175g/6 oz, cornmeal
½ cup/190g/3 oz, plain flour
1 teaspoon salt
1 teaspoon baking powder
½ teaspoon baking soda
2 eggs, lightly beaten
½ pint/300 ml, buttermilk
3 tablespoons olive oil

Heat oven to 400F/200C. Sift dry ingredients into a bowl. Add eggs and buttermilk; stir just enough to blend. Heat oil in 9-inch baking pan, allowing sides to be coated. Pour excess oil into cornbread batter. Pour batter into hot pan and bake for 25 minutes or until brown. Cut into desired serving sizes and serve hot.

Sweet Potatoes glazed with Orange Sauce

Peel and simmer 4 large sweet potatoes, cut into halves. While they are cooking prepare the orange sauce below.

Orange Sauce
Combine and stir in a double boiler over boiling water until thickened:

¼ cup/ 4 tablespoons sugar	1 tablespoon cornstarch
1 cup/½ pint water	

Remove sauce from heat and stir in:

2 tablespoons butter	1 teaspoon grated orange zest
3 tablespoons orange juice	Dash salt

Drizzle sauce or cooked, drained potatoes and serve.

5:36 p.m. Good Friday, Alaska, 1964

Mrs. Edens and I had just sat down in the kitchen for an early dinner when the table began to wobble. A tremor? We had had them before. Pete, the parakeet perched on the gray haired widow's shoulder, began to squawk. Mrs. Edens leaned her wrinkled bespectacled face towards her pet, "What is it, Pete? Tell Mama."

Pete flew off to another perch in the room screeching as the wobbling became vigorous shaking.

We sprung from our chairs and raced for the door, trying to keep our balance. The dinner plates slid off the Formica table and broke. The silverware hit the floor. Pots and pans flew off the stove splattering gravy and mashed potatoes down onto the broken dishes splayed on the linoleum.

Spruce trees swayed violently from side to side, lower limbs touching the snow-covered ground. There was loud crackling as tree trunks split. Cars lurched backward and forward as if ready for takeoff. The Homer hillside was topsy-turvy and seemed to be roaring.

Time seemed suspended. Was this the end of the world? My nerves were still on edge since the assassination of President Kennedy and the escalation of the Vietnam War. Each Sunday I accompanied Mrs. Edens to Homer's Christian Community Church. As the lonely widow's lodger, I was expected to attend the services. The fundamentalist preacher there urgently reminded us of Christ's imminent second coming. The warning made me feel more concerned. Good Friday—dark clouds above—violent shaking of the ground. What was happening? Finally, we were able to stand as usual and saw that the cars and trees were still again.

"Quite an earthquake. Praise God it's over," Mrs. Edens said gripping her shaking hands. "Let's get back in and turn on the radio. Wonder how widespread it's been?"

Stepping into the house, we were confronted with heaps of

broken jars which had collided and dripped onto canned vegetables spilled out from the pantry.

Mrs. Edens made it to the radio and switched it on.

As she moved, she looked around and called out, "Pete, Pete." No response. She whistled. Nothing. No fluttering of wings. Then the cage started to rattle as the first after-quake hit. We braced ourselves, but I skidded on a glob of mayonnaise and almost fell.

The radio blared: ninety five per cent destruction in Anchorage; the earthquake had lasted 4.38 minutes. We shook our heads, and I felt despair.

"Oh, gosh—my family? Gail?" She was higher up on the Homer hillside. "Mom, Dad, Jerry, Brent?" They were on the homestead. There was no phone at Porcupine Lake for me to ring. I would have to wait for them to contact me.

Mrs. Edens said, "My boys? Gwen? My grandkids?"

The phone rang. It was my pregnant sister, Gail.

"Judy. It's you. Ok?"

"Yes," I said trembling.

"I thought I would give birth on the spot with all the shaking. Our car moved ten feet. We're heading down to check on Jack's mother. Since you're ok, we won't stop. I'll call with any news from the folks. Dad will try to get to a phone. They should be all right. Must rush, bye." That alleviated worry for Gail and her family, but what about the others?

From the radio, a tsunami warning for the Alaskan, Hawaiian, Washington State, Oregon, and Californian coasts was given several times. People living in the low areas were urged to flee to higher ground. On the Homer hillside we were out of danger. The homestead was also ok as it was high, but many Alaskan villages were beside the Pacific Ocean.

We started slowly to clean up the mess. But the tremors kept coming and prevented us from planning our next step. Would the next one turn into another massive quake? Some were ten to twenty seconds long and quite strong.

The phone rang three more times. Each of Mrs. Edens' two grown sons were concerned for us and wanted to relay that they and their families were ok. Her daughter had a similar message.

These calls seemed to help comfort the older woman.

She said, "Praise the Lord," when hearing from each of her children.

I prayed silently that God would spare us from another violent quake and that Mom, Dad, Jerry, and Brent were safe.

With each call, Mrs. Edens wailed into the phone, "Pete has gone." Neither of her sons nor her daughter could say the reassuring words she longed to hear about the bird. He must have flown out of the house when we left the door open.

Mrs. Edens kept repeating, "My bird, my bird, my Pete."

There was non-stop news from the radio. The earthquake was the second largest recorded in the world at 9.2 on the Richter scale. Only Chile had one stronger at 9.5 in 1960. The destruction in Anchorage was not as bad as first feared, but it was severe. Fourth Avenue, the main street, had sunk several feet on one side, causing buildings to subside. On the other side, buildings were undamaged. Many homes in the prestigious Turnagain Heights district, with its famous view onto Cook Inlet, had slid into the water.

We continued to clean in spite of relentless after-quake tremors. Many times we headed towards the door, but then turned around when the shaking stopped.

Late that night we were exhausted but also fearful of what destruction around the state would be revealed on our waking. Mrs. Edens went to her bed still distraught about Pete, and left the window open in case he came back and tried to get in. I was worried as I climbed into bed, and prayed over and over for Mom, Dad, Jerry and Brent.

"Let them be safe. Let them be safe," I murmured. Were they in bed sleeping? Had any of them been injured? My hope was that Dad would get to a phone early in the morning to tell me how they were. Sleep was broken by tremors so neither of us felt rested in the morning.

We woke up to knocking at the door. There stood Mom and Dad. Mom's hair fell in wisps around her shoulders rather than up in her usual neat French bun.

"Judy, Judy," Dad said hugging me.

"Where are Jerry and Brent?" I almost screamed.

"With Gail and Jack," he said patting my back. "We drove up there first to see how she and Jack weathered it with little Jamie. This is a quick stop to see how you are and take you back to the homestead for Easter."

"Come in," Mrs. Edens said standing at my side. "It's good that you came, Henning. Judy has been so worried. "Hello, Ruth."

Mom stepped into the kitchen and said, "What Hell we've been through." She looked weary and had still not recovered from the shock of yesterday's events.

"Yes, terrible," said Mrs. Edens. Then, pulling out kitchen chairs, "Sit down."

"Great that I'm going with you," I said. "I'll grab a few things."

As I came back into the room with my overnight bag, Mom began telling what happened during the earthquake on the homestead. I sat down to listen.

"I had just sent the boys to the root cellar for eggs to dye for Easter. I was standing by the kitchen table thinking about what else to prepare. I was expecting John—my name for Henning—at any moment and knew he would want to eat. Suddenly the table started shaking and the kerosene lantern slid to the edge. I grabbed it and rushed outside. Behind me the gallon jars slid off the shelves. The dishes and glasses just flew from the cupboards. Also the books came down from the shelves. I thought the whole cabin would fall in."

Mrs. Edens looking concerned, stated, "Praise the Lord it didn't."

"The cabin was second place in my mind," Mom continued. "I was far more anxious about the boys under the mound of ground over the root cellar. I ran out down the path towards them. My heart was racing. I kept calling out, Jerry…Brent…"

"You poor woman," Mrs. Edens said, shaking her head.

"Scamp came running towards me barking," Mom went on. "He usually goes into the cellar with the boys. The door must be open, I thought. Louder than Scamp's barking was the roar of ice breaking up on the lake. It sounded like a speeding train descending down a mountain. I thought, the trees would all come down, too. I heard Brent shout, 'It's the end of the world.' Jerry yelled back, 'No it isn't, you idiot. It's an earthquake.' Ok, I thought, my boys are safe."

"Praise the Lord that they were not buried in the cellar," said Mrs. Edens.

"And it is still standing," said Dad. "But, yes, we are very thankful that no one was hurt. They say scores of people around the State will be dealing with the loss of loved ones. I had it quite good. I was driving home after visiting a client when the quake hit. That meant me stopping until the shaking was over. I got back in the car and bounced over a few cracks in the road, but got home. Needless to say, our meal was delayed with all the cleaning we had to do."

"We have so much to be thankful for," said Mrs. Edens looking at my parents. "But, I'm so very worried about Pete. I'm afraid he's gone for good."

I lived with Mrs. Edens to the end of the school year, and then returned home to fish for the summer by which time many signs of the earthquake had been cleared away. But the damage to roads and bridges further along the Sterling Highway would challenge our family's travel in summer. Some areas of the State would never completely recover despite millions of dollars being poured in.

Pete never returned.

An Inspector Calls

Mom welcomed me back home for the summer, waving a letter. It was from the Land Department with the date for a Federal Homesteading Inspector to come to check on our planted fields and livable house. An inspection could mean the end of life on the homestead. Would we meet the requirements laid out in the Homestead Act? What did a livable house mean and how would it be interpreted? I climbed upstairs and hung my school dresses on the rail on my side of the curtain, knowing that blue jeans and sweatshirts would be worn in the month ahead to help prepare for the all-important deadline.

In the morning, Dad had us all out pulling weeds and hoeing in the gardens. Rows upon rows of potatoes had to be hilled, and all the root vegetables—carrots, parsnips, and turnips—plus broccoli and lettuce, needed attention. Jerry and I also took turns on the tractor tilling the fields. At the end of each day, I crashed into bed early with my back aching. Not even hard, persistent rain interrupted us.

I could hear my parents into the early hours from the round greenhouse nearby. It is still a mystery to me why Dad made it round. By putting a stove under the floor, he created conditions perfect for growing vegetables needing a more temperate climate than Alaskan summers provided. Heat rose through the soil making the inside like a Brazilian rainforest. Leafy stems with red clusters of tomatoes crossed the ceiling; and underneath, vines of squash, cucumbers, and once a pumpkin, burst forth.

As I lay in bed, they sifted, mixed, and planted to get it going. I heard Dad, "Ruth, what is the amount of bone meal... manure...what else do I add to mix with the soil? Got the sand in...Do you hear me for Christ sake? WHAT the hell?"

Mom, "Idiot. Be patient God Damn it. I don't remember...the Extension Service Pamphlet...I'm looking...HERE it is." They argued and contemplated. Their bickering was a continual irritation to me, but I thought perhaps the work in the warmth took their minds off the looming inspection and relaxed them for sleeping.

The small amount of grains that matured in the cleared swamps, and even the couple of fields on hills was not sufficient to justify the expense of harvesting equipment. The cleared land did diminish the nuisance of mosquitoes, and that was a welcome change. Before, we often wore mosquito nets to protect our faces from their incessant bombardment.

I disliked doing my share of gardening anytime, but now in preparation for the Government Inspector, I knew that it was vital so that we would retain the homestead. I was living the school year in Homer with the Andersons, Mrs. Edens, and Gail and Jack; and only back at Porcupine Lake for summers. But, this was home for Mom, Dad, Jerry, and Brent. As I pulled and chopped, I worried. Dear God, help us, I prayed.

Mom was beside herself on inspection day. At breakfast she ate little oatmeal. She put down her spoon, and covered her face with her hand. "God let's hope Lincoln's requirements are met. With this shack for a house and cleared swamps for fields..."

Dad frowned, and also seemed tense. "How can they throw us off the land? I'm glad we saved the trees. You didn't want to cut down the spruce and birch. But, who knows what a Government man will think or do?"

I rose from the table fearful of what could come. I saw that the sofa was down into a bed—still unmade from my parents' night there. Mom would soon fold the sheets, covers, and sofa. The tiny cabin was well organized and clean. I leaned on a step of the steep stairs and pulled on my rubber knee boots. Dear God, help us, I prayed over and over. We could not all fit in the small trailer Dad now rented for a Homer office if our one hundred and sixty acres and cabin did not pass the inspection.

Jerry coughed and asked, "Shall I go to the cabbage patch and hoe?"

"Yes, and you, too, Brent. Let's all be busy when he comes," Dad instructed.

Mom yelled, "Pick some rhubarb first. Bring it right in. Hurry.

Judy, you start mixing up the crust."

"Ok, but Judy needs to get out soon, too," Dad said.

I would be on the tractor tilling the field across the lake when the Federal Inspector arrived. Mom and Dad thought it would be best for them to welcome him with coffee in the cabin and then let him look at our fields—first the two on high ground. Dad rowed me across in our small boat, and I hurried up the hill to that field. I became more anxious wondering what the Inspector would put on his report after sizing up our tiny house with only tarpaper on the outside. Oh, God.

This field was higher up than our other clearings, so probably ok...but the ones in the swamps? I feared the Inspector. I imagined him to be stern, even cold. Hopefully, Dad's warm smile and positive attitude would help soften the man's strict adherence to rules and regulations. Even the title of "Government Inspector" brought up foreboding in me.

Mom would tell me after he was gone, that over coffee with her and Dad, the Inspector seemed more interested in learning about the Lewis' homestead next to us than about ours. Charlie and Frieda were well known in the community as they led the Friday night square dances; she was a Post Mistress; and he worked for the State. They were older than my parents and had made the decision to make a claim on relinquished land on Swan Lake. Money seemed no object as they hired workers to erect a small Lindal Cedar house close to the spot Dad had shot the moose our first year when we still lived in a tent.

"Do you see evidence that Mr. and Mrs. Lewis occupy the house there?" the Inspector questioned.

"Oh, they are away in jobs during the day, but I see their car when I drive past at night," Dad said.

"Oh, well, thanks, and what about their..."

Dad cut him off, "I'll row you across the lake to see the field there."

The inspector was reluctant replying, "Can't I just stand here and use my binoculars?"

"Too many trees in the way," Dad said.

They did come and tramp around as I was busily running the

tractor. I pretended to be totally engaged pulling the disk to till the field. Actually, most of my attention was on the Government Inspector, but I did not learn a thing bouncing around on the seat of the noisy Allis Chambers. Instead of waving, he nodded at me under a baseball cap shielding his eyes, and arms folded. Glancing again, I saw that he was stocky and walked slowly as he jotted on a clipboard. I tried to imagine what he would be writing: height of the canary grass? I really had no idea and was relieved to see him and Dad exit the field. Looking down from the tractor, I saw that the Inspector's boots were flopping about. He had not bothered to lace them properly, and they were probably full of grass and weeds.

A couple of hours later, we were all back at the cabin around the table for lunch. It was Mom's duty to feed everyone—even the Federal Inspector.

The man was all smiles. "Very nice of you to ask me to join you," he said looking at Mom.

"Oh, no trouble. It's only a moose roast that we had left in the freezer. I always add our own homegrown vegetables to the pot."

"Ruth's cooking is special," Dad said with a big smile.

"Looks wonderful." He smiled back at Dad, and looked at Mom with appreciation. But, after this chitchat over the meal, would he leave saying that it would all be in his report—to come later in the mail? Oh God help us, I prayed again.

The Inspector chewed a few bites along with the rest of us, and then put down his fork and wiped his mouth with a paper napkin. Looking first at Mom, then Dad, and each of us kids he said, "I'm not here to take your homestead away. It is clear that you've all put in a lot of effort. I'll make my report saying that all obligations have been met."

Suddenly I loved the Inspector…a human being. Yes, we had worked hard to make the 160 acres around Porcupine Lake home. Mom had soldiered on, alone, with Dad away much of the time surveying. Homesteading was a tough job even for a man. I turned on the bench and pain shot up my back. "Worked hard," was an understatement, I thought. More appropriate would have been, "You've practically killed yourselves." But, I joined the rest of the family to smile at the Inspector. His favorable comments were as good to hear as the next course tasted: rhubarb cream pie.

A couple of months later our deed arrived in the U.S. mail. Mom was disappointed that her name was not on the document.

Rhubarb Cream Pie

Pre-heat oven to 350F/177C
Prepare enough short-crust dough for a two-crust pie.

Filling ingredients:
3 to 4 eggs, depending on size
1 scant cup/5 ounces, white or brown sugar
Dash salt
Dash nutmeg
Dash powdered ginger
¼ to ½ teaspoon cinnamon
4 cups/one liter, washed and drained, rhubarb, cut into small pieces.
1 tablespoon lemon juice, plus roughly ground zest of the lemon
1 tablespoon butter, cut into about 4 pieces

Whisk eggs, sugar, salt, and spices. Cover a 9-inch pie plate with rolled dough. Fill with prepared rhubarb and sprinkle with lemon juice and zest. Pour over whipped ingredients and place dots of butter on top. Cover with rolled dough to size. Secure edges with bottom dough by fluting. Cut slashes in the top to make your own design for steam to escape. Bake until golden brown.

Another Letter

Soon after the Inspector's visit, another important letter arrived. Grandma Dabbert was hospitalized with uremic poisoning. Mom put down the letter and exclaimed, "My God, this could kill her. I'm leaving for Florida."

"Of course," Dad replied, "but we will miss you. The kids and I…"

"What's uremic poisoning?" I interrupted.

"Toxins in the blood that should pass out in the urine," Mom replied.

"What causes it?" I asked.

"Weak kidneys," Mom said.

She was gone the next day on a flight from Kenai, the area's main airport, to Anchorage and then on to our grandparents in the sunshine state. Dad seemed gloomy, "I can't leave you kids to go surveying, but I will make a few improvements for your mother." He started on a unique kitchen table that would have a spruce trunk supporting the table top. Jerry and Brent helped peel, sand, and nail. The project took over the downstairs which made it crowded around the stove and sink for lunch and dinner preparations. Helping clean up the sawdust was added to my list of chores. Dad kept up his cheerfulness, but underneath he seemed a bit forlorn. I knew he missed Mom as I caught him staring into space at times. I had watched them over the years do every project together except when he was away surveying. I wondered how much mother being gone had taken out of him.

Another letter arrived from Mom that Grandmother was home from the hospital, and Mom would stay on to nurse her. That night after my brothers were in bed and I was washing the dishes, Dad confided, "Judy, I worry that your mother will not return from Florida. We work so hard here, and she is unhappy with this house. I know that she was upset that her name wasn't on the deed."

I went to bed that night to worry, too. Mom was still attractive, probably worn out and exhausted. Would she find another life in Florida? How much were we kids in her thoughts? My chest became tight. Surely she wouldn't abandon Brent, Jerry, and me? Please God, bring her back, I prayed. If she did not return, I would need to take over many of her responsibilities and perhaps leave high school in Homer to help on the homestead. I so wished that she would return.

Fourth of July picnic

194

A Fourth of July

A strong mid-June breeze made me shiver as I waited with Dad, Jerry, and Brent at the Homer airport. I was stupid to have left my jacket in the car, but we had rushed from where we parked in front of the small terminal, knowing that Mom's plane was due. She was returning from a six-week stay in Florida where she had been visiting our ailing Grandmother Dabbert. Hunching my shoulders and folding my arms, I was slightly warmer, but not comfortable. Mom's lengthy stay with her parents had worried me. Would she leave us for an easier life with her parents? I sighed with relief when the Pacific Northern Airline plane appeared on the horizon. The roar of the engines became deafening as it descended and touched down. It came to a rolling stop a few yards from the barrier where we waited on the tarmac. A young man in airport overalls rolled the metal stairs into place. He ran up and waited a couple of minutes before the door opened, and he bolted it to one side.

Travelers started descending carrying parcels. Some recognized family and quickened their pace. A tanned woman in a green, white, and yellow striped shift-dress came through the door and started down. She looked out searching, and found us, and smiled and waved. Pride, joy, and relief swept over me all at once as I waved back. I rarely saw her in a dress—and never this slim.

A kiss for Dad and hugs for each of us kids from this glamorous woman—Mom. As she held me close, I flinched; and she sensed something was not quite right.

"What is it, Judy?"

I shook my head and said, "Nothing." I fidgeted from one foot to the other and pulled my dress down, as the hem flapped up in the wind. "I left my jacket in the car, and it's a little cold out here," I explained.

Actually, my side had hurt since breakfast. I was trying to ignore it and will the pain away. Please God do not let this be a recurrence of last winter's bad health. Please God...please. Mom was back. That made me happy. I just wanted to admire her and hear her chatter. I had been running the household with more cooking and cleaning responsibilities. Now she would plough into following recipes from *The Joy* and keeping the cabin cleanliness to a high standard. I would have more time to myself. We retrieved the one large suitcase from the baggage area inside the terminal and chatted on the way to the car.

Mom said, "So glad to see the snow has melted. After all, I've been in sunny Florida. Each morning while your grandmother was sleeping, Grandpa and I..."

Brent interrupted with, "We've built you a new kitchen table."

Jerry, calmer, but unable to contain his pride, said, "I took turns with Dad to peel bark from a tree we cut. I used a draw knife and a chisel."

"We have a few things to show you. Keeping ourselves busy helped pass the time these weeks you've been away," Dad said. He had slept in bed alone; had taken on projects alone or with us kids since Mom's absence. He had confided in me that he worried that she would not return.

Mom nodded and smiled as she settled into her seat. "It is good to be back. I look forward to seeing the table. Right now let's run up to Gail's. Gosh, the kids must have grown while I've been away."

In a few minutes we were on the East Hill overlooking a blue Kachemak Bay, tall mountains with patches of snow, and Grewink Glacier on the other side of the water. The glacier was one of the beauty spots all the locals and tourists enjoyed.

Holding two-month-old Bryan, and with her toddler, Jamie Lynn, and small, hairy dog, Pepe, standing by her side, Gail greeted us at the front porch. It was more hugs for Mom and inquiries from Gail about our grandparents.

"Your grandmother is much better," Mom reassured us over a cup of tea at the kitchen table. "Jamie, come here and see what I've brought for you. Open."

Gail noticed that I was not myself, and took me aside saying, "Judy, you're looking a bit pale. Everything ok?"

"Well…my side hurts. It will get better."

"Not more of your old trouble?" Gail asked.

"I don't think so." I knew that she was remembering the past winter when a cyst burst on my ovary. It had brought me to my knees in agony as I clutched my abdomen. The only doctor in town came to administer morphine. I was bedridden for two weeks and under Mrs. Eden's care. Today's pain was different. Perhaps it was indigestion.

We kept the visit short so as to get started on the sixty-mile drive to the homestead.

"Ok, everybody ready?" my dad asked as we were climbing into the car and saying goodbye.

Gail blurted out, "Judy is having pain on her side."

"Oh no, maybe we should take you to the doctor now before going home?" Mom said.

"No, no," I forcefully stated, still holding firm with my decision to ignore the pain, hoping it would subside. It was mind over matter. I was pleased at Mom's and Gail's concern and attention, but was determined. No way did I want a repeat of last winter's ordeal.

Dad turned to look at me in the backseat and said, "If you're sure." I smiled, nodding my head to confirm. We started the journey. I continued to pray along the way. Help me, God. Keep me safe.

There was no mud anywhere like the mud our dirt road turned into during spring break-up. Dad could only drive one mile before asking us to leave the car and walk the one and a quarter miles remaining. Because the mud oozed over the width of the road in places, we were forced to tread cautiously alongside on the mounds of spongy moss called muskeg. With every step in my rubber knee boots, the pain stabbed me from within. The minute we entered the cabin, I slumped down on the sofa holding my middle.

"Oh dear, should have gone to the doctor," Mom said, shaking her head. She hung her jacket in the small stairs closet and sat down by me.

"See how you feel in an hour," Dad said, sounding concerned.

Jerry and Brent pulled Mom away to the kitchen side of the

cabin. They insisted that she admire the table they had constructed with Dad using timber from our own forest. "I love it," Mom said, rubbing her hand around on the satiny, smooth, sanded supporting spruce base. My brothers beamed.

Everyone changed into more comfortable clothes. Mom into her usual Bluebell jeans. My looser clothes felt better but not my side. It was good having Mom back, and I tried to chat with her. To myself I kept saying, "Forget the pain. Forget the pain."

"Where did you get the striped dress?" I asked.

"Oh, I sewed it up while your grandmother was resting," she replied. "I found the fabric on sale, and Mother had the white eyelet trim. I also walked on the beach barefoot and went for a swim most days. It was wonderful. I did miss you these past weeks. How are you now?"

"Not good," I said, regretting that I had not seen a doctor while we were in town. How stupid. So much for mind over matter. I was in agony. What was it? Dad had an easy time getting to the hospital in Chicago for his appendectomy as a young man. Was it my appendix? It was going to be uncomfortable and awkward making the journey back out. Guilt flowed into me knowing the trouble I had caused by not seeing the doctor in Homer before we made the journey to the homestead.

"*We are going,*" Dad announced.

That meant traveling twenty miles to Soldotna, the closest town. First we had to go back through the mud to get me to the car. The pain intensified at the thought. Dad, with me seated uncomfortably at his side, used our small tricycle gear tractor to drive out the road. We wound through the spruce and birch forest with Mom, Jerry, and Brent walking behind. Without suspension springs or shock absorbers, it was a bouncy ride. We lurched along until I could no longer bear the discomfort. I cried out, "Oh, God."

Abandoning the tractor at our homestead boundary, Dad carried me piggyback the remaining half mile to our red Land Rover. As I was joggled along, feeling like a knife was cutting into me, I remembered a worrying story Dad had told months ago. A moose hunter out in the bush had an appendicitis attack. It ruptured and his companions were unable to get him medical help before he died. Was this going to be my fate? Without a spoken word, but ongoing groans to Dad, I kept up a constant plea to God for me to get to the doctor in time. It was an easier drive on the gravel, yet bumpy Sterling Highway.

Doctor Isaac, a fellow Lutheran and an Alaskan of many years standing, examined me and administered a blood test. He decided that I should be kept close by the clinic for the next few days. A caring, soft-spoken man with a family of his own, his medical opinion was valued; and he was also a trusted surgeon.

Our kind town friends, Charlie and Katherine Parker, made up a cot for me in their living room. Charlie was a surveyor like Dad, and they had been friends since our Homer years. They tried to make me comfortable, but I knew that I was a nuisance. With a toddler of their own underfoot, they had enough trouble without sick me to nurse. Their youngster, blabbering away and wanting my attention, was irritating now, whereas on other visits she was cute and entertaining. After a couple of days, the pain had not diminished, and my white blood count shot up. Doctor Isaac decided he would remove my appendix. In 1964 the hospital in Soldotna did not have the facilities for surgery. My parents drove me the one hundred miles to the port town of Seward where there was a hospital with an operating theatre.

It was less than three months since the Alaskan earthquake so damaged roads lay ahead. Dad had to drive slowly crossing over temporary precarious bridges above the fast flowing Kenai and Snow Rivers. The water rushed around and gushed up large rocks as we crept above on thick wooden planks. The highway was full of bad patches which jarred and caused me to moan from where I lay across the back seat. Chicago, I thought. Why did we not live there? Dad dropped his speed over the rough areas trying to help.

We pulled up to the hospital late in the afternoon. It was a light green two-storey building, with no more than ten beds for patients, and a staff of half a dozen. Knowing my parents would not be staying in town, I was treated like royalty. A nurse in white starched uniform and traditional cap settled me into a private room. She took my blood pressure and temperature. I changed into a hospital gown, and Mom tied up the strings in the back. The appendectomy was scheduled for that evening.

I was anxious. I had not had an operation since my tonsillectomy at age six while we were still living in Chugiak. Mom and Gail had driven me to Anchorage one afternoon; and before I had a chance to worry, the op was over and I was back home in Mom's care to recover.

Much of the time during my appendectomy I was awake. The doctors peered down over my abdomen wearing head covers and gowns working under a bright light. They murmured to each other through green cloth mouth protectors. Concern ebbed behind their muffled utterings and rose within me. What were they saying? There was rattling and clanking as they laid down tools on a stainless steel tray and picked up others. I longed to sleep, but the anesthetic was not strong enough to put me under. Time stretched on and on as I lay unable to move any part of my body except my head.

A nurse stood looking into my eyes and glancing at the doctors. Her comforting comments and pats on my shoulders were reassuring. She asked about the family and school activities. When I questioned her about the size of the scar, she chuckled and said, "You'll probably want to wear a one-piece swim suit this summer rather than a bikini." I was not bothered by her comment at the time. In the '60s two-piece swim suits in Alaska were uncommon. I had never had one nor had my friends.

The appendix was swollen and inflamed but had not ruptured. Doctor Issac attempted to investigate my ovaries for cysts, but was blocked by adhesions. After two and a half hours he gave up. Mom and Dad were there as I was returned to my room, and reassured me that I would be fine. They tucked me into bed, and left for the long drive home. Recovery in the hospital would lag on for two weeks. The nurses came routinely to take my temperature and bring me broth and later solid food that was nutritious, but I missed moose meat. I lay looking at magazines and snowy black and white TV. The reception over the mountains from Anchorage was bad. The Women's program one day showed how to fold a fitted bedsheet, and I switched the set off. Doctor Isaac told me that I was healing nicely when he painfully removed the stitches, but he made no mention of possible physical alterations from diseased cysts and an appendix. Neither did the nurses. I knew of no reason to worry, and just thought of recovering and returning home. I asked no questions.

One morning in the Seward hospital, I was woken up with the window being washed and pleasantly surprised to see a familiar guy's face behind the squeegee. It was Steve MacSwain's who was one of the High School's starting five basketball players. Steve and I had become acquainted at games in Homer, Seward, and Anchorage. Players and cheerleaders were bused between towns. Our school's team had displaced his team from the state tournament the past season. He made a silly smile, gave me a big wave, and finished the window. How grateful I was to see this lanky guy sitting beside me soon after he recognized my face.

His chatter about weekend basketball games and sock hops during the past winter lifted my spirits. "You're the prettiest cheerleader, Judy."

"Oh, gosh," I said, embarrassed. Fortunately, he did not bring up the name of the star player on the Seward team that I had a big crush on. My hope for the romance with the star eventually faded because the 100 plus miles between Homer and Seward meant we rarely saw each other.

Getting home once I was up to traveling again was the next detail to be worked out. I thought Mom and Dad would return with the car to drive me. However, Doctor Isaac came in to see me, checked the wound, and announced that he would be flying me back. He was not only a medical doctor and surgeon, but also piloted his own bush plane. I had flown in one at the age of ten, traveling from Homer across the bay to Seldovia, to see the dentist. This time, at sixteen, my childhood fearlessness was gone, and I felt anxious as I fastened the seat belt strap snugly over my tender abdomen.

It was a scenic, noisy journey in the two-seater Piper Super Cub with almost constant dipping and climbing. Below, white patches of snow remained on the Kenai Mountains. The green hills rolled along covered with spruce and birch trees interrupted with openings of wide mossy swamps, river valleys, and lakes. It was spectacular to see the territory of my home from the air.

I gazed down at shapes on the ground. "Looks like moose below," I said.

Doctor Isaac appeared startled and asked, "What? Planes?"

"No, no, moose," I yelled. He shook his head and frowned as he peered down.

The deafening roar of the engine and propeller made me give up conversation. I decided instead to concentrate on keeping calm as my sense of equilibrium was affected with the up, down, and sideways movements of the plane. The rocky flight continued for about thirty minutes. Then, thankfully, I felt the light aircraft descend, and the gravel runway came into view amongst a clearing in the trees. We landed smoothly which did not surprise me. The expertise of the pilot was evident. It was quiet around the small hut which was the only building in sight. My parents were waiting by our Land Rover. Doctor Isaac's car was parked close by, ready for him to drive home. He hopped down from his side and helped me slowly down from mine. I walked cautiously, aware of each step, bent forward from the waist.

"Thanks, Doc," Dad said. "What do I owe you?"

"Judy, how are you?" Mom said as she rushed up putting a hand on my back." Her touch was reassuring.

"Ok," I said. As good as it was to see my parents, it was even better to be back on solid ground free from the noisy engine and bounce of the plane. Free from the boring hospital routine.

"She's doing fine. Soon back to her normal self," Doctor Isaac said. "Bring her in for a check-up in a week." He chuckled, "You owe me nothing. I was coming home anyway." With that he walked over to his station wagon, started the motor, and with a wave was gone. We drove back to the homestead. Tomorrow was the Fourth of July, and we were hosting a picnic for family and friends. It was easier traveling as "drying up" had occurred since I had been away, and Dad was able to drive directly to the cabin door.

By the next morning I felt much better and was ready to participate in preparations for the busy day ahead. We had much to do to get the cabin and yard ready for the guests. Dad built a small campfire in the yard. He, Jerry, and Brent cut and arranged tree stumps as stools where young people could sit and brought out folding chairs for adults. They cut willow sticks and carved each with a sharp end for roasting wieners. Mom shouted instructions from the door, and Dad returned by announcing all was in hand.

Gail and her husband Jack, with Jamie and Bryan, Margaret and Fred Anderson with Ricky and Maren, Charlie and Katherine Parker, and other friends arrived to join in the celebration. They brought carrot and raisin salad, coleslaw, deviled eggs, and Boston Baked Beans. There was a large quantity of food laid out on the front of the Land Rover. Mom added potato salad and corn pudding. Teriyaki Salmon starred as the main course. Dessert was strawberry shortcake buried in freshly made Dream Whip. I was not able to help much, still weak and bent over after my recent operation.

Dad performed a grand finale with a fireworks display beside the lake. The multi-colored bursts brought forth joyful exclamations. Afterwards on hot coals, using the same sharpened sticks, we kids heated marshmallows to golden puffs and made S'mores— hot marshmallows placed on Hershey squares between Graham crackers.

We all squeezed into the cabin for a cup of tea, coffee, or cocoa before everyone said goodbye. Dad turned the radio on for the news. Vietnam mentioned by the newscaster and everyone in the room voiced concern. These news bulletins were ever more frequent. "Then Itsy Bitsy, Teenie, Weenie, Yellow Pokka Dot Bikini" came on, and we all laughed.

It was a superb Fourth. Minute by minute my homestead health was returning.

Potato Salad
Serves 6—8

750g new potatoes, cooked and cut in half
1 red sweet bell pepper, diced
½ red chilli, seeds removed and sliced fine
a few torn mint leaves
a bunch of curly parsley, snipped into small pieces with kitchen shears
½ red onion, peeled and diced

1 teaspoon salt

Good shaking of coarse ground black pepper

4 tablespoons olive oil

Juice of one lemon

Combine all the above ingredients. Refrigerate until serving time.

Carrot and Raisin Salad

Serves 6

4 large carrots, washed, and coarsely grated

½ cup raisins

grated zest from one lemon

juice squeezed from one lemon

½ teaspoon salt or to taste

Dash of ground black pepper or to taste

1 cup/¼ liter mayonnaise

Place all of the above in a bowl and mix thoroughly. Adjust consistency desired with more lemon juice and mayonnaise. Refrigerate until ready to serve.

Coleslaw

Serves 6

To make the dressing, blend together in a small bowl: ¾ cup mayonnaise, ¼ cup white wine vinegar, and 1 tablespoon sugar.

Shred coarsely or finely chop 1 small head of green cabbage into a serving bowl. Into the same bowl add one head shredded red cabbage.

Stir in enough of the dressing to moisten the cabbage. More may be needed if your heads of cabbage are large. Season with salt, pepper, celery seeds, mustard, Worcestershire sauce, and chopped fresh chives or whatever spice/herb you prefer. Flaked almonds can be added if you desire. Refrigerate until ready to serve.

Deviled Eggs

Hard-boil 6 eggs; shell and halve lengthwise, remove yolks and place in a bowl and whites on a plate.

Mash the yolks with a fork and add 3 tablespoons mayonnaise; 1 to 2 teaspoons of Dijon mustard; Dash of salt and black pepper; Stir in more mayonnaise if necessary to make a thick paste. The addition of snipped fresh chives is nice if you have them. Taste to adjust seasoning.

Spoon the yolk mixture into each white. Sprinkle the 12 halves with paprika and refrigerate until serving time.

Boston Baked Beans

2.2 pounds/one kilogram, dried white beans

Put the beans in a large Dutch oven or heavy pot which has a tight fitting lid. Pour in 4 quarts/liters of water. Bring uncovered, to the boil over high heat and boil for two minutes. Turn off heat; cover and let stand on the burner for one hour. Repeat once more. Uncover the beans and bring up to barely simmering and continue to cook like this for 45 minutes, or until the beans are soft but still intact. Pour the beans into a colander and let drain completely.

Position the rack in the middle of the oven set to 250F/121C.

In the original pot, pour in the following ingredients and bring up to boiling:

  3 cups/¾ liter water

  1 cup/¼ liter molasses

  1 tablespoon salt, (to taste)

  1 tablespoon ground black pepper, (to taste)

  1 teaspoon cloves, (to taste)

  8 ounces/250g fatty bacon, cut into small pieces

  2 white or yellow onions, roughly chopped

Pour in the drained beans. Secure the lid onto the pot and bake about 5 hours or until the liquid is thick. Serve hot.

Corn Pudding

Drain:

2 x Can of kernel corn, to make 3 cups; reserve the juice. Melt

2 tablespoons butter in oven proof dish

Stir in 2 tablespoons flour; remove pan from heat

Combine and stir in slowly:

The corn liquid and enough evaporated milk to make one cup

Return to heat with stirring

When the sauce is thickened, stir in corn, and

½ chopped sweet pepper, green, red, or orange (membrane removed)

When mixture starts to simmer, add:

Two beaten eggs yolks; actually add a half cup of the sauce to the egg yolks and when mixed, pour back into the main pot of sauce

Stir and cook for a couple more minutes until thick; add to taste:

Salt, white pepper, and paprika

Whip two egg whites to form soft peaks and fold in.

Crumbled cooked bacon is good sprinkled on top if desired.

Bake for 30 minutes in a pre-heated 350F/180C oven.

Strawberry Shortcake

Serves 10 easily, but depends on the size of cutter used to cut dough. This dessert is famous in Alaska and every one of the fifty states of the U.S.

First slice enough strawberries to fill a large bowl. Sweeten with a little sugar if desired or use a powdered artificial sweetener. I like to add 2 to 3 table-spoons Amaretto. Refrigerate.

Prepare Baking Powder Biscuits (Below)

Biscuits Supreme

2 cups sifted, plain white flour or potato flour

4 level teaspoons baking powder

½ teaspoon salt

½ teaspoon cream of tartar

2 teaspoons sugar

½ cup (8 tablespoons) unsalted butter

⅔ cup milk

Sift or stir together the first five ingredients in a mixing bowl; cut in butter with a pasty blender or fork until mixture resembles coarse crumbs. Make a "well" in the center and pour the milk in all at once. Stir briefly until dough leaves the sides of the bowl.

Turn out on lightly floured surface and knead about 10 seconds. Pat or roll to ½ inch thick; cut rounds of desired size with cutter. Bake on ungreased baking sheet at 450F/200C for 10 minutes or until golden.

Whip enough whipping cream to fill a medium sized bowl.

To assemble the Strawberries Shortcakes:

Break a baked biscuit in half. Place in an individual dessert bowl; spoon over sliced strawberries with juice; top with a spoon of whipped cream. Repeat with other biscuits, strawberries and whipped cream. Serve immediately.

A Sense of the Future

At the homestead one weekend, we were listening to a news report about the situation in Vietnam and the possibility of being called up. "Gosh," Dad said. "What about Jerry and Brent? They could be drafted at nineteen. Birthdays creep up." Both of my brothers looked at Dad, Mom, and me. They did not say anything, but they frowned and looked down. Jerry reacted with his nervous cough.

"Oh Dad," I said, They're young. Surely the war will be over before Jerry and Brent are old enough to go. Jerry is twelve…Brent nine."

Listening to the radio we learned that thousands joined peaceful protests from Berkley, California, to New York, by marching with anti-war placards and participating in sit-ins against the Vietnam War. There were hourly updates about the escalating situation.

The guys in World History had been right to worry…it had become life or death war. Johnson won by a landslide and was re-instated as President. Early in 1965, the United States was bombing North Vietnam and sent in ground troops.

One day in January, Gail and I heard Malcolm X quoted on the radio broadcast as we sat at her kitchen table. "The defeat of the United States in South Vietnam is a matter of time. The French gave up years ago and withdrew knowing it was hopeless."

I was surprised as I thought our American Army could defeat any enemy. "Gail, what do you think?" I asked, meeting her eyes over my coffee cup.

"Judy, I am so glad that my kids are not in school yet and that Jack has done his military service. Why should they risk their lives over there?" She got up and poured herself another cup. "More?"

"No thanks, I'm fine. It's so far to send our soldiers to fight, be injured, or die. For what?"

"Dad put on an army uniform gladly when he was drafted into World War II," Gail added, But this war—it's so far away. I just can't identify with it."

"I know," I said, as I drained my cup and put on my coat. I met Gail's eyes again, and we shook our heads as I left. As I walked up Mission Road, I asked myself, what had the establishment got us into? Maybe yelling my lungs out at tonight's basketball game would lighten my spirits.

Dad drove me to the homestead for a weekend visit in April, 1965, and over the radio we heard that the Students for Democratic Society (SDS), and others, had organized a march on Washington, D.C.

Dad raised his voice and said, "Twenty-five thousand participants. Wonder if those will join in the others burning their draft cards?"

"My word," I exclaimed, thinking how extreme it was to do such a thing.

Dad replied as he drove us along, "It's a sad time. Senator Ernest Gruening was one of two Senators to vote against Johnson's Tonkin Resolution to escalate. What an Alaskan. What do you think, Judy? What courage." Hearing this broadened and reinforced my sense of what it meant to be an Alaskan. We were pioneers after all, and that meant going where nothing existed before.

"Great, Dad, but the draft. I worry about guys I know who could be sent." I thought grimly about the war, but brightened listening to a current hit on the car radio—"Sweet Talking Guy".

When we were alone in the cabin, Mom took me aside. "Judy, Dr. Fenger had the nerve to blurt out news of your operation to your father in front of other men on the Homer dock. He said that you will never have children. What a horrible, inconsiderate thing to do. Your father was embarrassed, and worried that those around him might believe such a lie."

I shrugged my shoulders and did not think much about it as my health had been fine since the operation. But, why would Dr. Fenger be so unprofessional? He had not told me there was any internal problem; and since it was my appendix that was removed, I had no reason to worry. I felt fine, but felt embarrassed for Dad.

The seniors graduated in spring. Most of the basketball players went on to university. Ray stayed in Homer and learned to fly Bush planes, and received his pilot's license working for a local company.

In a few months I would be a senior, and more than the war, my ability to have children or not was my preoccupation.

Mom and Dad with Sherry and Gail

The Senior Prom and Going Steady

We girls were more likely to have a "steady" if we were cheerleaders. The enviable "steady" status was evident when the girl wore a guy's class ring around her neck on a chain.

No fate was worse than being regarded as a "wallflower" at a dance. We girls all dreamed of being asked to the prom—the date, the dress, the corsage, and the photos in the school yearbook and for her personal album.

I did get asked to spring proms even though I never was given a guy's ring to wear. The first time was my freshman year when a graduating basketball player, Jackie Alexander, whom I had briefly dated when first in high school, invited me. Or did he? I put on an evening gown with matching high heels and fixed my hair in a French twist, but the clock ticked past the hour he was to come. I thought I had misheard his invitation, as I desperately wanted to go, and very much needed to be seen as one of the "in crowd."

The evening was especially embarrassing as the Andersons, with whom I was staying, hovered around waiting for my date, and voiced misgivings about him and his family as the clock ticked. They even suggested that I call him, or they should call his mom or dad. The Alexanders ran the town bakery, and the Andersons collected the daily hot loaf for dinner; thus, knew Jackie's family. With my parents, I could have told them to back off, but with Margaret and Fred, I had to be polite and appear to be ok even though I was suffering a massive letdown.

Jackie's mom or dad must have been told by the Andersons because he made a feeble excuse when we ran into each other at school. It was something like, "When we spoke in the hall before the prom, I just said I would like to go, but I didn't invite you because..." He may have said sorry for the mix-up, but I did not listen closely. I knew that basically he could not be bothered to take me. I nodded and escaped down the long corridor to bury my head behind the metal door of my locker. Tania came by ready for the next class. We walked in together, and I whispered what had transpired with Jackie. Her interest as she shook her head and looked sympathetically into my eyes was comforting, although I knew Tania had never been to a ball. Her thick glasses and gangly physic put guys off. Confidence and beauty would emerge later for her.

The next year the Andersons arranged my prom escort, as they knew a couple with a son. Skip had been expelled from an Anchorage high school and shipped down to Homer for relatives to sort out. He strutted around the halls and into classes quite sure of himself with a big dose of cockiness and verbal dribble that annoyed the teachers and many students. I did not totally dislike him, but found ways to skid around his attention-demanding gyrations and shoe shuffle.

Prom night he was punctual and seemed to enjoy wearing a tux, pinning on my corsage, and standing for me to pin on his boutonniere, and for our picture. His golden blond hair (obviously dyed) was slicked back, and he wore heavy black framed glasses that made him look like he belonged in Hollywood. That evening he was confident instead of cocky, and looked worldly rather than small town. I took his arm and left the house with Margaret's and Fred's approving eyes and smiles.

Girls in steady relationships sat very close to the side of their guy behind the wheel. My dad proclaimed once, "I thought there was only the driver in a car today. I got closer and saw there were two people in the front. Gosh, true love." With the introduction of seat belts soon after, driver and passenger had designated spots to enable buckling up. It meant the end of one of the standard proclamations of a steady relationship.

I decided to be cautious and sat fairly close to the passenger door. Small talk flowed from Skip's mouth as he drove us to the high school gymnasium. He broke into song and swayed behind the wheel as "Can't Buy Me Love" played on the radio.

On the dance floor he was right on beat, whether the music was fast or slow. We rotated our bodies to "Let's Twist Again". I wore a below-the-knee, white satin dress that was a hand-me-down from one of Gail's in-laws; and moved my hips back and forth. A few of the girls in long evening dresses accomplished the hip action, but caught their high heels in the hem of their floating gowns as they shifted weight from one foot to the other. To "The End of the World", Skip led me smoothly around the floor between other couples enjoying the special night beneath dimmed lights and grey paper streamers. His embrace was elegant, and he never smothered me. My eyes caught the sight of others in a "steady" relationship in such tight holds that I was embarrassed. It was evident that the blue tinge on a few girls' faces was not only eye make-up, but they were suffering from lack of oxygen. I was proud to be seen at the prom and accompanied by Skip whose troublesome personality seemed to be transformed by my presence.

Going home in the car, I sat closer to him than to the passenger door, but made no move to snuggle. We sang along to "I Get Around". Skip walked me to the door, and with a light touch of his lips to mine said, "Good night. Thank you, Judy." He turned slowly, and strode back to his car, humming more of the Beach Boys and was gone. I crept quietly into the house and to bed, thinking…what a gentleman. What a night.

Neither before or after the prom did Skip participate in school sports. That fact made me cross him off as a guy to consider dating. As a cheerleader I was keenly interested in the talented fellows who became athletic dreamboats. I yearned to be taken to a prom with such a guy. During the next few months my dreams would materialize, although not in quite the way I anticipated.

The Game and How It Played Out

It was a Saturday night in 1966, and the high school gymnasium was packed with parents and friends of players. These people braved the winter cold to sit on wooden bleachers to support Homer basketball. The Pep band members, in blue and gold sweatshirts, settled on the far right of the bleachers with their French horns, trombones, clarinets, and drums. Tania was at the piano.

I walked over with our cheering squad to welcome the Kenai cheerleaders. Like us, they were all girls. There had never been a boy cheerleader. Their high school was larger than Homer and their cheerleaders more professional, I thought. It did not matter. We had bundles of enthusiasm. I introduced myself as did the others. After brief chit chat, the Kenai Pep Band started playing. We wished them well and returned to the Homer side.

The Kenai cheerleaders led their supporters in the Cardinals' theme song. They were on the mark with flips, cartwheels, and splits. Their red and white uniforms swished, swung, and flapped with every move. I was impressed and clapped as they ran off.

Then, the Homer Pep Band played the Mariners' theme song, and we belted out the words as we performed our routine.

Oh when the Homer Mariners fall in line,
We're going to win this game another time,
And for the high school team we love so well,
We're going to stand right up and yell and yell and yell...
We're going to fight, fight, fight for every score.
We're going to win this game and then some more.
We're going to roll 'ole Kenai
On the floor, Out the door
Rah, rah, RA-AHH-AH!!

Pride for the basketball team filled me as I moved with the others. It was an honor to wear the cheerleader uniform: this year it was white with blue and gold "Varsity" lettering to one side of the sailor top. I had sewn the wool uniform myself. Mothers of a couple of the others made theirs. We ended with a mighty jump while throwing the blue and gold pompoms overhead. The Homer crowd applauded and yelled, "Go Homer, Go Mariners," while our most talented cheerleader surprised the crowd with a couple of forward flips. More clapping as we yelled out the names of the starting five.

Everyone in the gym stood and placed their right hand over their heart, facing the American flag, with the start of the "Star Spangled Banner". Many sang along:

Oh say can you see, by the dawn's early light,
What so proudly we hail'd at the twilight's last gleaming,
Whose broad stripes and bright stars through the perilous fight
O'er the ramparts we watch'd were so gallantly streaming...

Overcome by emotion at these patriotic expressions of loyalty to our country, I would well up with tears. Even in remote Alaska, separated by Canada from the Continental U.S.A. on one side and by the Bering Straits from Russia on the other, I was proud to be an American. The National Anthem finished, and I clapped and cheered with the others as the drum beat roared.

The crowd became silent as one player each from the opposing teams crouched, ready to tip the ball to their teammates when the referee tossed it above their heads. A Homer player caught the tip and the game was underway, backed by cacophonic cheering from the crowd.

The blue and gold Homer Mariners battled the red and white Kenai Cardinals for the ball. Up and down the court they raced. One basket made by Homer, one by Kenai. Every move guarded closely. Heads in the audience turned left and then right and back again as the teams worked the ball up and down the floor. Energetic supporters stood and cheered.

At the end of the first quarter, the players of each team went into a huddle. Their bare arms glistened with sweat as they stood with arms around one another, and eyes that looked straight into those of the man talking to them. They leaned forward and strained to hear every word of their coach. I was fascinated with their display of trust and really admired him.

We ran out with another cheer followed by the Kenai girls.

The second quarter raced by. We guarded more closely and stopped their players getting around and sinking the ball. The first half ended with Homer a few points ahead because of scoring on free throws and super guarding. I thought, well done, guys, for listening to your coach.

Homer cheerleaders took a break to the ladies' room. I brushed my shoulder length flip and said, "How about, 'Go back into the woods'?"

Patty, the daughter of well-established Homer residents, applied lipstick and responded, "That old one?"

"Yeah," I said. "It's been around since my sister was cheerleading. Everybody knows it." We ran into position on the gym floor without interrupting the players doing half time drills, and led the Homer classic and same cheer that had been a winner for me in Freshman tryouts: Go back onto the woods.

The Kenai cheerleaders responded with more of their athleticism. Even backward flips. It seems that they were in the air more than on the floor. I felt outdone.

People left and others entered during the break. Tania got up from the piano and joined me. The cafeteria window was open with refreshments for sale. There were drinks and plates of brownies, chocolate chip cookies, and large popcorn balls. I chose a popcorn ball and paid my 50 cents with appreciation for the students who had sticky fingers from mixing and shaping the popped corn and hot syrup into balls. Neither Tania or I had entered into steady relationships. We had been active with interests other than boys. Tania was an honor roll student, on the cross-country ski team, as well as a member of the Pep Band. I had achieved decent grades and made the honor roll many times and enjoyed cheerleading. Weekends Dad drove me to the homestead to visit the family if there were no basketball games. Tania and I had each other's company while the steady girls flaunted their boyfriends' rings around their necks, and did not bother to make eye contact with the likes of us when draped around their guy. I chomped the sweet kernels and gazed around. Tania chatted away, but I suddenly lost concentration.

Homer's coach, Dewayne Johnson, reemerged from the locker room with the players. I felt an immediate glow radiate through my body as he smiled at me briefly with his piercing blue eyes under a head of neatly combed dark hair. His head turned quickly away to watch the players passing the ball in organized drills.

I was still glowing from seeing him in the gym with the players when the buzzer rang for the start of the second half of the game. Tania and I hastily said goodbye and got into our places.

With another jump ball, play began. Kenai and Homer pounded up and down the floor. We guarded closely, but could not stop their players moving around and sinking the ball time and again. A long shot by a Homer player made a swish as the ball went through the net just before the end of the third quarter. We were still slightly behind, but this great shot brought the locals onto their feet screaming, "Homer. Mariners." The cheerleaders chanted, "Yay Mike."

Our opponents' third quarter momentum carried on until the end. It was victory for Kenai. Their supporters went wild yelling, "Kenai. Cardinals." The final score lit up in yellow on the electronic scoreboard. This brought noisy foot stomping on the Kenai side of the wooden bleachers.

The Homer crowd clapped despondently, heads down. It was disappointing. I glanced over at the coach and tired players as they left for the locker room. I thought, Dewayne Johnson will make it happen for Homer next time. Dewayne was 25, six feet tall, and well groomed. He had driven me home from school a few times, and we sat talking. We lingered in his car chatting about school and upcoming games. I sat by the passenger door and shook my head while talking, bobbing my shoulder length light brown hair up and down, and coyly glanced at him through heavily applied black mascara lashes. His back leaned against the driver's door with his left arm hugging the steering wheel. He told me he collected albums of the country western singers—Patsy Cline, Loretta Lynn, and Merle Haggard. Johnny Cash was his favorite. He had all Johnny's records.

The chat became more personal as we discussed our family backgrounds. His youth was spent on a farm in South Dakota. "My dad was on a farm in Wisconsin," I said. Both of us were Johnsons and both Lutherans, although I had never been inside of a Lutheran church. My dad only told me we were Lutheran. Our mothers were of German descent and mid-westerners. He had worked with his two older sisters to help their parents plough, plant, and harvest crops on their rented farm. My mom was a city girl from Chicago, but we did not dwell on that family difference, nor the fact that we owned our 160 acre homestead at Porcupine Lake, and land in Homer.

During these times together I yearned for his kiss. I dreamed our first kiss would be not overly effusive but reserved and tender. My crush on the star basketball player who was long gone to Anchorage with his pregnant girlfriend had not ended—until now. I was interested in necking, with eventually more passion—no more than that. I did not want to end up pregnant and be forced to stay in Homer before getting out into the world. I had seen that happen in "steady" relationships numerous times.

I remembered Gwen, who had been an outstanding cheerleader last year and capable of high jumps, splits, and cartwheels. She was also both studious (on the honor roll) and attractive. A new routine required three of us to stand behind the three in front and lift the girl's middle as she jumped, touching hands to feet—the eagle spread. As I grasped Gwen's waist, the stays of a tight corset were rigid underneath her light cotton uniform. I was shocked at my suspicion, but knew that she was going steady with tall, good-looking Cliff. Poor girl. Gwen carried on smiling and yelling through the duration of the game.

The following Monday Tania and I were alone in the girls' restroom touching up hair and makeup. In a hushed voice I told her what I had learned about Gwen at the Saturday night basketball game. Tania looked amazed, and we both shook our heads in despair. "Not Gwen," Tania said. Naïve me said, "Maybe there is another way to get pregnant." Shrugging her shoulders, Tania said, "Yes, maybe so because—well—I just can't believe Gwen..." A few weeks later, Gwen left for Anchorage with her mother. She was not seen at school again.

I also knew Dewayne had plans. He was hell-bent to make Homer a winning team before leaving for the Continental US in a couple of years to teach, coach, and then work on a PhD in Physical Education. When he told me, I thought, seven years in age between us was not that much. I knew that I wanted to leave Alaska and go to university in the Continental US. Dewayne could be my exit card.

That night after the game, all of us cheerleaders went upstairs to the Home Economics room to change clothes. Gail had sewn a snappy dress for me out of black imitation alligator material. I was eager to show it off to Dewayne and, hopefully, catch a glimpse of approval in his eyes. Perhaps this carefully selected outfit over silver mesh tights would spur a bit of passion between us when he drove me home. We drove around before heading up the East Hill to Gail's. My hands became clammy. I waited with anticipation as he parked his second-hand Ford. It seemed like eternity for him to slide over and grab me into his arms. Heads together, our hungry mouths met, opened and we made up for lost time with that first kiss.

I was thrilled with Dewayne's interest in me and hoped for lasting affection. To be with someone intent on having a future beyond Homer and Alaska was wonderful. However, I was aware that a student dating a teacher was unusual. I was now more popular in the school, but carried a subdued element among animated curious smiles, and I avoided patter about Dewayne and me except with Tania.

But, it was not long before the principal called us into his office. I knew what it would be about and worried that this would be the end of us. I was stressed as I took my seat beside Dewayne. Mr. Ronda, with his glasses perched at the end of his nose, got directly to the reason we were there. "I guess you know people have seen you in Dewayne's car, Judy." There was a moment's silence. I was not sure whether to come clean or not. "Nothing derogatory has been said." Mr. Ronda continued, "And as far as I am concerned, what the two of you do outside school is your business." His words brought instant relief. I thought, Yippee! As I left with Dewayne, he smiled but walked away into the teachers' lounge. I sobered because what I already knew about our romantic relationship had just been reinforced. There was to be no display of any physical affection at school. I also knew that many times after dropping me home, he joined other teachers for a late night drink. He did not take me out to dinner, but we went to films; and I stayed in town rather than visiting family on the weekend when there were basketball games.

One night after a basketball game, when we were parking and just beginning to make out, Dewayne said, "Judy, there is something I need to tell you."

"What's that?" I asked.

He put his hands to his face to wipe away tears, and said, "I've been married."

"Married?" I said.

"Yes, I didn't love her and it didn't last long. But, I am divorced. No children," he said.

"Well, ok then," I said. I felt a bit let down, but did not want to break off the relationship with Dewayne.

When I did go to the homestead, I informed my parents I was dating the coach. I held my breath for their reply. Mom shook her head and chuckled and said, "Judy, your dad and I are in favor of you having a boyfriend. He isn't *your* teacher."

Yes, I had my man, but life had brought me anything but a typical "steady."

Pop Corn Balls

Ingredients:

½ cup popcorn kernels   2 cups white, granulated sugar

1½ cups water   ½ cup light corn syrup

1 teaspoon vinegar   1½ teaspoon vanilla

Dash salt

Procedure:

Pop kernels in popcorn popper. Pour into a large bowl. Set aside.

In a large saucepan, with candy thermometer attached, boil sugar, water, and corn syrup over medium heat. Stir occasionally with a wooden spoon.

Continue, heating syrup at simmering, until it reaches 260F.

Add vinegar, vanilla, and salt. Stir and pour over popcorn. With the wooden spoon stir to coat all kernels. Cool briefly.

Coat your hands with butter, margarine or oil, and shape the popcorn into the size of balls desired.

Place on a tray lined with parchment paper.

Judy in high button shoes costume as Eliza in "My Fair Lady".

Miss Homer Pageant, 1966: Coming of Age

I woke to a freezing cold 13th of February and then remembered it was my 18th birthday and leaped out of bed. I was one of six contestants competing for the crown of Miss Homer that night.

Town folks gathered to sit on wooden bleachers and folding chairs in the High School gymnasium for the pageant. All 300 seats were taken. Even my parents with Brent and Jerry were in the audience in spite of Mom moving us to the homestead to leave the small town mentality of Homer which was so alien to her Chicago upbringing. She and Dad had been against me entering the contest as Gail had years before and had "felt degraded" selling enough Homer Winter Carnival tickets to run for queen. Lights went out except for bright blinding ones projected onto the stage. Dim desk lamps lit up a nearby table. There sat six Miss America qualified judges, made up of both men and women from Anchorage, pencils raised.

As I changed into my black one-piece swimsuit for parading the catwalk, thoughts buzzed in my head of the preparation for this night over the past six weeks. We had all dieted, had hair styled, enjoyed make-ups, selected and practiced a talent, and had chosen a white ball gown designed to accentuate our best assets. On day one we were critiqued by our older, red-headed leader, Mrs. Doris Shultz, and her assistant. Mrs. Shultz had been in Homer for years and a leading organizer. I had more "corrections" suggested than any of the others. These included being slightly overweight, bad posture, the wrong hair style, and applying incorrect make-up. Even now these corrections trigger a lack of confidence. Back then, I faced these bravely, determined to overcome each defect, or at least show improvement.

Slim, bouncy cheerleader, Suzie, had the least alterations. She was a very pretty girl with a mother active and popular in Homer. My mom was sixty miles away on remote Porcupine Lake. Mrs.

Shultz and her assistant could not help themselves. Suzie was their favorite and all of us contestants were acutely aware of it.

Each of us had been responsible for ticket sales to raise money for the Homer Winter Carnival which held the beauty pageant. Luckily, my sponsor, Pacific Northern Airlines, took over that grueling headache from me after I did just one exhausting swing around town, knocking on doors up and down Pioneer Avenue. Ace Gribble, the kind manager of the Homer branch, with a son on the basketball team and a daughter on the cheerleading squad, said, "Judy, you spend your time practicing your singing number for the talent show. We'll sell plenty of tickets." What a relief.

Once into the swimsuit, we all zipped up real fur parkas for the first parade down the catwalk. There was a holdup getting onto the stage, and I became overheated and stressed with the delay. I just wanted to get it over. Then the command was given and we strode out, paced as directed by Mrs. Schultz. Giving a big smile, my lips quivered; I hoped that the bright red lipstick painted on generously would not smear onto my teeth. Back in the girls' locker room, which served as our changing room, I was happy to unzip the heavy parka and hand it to Mrs. Schultz's assistant. "Good going, girls." Mrs. Schultz beamed. "Now it is time to step out for the swimsuit competition."

I was ready, but then hesitated as I saw my reflection in the wall to wall mirrors. My figure was not as splendid as petite Suzie's, but it was presentable. What mortified me was that while overheated in the parka, red blotches had developed on my bare chest above the cut of the bathing suit. What could I do? Nothing, and they were nearly as bright as my Revlon lipstick. With a quick glance at the others, I saw no one with a similar affliction. Several were looking at me with raised eyebrows. As our eyes met, they looked away. With trepidation I followed a few strides behind another competitor entering the stage. I put on a big smile again, and was thankful that I could not see a soul in the pitch black darkness of the audience. Mom, Dad, Jerry, Brent, Gail, and her husband Jack would probably be showing concern and sympathy at my plight. Thank God Dewayne was away at an out-of-town basketball weekend.

The judges were busy with their pencils as we strutted our stuff. I walked with misgiving, knowing that the red blotches were evident. I was happy to exit the stage and get back in the changing room. One of the other contestants cattily said, "Don't worry about the blotches. No one saw them." Fat chance, I thought. Bitch. Oh well, KEEP GOING.

Next was the talent competition. For weeks I had practiced my dramatic interpretation of "Just You Wait" from *My Fair Lady*. The music had captivated me with Julie Andrews' singing. On the run-up to the pageant, I lucked out with help from Sister Ruth of the Barefoot Gang. This communal group from California made Homer its base a few years earlier. They were people with various talents and opened a machine shop on Pioneer Avenue where they welded and also lived off donations made by people who joined them. They seemed like older hippies to me. We were uncertain as to their claim to religion, but felt sorry for them walking around in bare feet on frozen ground. Sister Ruth must have been of lesser faith as she wore boots when we met to practice.

Friends and family had helped me assemble a black outfit similar to the one worn by Audrey Hepburn in the film. I even had button-up black leather boots with heels from June Uminski, Tania's mother. The outfit was complete with a straw hat Gail found.

Sister Ruth played the piano softly, wanting me to have full stage with my voice. I belted it out while moving my hands in meaningful coordination to the lyrics. I looked angry at times as was needed to express Eliza's feelings for Professor Higgins. I got ahead of Sister Ruth's soft, background playing, but we quickly rectified the situation. When I finished, there was a lot of clapping. I was happy for the hearty response, but worried it might just be out of sympathy. All must have seen and heard the bit where I had jumped ahead. I ran off the stage feeling that I had blown it.

Suzie's talent was looking great in a smart, short length dress as she mimed the very popular, "Ebb Tide". The recorded music was lovely, and she looked fabulous as she mouthed the words in sync. The audience clapped enthusiastically when she finished. Her mother had a large contingent around her. The other contestants performed, and then we moved on to the ball gown competition.

Wearing the sweetheart, beaded, long taffeta gown made me feel elegant. The red blotches had disappeared. We all stepped and turned, and the judges made their notations and nodded us off in single file from the stage.

Last were the questions. The judges compiled these from questionnaires we had completed and returned. When called, each contestant stepped up to the microphone beside the dark curly headed man acting as Master of Ceremonies. I came about midway in the group. Having only performed memorized pieces for church programs, cheers for high school basketball games, and once in a while, readings before an English or History class, I was tense. My hands were clammy in my opera-length pearl button gloves.

The MC, in a white sports jacket, read out to me, "Judy, why have you chosen home economics teaching as your desired profession?"

Smiling, I quickly replied, "Because I enjoy sewing my own clothes, creating beautiful, tasty meals, and working with children."

"Thank you, Judy." There was a lot of clapping from the audience as I moved back into the line of contestants. I felt relief that it was over, and I had not stumbled or rambled with my answer. I was disappointed about my loss of rhythm with Sister Ruth in the talent section. All consideration by the judges must now be with Suzie. She was right to play it safe with her routine of miming words to a popular song. Then there were my blatant red blotches in the swimsuit competition. Ugh. Strangely, I had enjoyed the contest. Yes, I felt sorry for myself, but good luck to Suzie. She had not made any blunders.

The Master of Ceremonies picked up the sealed envelope from one of the judges stepping up to the stage with an outstretched hand. All was quiet as he walked back to the microphone. He removed the message slowly, with care, then read loudly, "First Runner-up is Miss Suzan Hurley. The winner...Miss Homer, 1966...Miss Judy Johnson." The gymnasium erupted with clapping. The MC broke in with the famous, pageant song: "Here she is, Miss America, here she is, your ideal..."

I felt bewildered, attempting a smile as the long red velvet cape with ermine trim was draped around my shoulders. Was it a mistake? Me? Miss Homer, 1965, tried to secure the sparkling light rhinestone crown on my head, but it slipped, lopsided, messing up my coiffured hair.

One of the contestants said, "Judy, aren't you going to cry?" I thought maybe I should. Was it expected? I did not want to break the spell. I felt elated—too happy for tears. The night had turned magical.

The MC read off my gifts as queen: A $300 university scholarship; a $500 wardrobe; a $500 mouton fur parka, trimmed with seal and wolverine made by Mrs. Bea Watson (Gail's mother-in-law); an ivory bracelet; and gifts from every store in town. Most importantly, in two weeks I would represent Homer in the Miss Alaska pageant during the Fur Rendezvous in Anchorage which was a winter carnival much grander than Homer's. The 938-mile Sled Dog Race—from Anchorage to Nome—was part of it, and still continues to this day, drawing people from all over the world. Wow. I would be flown to Anchorage by my sponsor, Pacific Northern Airlines.

As people filed out of the gym, many came up to congratulate me. Gail made her way through the crowd, and gave me a big hug. "Good going, little sister."

I stepped down from the stage and waited briefly to look around and take in what had unexpectedly happened. Mrs. Shultz came up. "Judy, you are a first in that every judge gave the talent vote to you." I thought, gosh, I guess taking a risk and belting out something is better than playing it safe. Suzie was all smiles as she congratulated me before leaving. Having been relieved Dewayne was away, I now sorely missed his presence. He would have to hear about it all second hand and wait for photographs to be developed. With or without him, I felt that I had come of age.

From Porcupine Lake to the Miss Alaska

Pageant

The flight from Homer to Anchorage made me feel like a celebrity. I felt that I was stepping up to a bigger stage.

The first person I met was Miss Kodiak. Elana was the chatty one who seemed determined to become acquainted. She would go on to win Miss Congeniality. Kodiak Island lay between the forlorn Aleutian Chain and us on the Kenai Peninsula. Winds were known to sweep across, and although I had never been there, knew that it was a hearty Alaskan king crab and salmon fishing community. I thought supportive Elana had the grit to stand up to nature's worst gales. She and I were two of nineteen Miss Alaska contestants from around the state who had ploughed through the first rehearsals.

"I love the way you just belt out your song, Judy."

"Thanks, Elana, but actually I'm uncomfortable with the pianist. I so wish I could have mine from Homer. I've practiced and practiced with Sister Ruth," I replied with slumped shoulders and knots in my stomach. "I'm worried about performing in front of everyone when I can't even hear the piano."

"Then ask for her. Why not? My hostess would."

My own hostess/chaperone had been hovering and sprung over. "What did I hear, Judy? You aren't comfortable with the pianist? Come and we'll talk to Mrs. Linton...I see her with lovely Miss America." I looked over and saw our celebrity looking slim and confident in a rose boucle suit and striking in appearance. She had won the crown in 1948, the year I was born, and had managed to keep her good looks.

With a forthright face and determined eyes behind nondescript glasses, my grey-haired hostess approached her leader. "Say, Mrs.

Linton, Judy…" and before I could do more than nod in agreement, my hostess had me on the phone with my Homer sponsor—Pacific Northern Airlines.

Ace Gribble's familiar voice asked, "Judy, how are you? What? You need Sister Ruth…OF COURSE, I'll fly her to Anchorage. She will be delighted. Hey, Gal, don't get ahead of her this time. We're all pulling for you. Good luck."

Preliminary night I was hopeful, standing in front of the packed house with Sister Ruth seated erect at the piano, observing me carefully from under her loose grey bun. She had traveled in the old boots worn at our Homer practice sessions, but now had slipped into flat evening black slippers. There was no evidence of her being from the California Barefooters. She smiled, lifted her head, and I started on cue; but then looked away from her reassuring presence squarely at the hundreds of faces staring back at me, and felt my entire body go numb.

All those who had watched the morning parade with me in fur parka perched on the hood of an Oldsmobile Toronado striking the pose of a harbor seal resting on a black iceberg, now filled West High Auditorium. Heat from the bright lights baked my flesh under the black tatty jacket and ankle length skirt. Perspiration rose on my back, neck, and brow. Did the straw hat conceal the strands of hair becoming damp around my made-up face? Oh, please someone open a door and let in a winter blast. I refilled my lungs, and with greater determination proceeded with the dramatic interpretation of Liza Doolittle's "Just You Wait".

The stage lights burned hotter, and the faces in the audience appeared as if they sensed my discomfort. Perhaps instead of hundreds there were thousands out there—all embarrassed on my behalf. This experience required skills that I had not learned in all my talent practicing in Homer, or on Porcupine Lake. I leaped on and thought *keep going*. I blotted out the audience and the sound of the piano in the process. I rushed with determination, out of control, galloping ahead of Sister Ruth, AGAIN. Oh dear, I've let them all down, I thought as I made my exit back stage. No chance of making it into the top ten final tomorrow night.

I realized how lucky I was to have actually met Miss America

1948. It made me feel a part of the Miss America pageants, and my roots in Porcupine Lake suddenly felt very small. Mom, Dad, Gail, Jerry, Brent, Tania, and Ace Gribble had all been so hopeful that I would make it to this year's pageant in Atlantic City. Had Dewayne made it up from Homer? I would not know until I returned to Homer, and I worried that he had seen me jump ahead of the music.

My hostess looked at me frankly as we pulled on our coats. "Honey, you were great. One of the judges told me after your interview, 'That girl is going places'." Being only eighteen, I thought 'how nice,' but I knew I had been out of my depth on the stage.

The girl who won Miss Alaska that year was twenty-two years old, and it was her second time to run. She had the advantage of more experience, and had developed her singing talent to a much higher professional level than mine.

A couple of months after the Miss Alaska pageant, Dewayne drove us to Anchorage to see the film, *My Fair Lady*, on its opening night. We attended the champagne reception with the middle-aged couple who had been my pageant hosts/chaperones. I loved the film, and took special interest in the singing of "Just You Wait" and Audrey Hepburn acting the part of Eliza Doolittle. We all knew that the voice was another's as Audrey Hepburn was a great actor, but needed the singing voice dubbed. I had tried to copy Julie Andrews' voice from her record when I did my dramatic interpretation in both the Miss Homer and Miss Alaska pageants, listening to the record repeatedly.

The couple welcomed us with home-cooked meals and a tour of the man's executive office at the Gas Company. Having no children, they seemed pleased that I had come back to visit them with my boyfriend, and did not voice any concern about me dating a high school coach. On our drive back to Homer, I said, "Dewayne, thanks for taking me to my hosts."

"No problem, Judy. It was cheap. All I had to do was fill my car up with gasoline." I thought, if it was that cheap, maybe he could have at least brought them flowers.

Dewayne

Dewayne came down with mumps in April. Les, the junior high school teacher with whom Dewayne shared a house, told me at school. "When can I see him?" I asked.

"Tomorrow," Les replied. "I'll tell him." So, the next afternoon I walked to his small rented house a half mile from the high school. It was the first time that I had been there. As I approached the door, I felt every bit Dewayne's younger girlfriend by eight years. He was a grown man living independently from his family. I was living with my sister, Gail, and dependent on my family. Summer fishing income provided me with spending money and savings for university. My school days were carefree by comparison to the daily requirements of Dewayne's teaching and coaching duties. Tearfully, he had told me in the winter that he was divorced. I was surprised by the news, but he said that he had not loved the girl. Still this meant that he was much more experienced than me. Neither one of us shared his previous marriage with anyone, and I felt my parents would be upset by the news.

Dewayne knew that I was coming, but did not come to the door. He called out, "Come in." I opened the door which lead into a sparsely furnished living/dining/kitchen. There was no woman's touch. Seated at the table by a window looking out onto the calm waters of Kachemak Bay, he was unresponsive as he shuffled a deck of cards. What a disappointment. I knew he did not want to give me mumps, but he surely was not the man who mostly, on dates, wanted the closeness of making out in his car. We were sitting apart—me on the sofa—and I found myself lacking for conversation. I wanted a boyfriend, and he filled the role, but that day there was nothing to be bubbly about. He looked sick, unshaven, and with very swollen glands in his throat. A Johnny Cash record was playing in the background—*Folsom Prison.*

Dewayne looked up from his cards, "There is a danger of becoming infertile when a man has the mumps." This was an unexpected statement. But I did not bring up that I had been faced with the same potential challenge.

I felt flushed and wondered, "why is he saying this?" I was not ready to talk about having children even though I knew I wanted children after marriage. Gail already had two and Mom and Dad had produced five. His comment was premature and embarrassing, and I brushed it aside. We struggled through another half an hour making uncomfortable conversation. As I left his house and walked to the main road and on to Gail's, I was concerned about the possibility of the mumps making Dewayne sterile, but I was also feeling unhappy and unfulfilled. I had hoped for so much more from the visit. Looking back, this was a turning point in the relationship. It would never fulfil its early promise.

Miss Homer 1966

Fishing, Poetry, and Sewing

In May, 1966, I graduated and was proud of Tania being valedictorian. She gave a good speech, and we and the other twenty seniors embarked on the world. Tania worked in the store and prepared for university in Washington State. That summer I fished commercially again with Mom, Jerry, and Brent on the Clam Gulch beach for the last time. It meant long hours on fishing days, but the work had become an established routine over five summers: getting up at 4:30 a.m., rowing the boat across the lake, walking to the bluff, climbing down the other side; and then fishing patiently for hours before returning home.

The routine of fishing was interrupted by the fun of taking part in Alaska pageants. One pageant was in Nome, still a small native village, in 1966, in the far north close to the Arctic Circle. During the Alaskan Gold Rush, it had become a boom town of 20,000 people from around the globe. As I walked the streets with Jean Foter, Miss Nome, a dark haired slim girl, I was amazed to hear how animals such as polar bears meandered around houses and businesses in winter. "The first automobiles in Alaska," Jean told me, "ran on these streets; and the first telegraph in the United States to transmit over long distances began operating in Nome."

Seward, where I had my appendix out, was a lovely town to return to for their pageant. It was in places like this that I would encounter pageant queens from all over the state which I know now contributed to my sense of Alaskan identity. With Dewayne, identity meant the possibility of going further afield, but Mom and Dad did not say much about him. I sensed they regarded him as cold as he did not have much chit chat for them. They were practical people, and I knew that their long term expectation for me was to marry and become a housewife and mother, although Mom kept encouraging college. "Teaching is a great career for a woman," she insisted. I agreed. "Yes, and maybe I could major in music…" I had always loved singing in church and recently in the Miss Homer and Miss Alaska pageants.

"No, no. You should go into home economics. That is the best choice for you." I thought about her suggestion and felt immediate disappointment because I was determined to become a more accomplished singer. She usually supported my goals so I was also surprised. After thinking about it for a couple of days, I knew that a major in home economics made sense as I was confident sewing, cooking, and with childcare. Since I had not had a piano to practice, my voice was not developed enough to give me equal confidence compared to my household skills. "You are right," I said, still feeling sad with the practical decision. I was determined to investigate voice lessons at university, but did not share this with Mom.

Dewayne drove his trusty white Ford station wagon to visit on days that we were not fishing. He got us reading to each other in the crowded cabin sitting side by side on the sofa. His selected love poems by Elizabeth Barrett Browning brought us together intimately in a way I had never shared with anyone. What a welcome change from necking with the guy while the steering wheel pried into my back and the gearshift wedged into one leg with no place for the other leg.

Dewayne sparked joy in me with:

How do I love thee? Let me count the ways. I love thee to the depth and breadth and height my soul can reach, when feeling out of sight…

These romantic visits seemed to bring grunts and groans from Dad as he darted in and out between projects. There was so much for him to do while home on the 160 acres. His land surveying business required long absences. Mom's lot was to pick up the slack with reluctant help from my brothers and me.

Once when Dewayne was visiting, Dad worked alongside the cabin under the Land Rover hood trying to start the engine. It was a dry, cool day with the usual number of mosquitoes buzzing around. Dewayne sat next to me on the sofa reading aloud and sipping steaming coffee from a thick mug. The clatter of wrenches thrown into the metal toolbox outside grew in frequency as the morning progressed. "Oh, no," Dad yelled, gasped, and grunted. Dewayne kept reading in spite of what was clear to me: Dad was frustrated and angry—no luck with rectifying the motor problem. I could picture him with black grease smeared on his face gazing down at a hopeless situation. Suddenly the door flew open, and Dad stomped in. "Grab your coat, checkbook, and tax statement, Ruth. Payment deadline is 5 p.m. We must go. NOW." Mom looked over at us relaxing on the sofa and left her lunch preparation and said, "Judy, you will have to finish this." She poured her cup of tea into the sink as she shook her head.

I stood up feeling the urgency of my parents to get to town. Dewayne remained seated and took another sip of coffee. He mumbled, "Oh…ok.. See you." My parents barely looked at us as they said goodbye. I stepped over to the window and saw them walk past Dewayne's car and hurry up the homestead road. Slowly I sat back down. He began to read again from Sonnet 43:

I love thee to the level of every day's most quiet need,
  by sun and candlelight,
I love thee freely, as men strive for Right;

Elizabeth Barrett Browning's words of love were lost somewhere between the page and his lips. I felt concern for my parents. I could visualize them hitching a ride to Soldotna—twenty miles away. Why had Dewayne not offered to drive them? My stomach tightened into knots. I said nothing about it over lunch, but left food on my plate. I felt insulted by Dewayne's lack of helpfulness. How could he have continued reading poetry while my parents were under such stress? I knew that if they did not get a ride quickly into town by hitchhiking, they would miss the 5 p.m. deadline. That would result in a hefty fine which we could ill afford. Dewayne continued with Elizabeth Barrett Browning, but my enthusiasm had waned.

Hours later, Mom and Dad returned. They appeared exhausted after the rushed trip and the unusual need to hitchhike. Mom slowly removed her head scarf and jacket, but Dad threw down his coat and turned to Dewayne. In a firm voice he said, "You can leave now."

Dewayne did not argue, and rose from the sofa to put on his coaching jacket. He may have mumbled goodbye to my parents.

Walking with Dewayne to his car, I felt embarrassed and sad. He whispered, "Bye, Judy J" and kissed me before driving off, but I did not connect with any passion in his parting embrace. I mumbled "goodbye" and walked away. Browning's poetry rang sour—even Sonnet 43. Neither he nor I spoke of the day again. My parents said nothing about it to me, but the memory lodged in the back of my mind. The disappointment replayed over and over as I fulfilled necessary tasks of cooking and cleaning. In my heart I knew my dad was right, and wondered if the unpleasant episode was an omen.

I felt gloomy after Dewayne was asked to leave by Dad. Dewayne was my steady, and I planned to keep him as such. Over the next few days, in my spare time I buried myself in sewing for university. Wool trousers would be a must as it was well below zero in Fairbank, Alaska, during the winter.

I cut out the first pair of trousers and was buzzing up the long leg seams on the Singer when Dad turned to me and said, "Judy, the way you are roaring along I think we will have to put a muffler on the sewing machine." I could not help but smile at his comment even though I had not spoken to him much since Dewayne had left.

Mom laughed and said, "Judy is quite the seamstress now." With my sewing and cooking capabilities, I felt confident majoring in home economics at university. This helped lighten my spirits, but I knew neither the question of my singing nor the question of my steady had been resolved.

A Cardboard Box, a Metal Trunk, & Fitting In

"It's not fair," I shouted and banged on the kitchen table. "You gave Gail a three-piece luggage set when she went to college, and I have to buy my own. I remember Gail went on and on about the color—all white with light blue interior."

"We just don't have a dime to spare, Judy," Mom replied with downcast eyes and a slow shake of her head as she and I cleared the breakfast dishes. "But your dad has a letter from Ollie and Naomi saying that they'll purchase a metal trunk and ship it from Chicago in plenty of time. You'll be fine on the train from Anchorage."

"I bet you that I'm the only one going with a metal trunk. I just can't believe…I'm doing it all. Without the Miss Homer scholarship, dorm scholarship, salmon fishing money, and my plan to work in the cafeteria, I wouldn't be going. All my doing. Well, I don't want you and Dad to take me to the train either. I'll ask Dewayne to drive me to Anchorage."

"If that's what you want," Mom said with a frown and then looked away cupping her chin in her hand and shaking her head again. She said no more, but I knew that Dewayne's last visit was in her thoughts as it was in mine. He had not given my parents a lift when needed, yet I preferred him taking me to catch the train. I also knew that it was Mom who had instigated our commercial salmon fishing and kept it going for the past five years; but in my upset state, I was not able to voice any appreciation. The atmosphere in the cabin had turned somber with my outburst and was only slightly improved by the hearty aroma of the Swedish rye loaves Mom removed from the oven. As I tore into a slice, Dad came in.

"Judy is upset that we're not helping her more for university, and she has a right to be. Never enough God damned money," Mom said.

"Sorry, Judy, but you've done brilliantly on your own. I'll buy your return train ticket so that you can come home for Christmas. We'll look forward to hearing all about your first semester."

"Ok," was all I managed feeling unimportant. I was close to tears, and the warmth of the Swedish rye in my hands was comforting, but only slightly alleviated my distress.

My parents were polite to Dewayne when he drove into the homestead to take me to Anchorage. I wondered how things would change both on the homestead and in my new life while I was away.

Snuggled beside Dewayne on the five-hour car journey was pleasant, and I put disappointment and embarrassment of the metal trunk out of my mind. I studied his profile and reached to touch his clean-shaven face. We passed through the small towns of Soldotna, Sterling, Cooper's Landing; through forests made up of green spruce and autumn-yellowed birch trees; and along the rushing glacial water of the Kenai and Russian Rivers. An hour from Anchorage the expanse of blue ocean around Turnagain Arm and the sheer rock cliffs with circular-horned Dall sheep grazing, took my eyes off the road. The scenic drive and me sitting close to Dewayne had made me light-headed. Then we entered the city. Thoughts of missing him sobered me. A long-distance relationship would mean loneliness. No waiting for him to appear. There would be no need for much sewing in order to dress up. No driving around in his trusty white Ford, attending films together, or celebrating basketball wins. But, thinking of being a student at the university was exciting. I would make new friends and learn how to teach Home Economics. Back and forth my mood swung.

Dewayne said, "I'm proud that you've enrolled, Judy J, but I'll miss you." I chuckled and said, "You'll be busy coaching the team to win the State Basketball Championship." We promised each other a letter at least once a week and passionately said goodbye at the Anchorage station. He swiftly slid my metal trunk onto the luggage rack and was gone.

It was my first train journey and a long overnight trip on the Alaskan Railroad to Fairbanks. We passed through thick forests and across swamps, but slowed down nearing Mt. McKinley to traverse Hurricane Gulch. I gasped looking from the carriage window with the faint view of a stream about a mile below. The train crept along on the tracks without barrier railings. It felt as if we were in mid-air like the bald eagles hovering on the updraft above the bluff at our fishing site in Clam Gulch. I loved watching them, but this swaying along in the train over Hurricane Gulch gave me the sensation of riding one of those eagles and being about to topple off. The driver braked and the resultant scraping of the iron wheels on the track echoed in my ears. Suffering dizziness and vertigo, I was frightened; but after a few prolonged minutes, we reached the other side and regained speed.

We reached Fairbanks in early morning, and I climbed down from my carriage and into a taxi with a few other students. The drive took only minutes and then I was out dragging my trunk along a campus walkway. The sight before me was of students dashing around on well-groomed paths between buildings as dozens sailed through the Student Union doors. It reminded me of the worker bees darting around wild geraniums and bluebells on a homestead field, and then to one of Mom's strategically placed hives off to the side. The Student Union was in the middle of the buzz, and there I found directions to the Housing Department, and observed plastered notices for upcoming Freshmen events. One in bright pink letters was of a sock hop starting at 8 p.m. Come, Get Acquainted. Hmmm, fun I thought.

Passing my letter for dorm scholarship to the housing receptionist, I was pleased to learn that I would be in the new high-rise at the top of the hill over-looking the campus. It was co-educational although men and women were separated by floors. My shared room was on the fourth floor with a soft spoken Athabaskan from a small village. The only native village I had been in was Nome with its meandering streets around shack houses, but she assimilated so badly into university life I later felt her native village must have been much smaller than Nome. She struggled to socialize and was never at ease. A window divided—our sides—each with built-in bunk, desk, and mirrored wardrobe. As I unpacked, Dorothy told me that she was a Psychology major and that she was already homesick. She was meeting a friend from home for dinner.

Class registration meant lining up to enrol in each subject and to pay the necessary tuition which took the afternoon. As a freshman, I had the requirements of Inorganic Chemistry, English, Psychology, P.E., plus classes in Home Economics and an elective. Standing to wait my turn gave me a chance to meet other students and arrange for dining with a few, and afterwards moving onto the dance. It was a relief to get acquainted quickly. A guy from Seward whom I knew from basketball games joined us at the Student Union.

"How is Coach Johnson, Judy?"

"Fine. Already coaching cross-country," I said, and knew that my long-distance relationship with Dewayne would soon be known among those whom the Seward students hung out with. I did not plan to keep it a secret anyway.

Almost immediately I went to work in the one large cafeteria for two hours each morning making salads to pay for my meals. Between 5:30 and 7:30 a.m. the industrial kitchen had the sounds of me setting plates onto plastic trays on metal racks, opening and closing fridges, and hearing the laughter and chatter of the four cooks preparing scrambled eggs, bacon, and hot cakes.

My favorite Home Economics course was Clothing Construction under Miss Clark, an old grey-haired woman who had been teaching for decades. It was a relief from the dry Chemistry study of balancing formulas; the English 101 class, where I struggled to write the weekly essay; and the Psychology textbook with page after page on how personal toilet training affected one's later life.

The longed-for voice lessons began, and my voice became more controlled; and I was able to hit the high notes at a performance and witness broad smiles from my teacher and the head of the Music Department. My individual weekly lesson was with an accomplished pretty brunette, thirty years old, who had performed at the Starlight Theatre in Kansas City. I adored her because she was kind and confident teaching me to sing as a more mature soprano.

Sewing a shirtwaist dress and a two-piece green, navy, and white plaid wool suit from patterns I made myself was a new satisfying experience. The last day of class, Miss Clark stopped by each of us sitting at an assigned Singer to look at our completed garments.

Picking up my shirtwaist dress and suit, she studied the seams. "Nice work, Judy. Professional." I looked forward to modeling my garments in the fashion show as part of my final grade. She stepped away to look at the work of the others girls in our sewing lab. Most received her compliments, and only a few were instructed to make minor changes.

Disaster struck when Miss Clark stopped across from me to look at my friend, Terry Vance's work. Terry and I had become well acquainted as we were both Home Economics majors and lived on the same floor in the dorm.

Terry had attended a college in Colorado the previous year, but her parents stopped sending her out of state for financial reasons. Her boyfriend was a student in Colorado. Both Terry and I had long-distance relationships so our talk was often about getting that letter—or not—and sharing bits when letters came.

"My word, Terry, LOOK at your suit jacket. What have you done? Oh dear me, the sleeves...they're in backwards. You must put them right. Work quickly to be ready for tomorrow. The fashion show is a requirement." Miss Clark exited the room, but I knew she would return from her office just down the hall at any time as was her usual routine.

Poor Terry gasped and said, "Oh shit." She came over to me with the faulty jacket and whispered, "Judy, please help me. God, I can't bear redoing the sleeves. Will you, Judy? Please? I'll watch the door for her. I never want to sew anything again. I hate it." She hunched over her shoulders and covered her face with her hands. Would tears be next?

"Give me the jacket, Terry. I'll start. Keep watching, though, or we're both in trouble."

With the slim metal ripper, I removed the wool sleeves and turned them the right way round. Not wanting to take time for basting stitches, I pinned quickly, easing in the fullness around the shoulder so that each sleeve fit. Just as I started to sew, Miss Clark re-entered the lab. I gulped, stopped the machine, and tossed the jacket to Terry, who made believe that she was pinning. Miss Clark was called to the other end of the room and became engrossed in discussion. I grabbed the jacket back. Speeding along with one shoulder seam under the foot of the Singer, I almost completed it; and then Miss Clark turned her head as if she would walk back our way. With heart pounding, I quit sewing. Terry and I froze, waiting for Miss Clark's next move. I saw the girl ask her another question, so I commenced sewing the other sleeve, speeding as on the homestead when Dad would shake his head and proclaim that a muffler was needed to quiet things down. With a snip of the scissors, I cut the threads. The sleeves were in. I passed the jacket back over to Terry with split-second timing just as Miss Clark turned around. She walked over, looked at Terry, and picked up the garment. Studying it closely, she said, "Hmmm, sleeves in right. Needs a good press, but nice work, Terry. I knew that you could do it."

We walked back to our dormitory together. Terry said, "Thanks, Judy. You saved me. Miss Clarke…ha, ha, old goat. I'll never wear the jacket after the fashion show. Hate it; hate sewing."

"No problem. But, after awhile you may. The rose plaid is nice with your complexion. I like it. Oh well, wonder if we'll have letters, Terry?"

I waited eagerly each week for Dewayne's which often included a poem he had written. The poems and letters I saved in a pillow case inside the black metal trunk stored under my bunk. That trunk proved to be good for something. I shared much of his news with Terry as she did with her letters all the way from Colorado. I never read her any of Dewayne's poems because I felt that they were too personal, plus reading them sometimes made me feel confused. One I read and quickly folded back up and put away, as its words did not seem to be for me. As I shut the trunk, the gist of the poem made me uncomfortable. It had been about a girl, five foot two, with eyes of blue, 110 pounds, and long blond hair. Actually, I was five-four and my eyes were often more green than blue. My weight was never as low as 110 with all the doughnuts I was downing during my two-hour stint in the cafeteria, and my hair actually was light brown. Dad sang a song about Judy with the light brown hair that I loved. He adapted the real words of the song for me. Was Dewayne writing about me or some dream girl? I never read the poem again.

Terry and I comforted each other on the days when letters did not arrive. I wrote Dewayne regularly about my friends and classes and how in the heated Olympic size pool, I was learning the various swimming strokes that I had never managed in the cold waters of Porcupine Lake. Often my written words to him were about Marriage and Family Life class. All of us enrolled thought we were acquiring the knowledge to make a successful long-term relationship. In the 1960s that meant marriage. The teacher and textbook stressed that communication was the key. A couple must discuss problems before climbing into bed. It sounded easy. I would read a chapter, close the book, and dream about Dewayne. We would be companions sharing responsibilities in our own home. He would dry dishes as I tidied up the kitchen. In my dreams, domestic chores would be interrupted by kisses. Terry and I compared thoughts and expectations.

"Judy, you are so lucky. You are almost engaged," she said.

Her long-distance relationship had fallen apart when her boyfriend found another girl in Colorado. She and the other girls I knew in the dorm were more and more interested in my long-distance relationship, and asked me about Dewayne when we met in the communal bathroom to brush our teeth. Often the questions were, "Will you marry him soon, Judy?" I loved their interest and thought more and more about the fun and excitement of planning a summer wedding. After a grand honeymoon, we would start living the married life I had conjured up in Marriage and Family Life class. Marrying Dewayne would mean enjoying his close companionship as I looked after him and he after me.

My first roommate, Dorothy, did not integrate well into university life. After only a few weeks, she brought a gigantic cardboard box into our room and stayed in it for hours, even sleeping in it. I realized that this was not normal university behavior, but I did not know what to say to her. My reaction was to continue our polite "hello" and "goodbye" on entering and leaving the room. I felt sorry for Dorothy and assumed her native village had not prepared her for living at the University of Alaska even though she was on a fully paid scholarship with fees, tuition, and food. She left to return to her small village after a couple of months. Even though

I had never grown to understand her, this image of her in her box stays with me as a symbol of not fitting in, what we cling to, and what we let go of.

My new roommate was a perky Seward girl who had a steady boyfriend on campus. She spent much of her free time out with him.

Towards the end of term, Psychology class finished one day, and fellow student, Betsy, ran after me. "Judy, how would you like to go to the Spring Ball?"

"What do you mean?"

"I have a graduating friend who needs a date. Nice guy. Up for it?"

"Hmm. Ok," I replied.

Warmer weather was emerging with bare ground showing through the snow so I wore a light coat over my long gown. Above freezing temperatures were a welcome change from the minus 60F in the winter. The one time I had worn a dress on campus, the severe cold had cracked the material along the hem. That was not only a shock, but made me sad because Gail had selected the synthetic suede and sewn it specially for me.

The evening of the ball, I walked up to the log venue just outside Fairbanks on Richard, my escort's, arm. He impressed me straight away as a fun loving guy. He was handsome with dark hair and grey eyes. I immediately felt conflicted regarding Dewayne. With each step I became more elated and free to be out on a date, and realized that I had missed experiencing full university life because of my involvement with Dewayne. If he and I married in the summer, the chance for more dates like this would end. On the other hand, preparing for the picture perfect wedding would give me the chance for miles of creative sewing and planning with Mom and Gail.

Richard and I sat at a table with cheerful Betsy and her "steady" and others, savoring a steak dinner and dancing. When dancing, our light embrace enabled us to look around. The other couples held each other close in the slow ones, and watching them made my mind drift to Dewayne. I had seen him in February on my trip back to crown the new Miss Homer. He had successfully coached the Homer Mariners to the state basketball championship and was very happy.

Richard was a comfortable partner on the dance floor. I enjoyed the music, including hits of "Penny Lane", "Strawberry Fields Forever", "The Beat Goes On", and, "Girl You'll Be a Woman Soon", which then took me back to dreaming of walking down the aisle in a white princess-lined wedding dress on Dad's arm to the altar where Dewayne waited.

After the ball, Richard and I drove back to campus in a packed car, just as we had come. He told me that he was thinking of returning in the autumn to work on a Master's rather than to do his military service and risk being sent to Vietnam. Lots of laughter and suggestions to cram in a few more outings before the end of term. Richard walked me into the dorm, and we parted with a light kiss at the elevator. As I pressed the button to ascend, I was hoping for more socializing with that group and more dates with Richard.

I had written to Dewayne that I was debating what to do the next year—complete my sophomore year or return to Homer to be with him. His reply had not yet arrived.

In the student union the next day, I ran into Betsy with one couple who had been to the ball. They were chatty and full of fun as we drank cokes sitting on comfortable sofas. Finals were starting; thus, free time for all of us was limited before classes ended. It would be the autumn semester before we could make more arrangements. They asked if I would be back on campus. I did not know what to say, so smiled, hummed and hawed. More of their company would be wonderful, I thought. But, as Dewayne's wife, I would start living my dreams of us as newlyweds. I would transform the little house he rented to a more homey atmosphere with tied-back flowered curtains at the window overlooking the bay, tablecloths, and home-cooked meals, such as the lemon chicken which I knew he liked.

At the dorm, there was a letter in my mail box. I spun round the combination to open the door and pulled it out. My name and address was clearly in Dewayne's familiar handwriting. Ripping it open, I was keen to learn his long awaited reply. Would it help me decide what to do?

Swedish Rye Bread

½ cup, 4 oz. dark molasses

2 tablespoons caraway seed

1 tablespoon salt

2 tablespoons soft butter or margarine

2¾ cups stirred rye flour, 3 packages (tablespoons) active dry yeast

1½ cups water

2¼ to 2¾ cups sifted plain white, or bleached, flour

Combine molasses, caraway seed, butter or margarine. Then the rye flour with the dry yeast stirred in beforehand, and about 1 cup of the white flour. Blend in the water and mix until smooth. Turn out on a lightly floured surface (using some of the remaining flour) and knead till elastic, working in the remaining flour; 8 to 10 minutes. Place the dough in a lightly oiled bowl. Turning once to grease surface. Cover and let rise in a warm place until double (about 1½ hours).

Punch down and divide into two parts. Let rest, covered, 10 minutes. Round into two balls and place on a baking sheet sprinkled with cornmeal. Cover and let double; bake in a 375F/180C oven for 30-35 minutes.

Lemon Chicken

4 chicken breasts, skin on

3 tablespoons clear honey

3 tablespoons olive oil

Zest and juice of one lemon

Salt and freshly ground black pepper

Preheat the oven to 200C/400F/gas mark 6

Place the chicken in a small roasting tin, skin side up. Season with salt & pepper.

Pour over, honey, oil, and lemon zest and juice

Bake for 30 minutes or until cooked through

Serve with rice, green vegetable, grilled Portobello mushroom and small tomatoes on the vine.

End of the Vietnam War and Beyond

Whatever my personal trials and tribulations, the Vietnam War continued as Dad had worried it would. My brother Jerry came of age and joined the Nuclear Submarine Division of the U.S. Navy in 1970. He left Alaska to train in California for six months, and visited me in Arizona before going on to the Northeast. Jerry was upbeat. He was excited to be away from home and to see more of the U.S. He and I went to a drive-in film outside of Phoenix, and I felt very proud of him. He sat on the passenger side across from me—good looking with Swedish blue eyes and blond hair. He mentioned exercise drills, the mess hall, and a few guys with whom he had chummed up in boot camp. Listening convinced me that he was willing to give the service one hundred per cent. Jerry went on to submarine schools around Anaheim. All of us in the family were relieved with his choice of service because being "under" was better than fighting on the ground.

Jerry was stationed in Hawaii for three years. Other times his sub was below in the waters around Vietnam. It came up in Guam when the war ended in 1975. Jerry, with hundreds of American servicemen, erected tents in massive fields for a month. These provided temporary accommodation for the thousands of refugees fleeing the Viet Cong.

He told me later, that the refugees were eager to get into the tents with only the shirts on their backs. Some had family with them. Jerry would be able to look back at his contribution at the end of the war with positive memories. He had made life a little better by helping to provide safe shelter for many war-weary Vietnamese.

He ended his six-year Navy term pushing papers and enjoying the white sands of Waikiki Beach under his bare feet. Thankfully for him and our family, he was never involved in fighting except for a bust-up in Sydney. There he and a few other sailors were told to change out of Navy uniform for an evening out. Perhaps it was their American accent that brought on the unexpected hostility. Or, maybe young American military personnel can be spotted a mile away around the globe. After one sip of Foster's, Jerry looked up to see a fist coming, and then felt his jaw snap. He sank down and heard his colleagues bashed about the bar by a dozen or so hooligans. Many suffered multiple broken bones. One sailor was safe as he had gone to the toilet, heard the commotion, and stayed put with the door locked. Jerry was in the hospital in Sydney for a month recovering. He could only communicate with Mom and Dad through letters, and they were beside themselves with worry.

The U.S. Vietnam veterans returning home were often met with hostility in states including Alaska. They had to deal with ridicule for participating in the war as well as their own after-effects—usually mental and often broken family life. I talked to a friend in Kansas whose cousin returned defeated and withdrawn. Months later, there was no improvement. My friend asked, "How was it like over there, buddy?" His cousin's eyes looked vacant as he said, "I shot Gooks. I shot Gooks." A couple of years later he committed suicide.

Many had fathered children in "Nam" that they would never see after returning home. Inevitable guilt caused tension and stress with those servicemen and their U.S. wives. People questioned why they had not opted like others to emigrate to Canada or Scandinavia to escape the draft. There were hard-nosed employers who threw veteran job applications straight into the wastebasket.

I heard that Ray, the popular basketball player in Homer High, had safely returned to Anchorage and met a girl called Dianne. They married, moved to Homer, and had two sons. The couple bought Homer Air, a small aviation company with only a few planes, and he flew passengers and cargo. He had survived the deadly artillery fire at his helicopter on many rescue missions in faraway Asia. The job back home was duck soup in comparison. On a brilliant sunny afternoon, and only having returned to his native Alaska for a few years, Ray piloted a plane across the bay from Homer, planning to land in Jakolof Bay, which is next to Seldovia. He lost power and crashed and died of internal injuries.

He was twenty-nine. Ray had been lucky in combat, but quite unlucky in civilian life.

Post-Vietnam War in the U.S. was not a time to belt out Frankie Valli and the Four Seasons' song, "Walk Like A Man". More appropriately "Bohemian Rhapsody" by Queen became a hit. I was living in Tennessee getting a Master's in Nutrition and identified with its melancholy mood and lyrics which were more in tune to the time.

"Mama, just killed a man…carry on, as if nothing really matters."

We did carry on, but of course all this did really matter and the long shadow of the Vietnam War still lingers to this day, touching the lives of so many families.

Epilogue

Dewayne and I were married in 1967 and lived in Homer for a year, and remained together for seven additional years. We reached our goals of further education. He earned his PhD in physical education, and I a teaching degree in home economics and a Master's of Science in nutrition. We each found other partners years later.

Tustumena School enrollment rocketed as more residents settled in Clam Gulch, Coho, and Kasilof. Completion of the Coho Loop road reduced our private drive to one mile.

Jerry returned after six years in the U.S. Navy, and built my parents' dream house they had planned for most of the 28 years we lived in the original cabin. Jerry worked with Dad in "Johnson Land Surveying," and Dad retired and passed the business to him. Today the business is busier than ever, although it is still a two-person operation—Jerry and a helper; and it has developed into a steady income for them.

After the many fishing seasons, Mom sold the site to a beach neighbor.

Brent is a busy Alaskan fisherman. He also serves on local committees, and is a Kenai Borough Assemblyman. Brent has self-published two poetry books. He and his wife Judy have six children, and six grandchildren.

Tania and I have enjoyed a lasting friendship in spite of my living away from Alaska since the age of 20. She made Anchorage her marital home after university teaching high school biology, rearing two sons, and completing her PhD in marine biology late in life. Her Norwegian husband, Tobben, recently told me with a laugh, "Tania never did learn to swim."

Gail completed a two-year degree through local university classes and correspondence courses. In the process, she started the community college in Homer. It became a branch of the University of Alaska. She sat on the board of directors for many years. While she was a secretary at Homer High School, she organized a union for non-classified employees—custodians, and secretaries in the school district. In retirement she and her husband, Bob Ammerman, are contract mail carriers for the U.S. Postal Service which means they each drive a Jeep and deliver letters and packages into mail boxes at the end of drives. They winter in St George, Utah.

My parents lived on the homestead to the end of their lives. Dad died at the age of 77 and Mom 96. They were blessed with ten grandchildren and seven great-grandchildren to date. The grandkids and many of the great grandkids have enjoyed swimming, skating, sledding, and fishing on Porcupine Lake. The land surrounding the lake is owned by Jerry, Brent, and me.

I married a Jewish British man from Libya 35 years ago and made London our home. This move across the Atlantic led me to encounter faiths and experiences I never would have encounterd in the 49th State.

I worked at his Micro-Rent computer company, until giving birth to twins through IVF. My twins, Adam and Suzanne, fished six summers with their Uncle Brent. The rough manner we handled the salmon in the '60s was different from Brent's operation on a separate section of Clam Gulch beach today. He fishes with a maximum of thirty-three nets and uses three to four skiffs to work the nets. Brent has a Styrofoam box called a tote holding a layer of crushed ice and seawater on each boat. Adam worked in a boat with his cousin Jason and Brent (operating the motor) to pick fish from several nets. In another boat, with cousin Chris driving, Suzanne and her friend Denise, picked additional nets. They broke the gills to bleed every salmon before placing them by hand into the icy water of the tote. This ensures maximum freshness before fish are delivered to market. Brent is paid by the weight of the different species of salmon in their catch.

Adam and Suzanne have dual U.S. and U.K. citizenship, and enjoy spending time in both countries. Adam works in New York City and Suzanne in London.

I was a member of the Cancer Research Totteridge Society fund-raising committee for twenty years. We sold tickets for our home-prepared buffet lunches in private homes, restaurants, and hosted several balls. We raised over £500,000 for cancer research. As Gail and I are both breast cancer survivors, it is a cause with which I have always identified.

To this day I feel that my youth and upbringing in Alaska made me who I am and gave me extra motivation to take risks. Although I have traveled far from the homestead, part of me remains there—fishing, skiing, skating, gardening, and walking around the placid waters of Porcupine Lake.

Baked Alaska

Start by preparing the brownies at the end of the "Moving On" chapter. After baking, lay the brownie cake out on an oven-proof tray. Mound vanilla, or another flavor, ice cream over; cover with a double batch of the soft meringue topping which is also at the end of the "Moving On" chapter. Place in a preheated 450F/220C oven until golden brown. Remove from oven and cut into eight servings. Serve immediately.

250

Acknowledgements

First, thank you to my husband, Bob, who supported me.

To my daughter, Suzanne, who learned to write long before me and designed the book cover.

My son, Adam, wrote in his Christmas card as I started, "I am impressed and inspired by your quest to be published. Never give up. Keep going."

To my sister, Gail, and brothers, Jerry and Brent, who shared many recollections of our family life through frequent emailing and Skyping.

Mom, deceased, lived to ninety-six, with two hearing aides, was always willing to listen and give her thoughts and recollections. My memories of the last two years of our daily conversations are precious. She would say a few words as: "Did Helen Edens ever find Pete, her parakeet?" Off I would go to write a chapter.

Friends to thank: Norma Jean Ramel, Robin Kent, Maggie Tyler, Jenny Shulman, Johanna Arden, Linda Thompson, Tania Spurkland, Madonna and Jim Robins, Sarah Sanderson, Anne Nickolson, and Margaret Aspinall.

I have much appreciation for fellow writers in the creative writing course at the Institute. There, all sixteen of us started writing through our teacher, Elizabeth Sardany.

Those in the East Finchley Writers', White Lion Writers', and the writers who met in my home, have been enormously helpful in shaping me as a writer. Thank you, also, to Caroline Natzler, who taught me autobiographical writing at City Lit, London, and also in her small workshops.

Thanks to Nick Barlay for editing the book.

Last, my gratitude to the organizers of the Kachemak Bay Writer's Conference, 2013.

Thank you all.

About the Author

Judy Johnson was born and raised in Alaska. When twenty, she moved to the Continental U.S. and completed university education. She taught nutrition at Middle Tennessee State University and worked in hospital food management. For the past 35 years she has lived in London, married to Bob, a British citizen. She worked in sales at Micro-Rent, a company started by Bob and two others in the 1980s. They have adult twins: Adam and Suzanne.

Judy received her Bachelor of Arts in teaching in 1973, and a Master's of Science in Nutrition, in 1975.